Uncover 3 Combo

Ben Goldstein • Ceri Jones
with Susan Banman Sileci

Student's Book

CAMBRIDGE
UNIVERSITY PRESS

University Printing House, Cambridge CB2 8BS, United Kingdom

One Liberty Plaza, 20th Floor, New York, NY 10006, USA

477 Williamstown Road, Port Melbourne, VIC 3207, Australia

314–321, 3rd Floor, Plot 3, Splendor Forum, Jasola District Centre, New Delhi – 110025, India

103 Penang Road, #05-06/07, Visioncrest Commercial, Singapore 238467

Cambridge University Press is part of the University of Cambridge.

It furthers the University's mission by disseminating knowledge in the pursuit of education, learning and research at the highest international levels of excellence.

www.cambridge.org
Information on this title: www.cambridge.org/9781316643662

© Cambridge University Press 2017

This publication is in copyright. Subject to statutory exception and to the provisions of relevant collective licensing agreements, no reproduction of any part may take place without the written permission of Cambridge University Press.

First published 2017

20 19 18 17 16 15 14 13 12

Printed in Poland by Opolgraf

A catalog record for this publication is available from the British Library.

ISBN 978-1-107-49340-7 Student's Book 3
ISBN 978-1-107-49342-1 Student's Book with Online Workbook and Online Practice 3
ISBN 978-1-107-49347-6 Teacher's Book 3
ISBN 978-1-107-49345-2 Workbook with Online Practice 3
ISBN 978-1-107-49352-0 Presentation Plus Disc 3
ISBN 978-1-107-49348-3 Class Audio CDs (3) 3
ISBN 978-1-107-49350-6 Video DVD 3

Additional resources for this publication at www.cambridge.org/uncover

The publishers have no responsibility for the persistence or accuracy of URLs for external or third-party Internet websites referred to in this publication, and do not guarantee that any content on such websites is, or will remain, accurate or appropriate. Information regarding prices, travel timetables and other factual information given in this work is correct at the time of first printing but Cambridge University Press does not guarantee the accuracy of such information thereafter.

Art direction, book design, photo research, and layout services: QBS Learning
Audio production: John Marshall Media

Acknowledgments

Many teachers, coordinators, and educators shared their opinions, their ideas, and their experience to help create *Uncover*. The authors and publisher would like to thank the following people and their schools for their help in shaping the series.

In Mexico:

María Nieves Maldonado Ortiz (Colegio Enrique Rébsamen); Héctor Guzmán Pineda (Liceo Europeo); Alfredo Salas López (Campus Universitario Siglo XXI); Rosalba Millán Martínez (IIPAC [Instituto Torres Quintero A.C.]); Alejandra Rubí Reyes Badillo (ISAS [Instituto San Angel del Sur]); José Enrique Gutiérrez Escalante (Centro Escolar Zama); Gabriela Juárez Hernández (Instituto de Estudios Básicos Amado Nervo); Patricia Morelos Alonso (Instituto Cultural Ingles, S.C.); Martha Patricia Arzate Fernández, (Colegio Valladolid); Teresa González, Eva Marina Sánchez Vega (Colegio Salesiano); María Dolores León Ramírez de Arellano, (Liceo Emperadores Aztecas); Esperanza Medina Cruz (Centro Educativo Francisco Larroyo); Nubia Nelly Martínez García (Salesiano Domingo Savio); Diana Gabriela González Benítez (Colegio Ghandi); Juan Carlos Luna Olmedo (Centro Escolar Zama); Dulce María Pascual Granados (Esc. Juan Palomo Martínez); Roberto González, Fernanda Audirac (Real Life English Center); Rocio Licea (Escuela Fundación Mier y Pesado); Diana Pombo (Great Union Institute); Jacobo Cortés Vázquez (Instituto María P. de Alvarado); Michael John Pryor (Colegio Salesiano Anáhuac Chapalita)

In Brazil:

Renata Condi de Souza (Colégio Rio Branco); Sônia Maria Bernal Leites (Colégio Rio Branco); Élcio Souza (Centro Universitário Anhaguera de São Paulo); Patricia Helena Nero (Private teacher); Célia Elisa Alves de Magalhães (Colégio Cruzeiro-Jacarepaguá); Lilia Beatriz Freitas Gussem (Escola Parque-Gávea); Sandra Maki Kuchiki (Easy Way Idiomas); Lucia Maria Abrão Pereira Lima (Colégio Santa Cruz-São Paulo); Deborah de Castro Ferroz de Lima Pinto (Mundinho Segmento); Clara Vianna Prado (Private teacher); Ligia Maria Fernandes Diniz (Escola Internacional de Alphaville); Penha Aparecida Gaspar Rodrigues (Colégio Salesiano Santa Teresinha); Silvia Castelan (Colégio Santa Catarina de Sena); Marcelo D'Elia (The Kids Club Guarulhos); Malyina Kazue Ono Leal (Colégio Bandeirantes); Nelma de Mattos Santana Alves (Private teacher); Mariana Martins Machado (Britannia Cultural); Lilian Bluvol Vaisman (Curso Oxford); Marcelle Belfort Duarte (Cultura Inglesa-Duque de Caxias); Paulo Dantas (Britannia International English); Anauã Carmo Vilhena (York Language Institute); Michele Amorim Estellita (Lemec – Lassance Modern English Course); Aida Setton (Colégio Uirapuru); Maria Lucia Zaorob (CEL-LEP); Marisa Veiga Lobato (Interlíngua Idiomas); Maria Virgínia Lebrón (Independent consultant); Maria Luiza Carmo (Colégio Guilherme Dumont Villares/CEL-LEP); Lucia Lima (Independent consultant); Malyina Kazue Ono Leal (Colégio Bandeirantes); Debora Schisler (Seven Idiomas); Helena Nagano (Cultura Inglesa); Alessandra de Campos (Alumni); Maria Lúcia Sciamarelli (Colégio Divina Providência); Catarina Kruppa (Cultura Inglesa); Roberto Costa (Freelance teacher/consultant); Patricia McKay Aronis (CEL-LEP); Claudia Beatriz Cavalieri (By the World Idiomas); Sérgio Lima (Vermont English School); Rita Miranda (IBI – [Instituto Batista de Idiomas]); Maria de Fátima Galery (Britain English School); Marlene Almeida (Teacher Trainer Consultant); Flávia Samarane (Colégio Logosófico); Maria Tereza Vianna (Greenwich Schools); Daniele Brauer (Cultura Inglesa/AMS Idiomas); Allessandra Cierno (Colégio Santa Dorotira); Helga Silva Nelken (Greenwich Schools/Colégio Edna Roriz); Regina Marta Bazzoni (Britain English School); Adriano Reis (Greenwich Schools); Vanessa Silva Freire de Andrade (Private teacher); Nilvane Guimarães (Colégio Santo Agostinho)

In Ecuador:

Santiago Proaño (Independent teacher trainer); Tania Abad (UDLA [Universidad de Las Americas]); Rosario Llerena (Colegio Isaac Newton); Paúl Viteri (Colegio Andino); Diego Maldonado (Central University); Verónica Vera (Colegio Tomás Moro); Mónica Sarauz (Colegio San Gabriel); Carolina Flores (Colegio APCH); Boris Cadena, Vinicio Reyes (Colegio Benalcázar); Deigo Ponce (Colegio Gonzaga); Byron Freire (Colegio Nuestra Señora del Rosario)

The authors and publisher would also like to thank the following contributors, script writers and collaborators for their inspired work in creating *Uncover*:
Anna Whitcher, Janet Gokay, Kathryn O'Dell, Lynne Robertson, Dana Henricks

Unit	Vocabulary	Grammar	Listening	Conversation (Useful language)
1 Life on the Edge pp. 2–11	■ Extreme weather ■ Basic needs	■ Simple present and present continuous review ■ Simple past and past continuous review ■ *used to* Grammar reference p. 106	■ Biking the Pan-American Highway	■ Agreeing and disagreeing
2 First Things First! pp. 12–21	■ Priorities ■ Emotions	■ *have to/don't have to* ■ *must* ■ Modals of obligation – *should, ought to, had better* ■ *It's* + adjective + infinitive Grammar reference p. 107	■ Take it easy!	■ Helping someone to do something
3 Art All Around Us pp. 22–31	■ Visual arts ■ Musical instruments	■ Verb + *-ing* form (gerund) review ■ *-ing* forms (gerunds) as subjects ■ Verbs + prepositions + *-ing* forms (gerunds) Grammar reference p. 108	■ Leo the one-man band	■ Inviting a friend and arranging to meet
4 Sign Me Up! pp. 32–41	■ Adventure travel ■ Phrasal verbs related to travel	■ Present perfect with *already, yet,* and *just* ■ Present perfect questions ■ Present perfect with *for* and *since* ■ *How long . . . ?* and the present perfect Grammar reference p. 109	■ Adventure travel experiences	■ Signing up for an adventure activity
5 Yikes! pp. 42–51	■ Fears ■ *-ed* and *-ing* adjective endings	■ Future review – *will, be going to,* present continuous ■ First conditional ■ Modals of probability – *must, can't, may, might, could* Grammar reference p. 110	■ Conversations at an amusement park	■ Expressing disbelief

Unit 1–5 Review Game pp. 52–53

Writing	Reading	Video	Accuracy and fluency	Speaking outcomes
A persuasive email	*Freezing in Siberia* Reading to write: *A fun vacation* Culture: *Tristan da Cunha*	*The Long Winter* *Which do you prefer, towns and cities or the country?* *An Island Flood* *The Khomani San of the Kalahari* (CLIL Project p. 116)	Not using *a* to talk about the weather Pronunciation of *used to*	I can . . . talk about extreme weather. discuss how my environment affects my life. talk about past incidents and habits. ask for agreement. discuss a faraway place.
A blog post about solving a problem	*Getting Some Shut-Eye* Reading to write: *Stories of Stress* Culture: *Ten Things I Bet You Didn't Know About . . . Cheerleading*	*Get Up and Go!* *What makes a good friend?* *Irish Dancing*	Using *to* after *ought*, *should*, and *had better* The letter *c*	I can . . . discuss my priorities. express obligation and prohibition. make strong recommendations. offer help to someone. discuss a sport or cultural activity.
A blog post about a concert	*Everyone's an Artist* Reading to write: *Fantastic Free Concert* Culture: *A Temporary Desert City*	*Original Art* *Have you ever been to a concert?* *A World of Music* *Art in Perspective* (CLIL Project p. 117)	Using the *-ing* form after *enjoy* Word stress with *love* and *hate* Spelling the *-ing* forms	I can . . . talk about visual arts. express my likes and dislikes. discuss music. make invitations and arrangements. discuss a cultural event.
An email comparing different customs	*Anchors Aweigh!* Reading to write: *Tipping help!* Culture: *Five Good Reasons to Visit New Zealand*	*The Age of Discovery* *What's the most exciting thing you've ever done?* *Fun in Australia*	Using *go* before activities that end in *-ing* Word stress with time words	I can . . . talk about adventure travel. ask and answer questions about personal experiences. ask and answer questions about the duration of activities. talk about signing up for an adventure activity. discuss reasons to visit a place.
An email to a friend about plans and problems	*Ask Maria* Reading to write: *Afraid to fly!* Culture: *Superstitions? Who needs them?!*	*Creepy Creatures* *What are you afraid of?* *Calendars of the Ancient Maya* *City vs. Country* (CLIL Project p. 118)	Pronunciation of *I'll* as /al/ Not using *must* for future probability	I can . . . identify and discuss common fears. talk about future events. talk about things that are possible and not possible. express disbelief. discuss superstitions.

Unit	Vocabulary	Grammar	Listening	Conversation (Useful language)
6 Difficult Decisions pp. 54–63	■ School life ■ Expressions with *make* and *do*	■ Second conditional ■ Second conditional *yes/no* questions ■ Second conditional *Wh-* questions Grammar reference p. 111	■ Would you tell the teacher?	■ Asking for and giving advice
7 Smart Planet pp. 64–73	■ Materials ■ Eco-construction verbs	■ Simple present passive ■ Infinitives of purpose ■ Simple past passive Grammar reference p. 112	■ Tour of a museum EcoHouse	■ Apologizing
8 Run for Cover! pp. 74–83	■ Natural disasters ■ Survival essentials	■ Past perfect ■ Past perfect *yes/no* questions ■ Past perfect and simple past Grammar reference p. 113	■ Survival story	■ Explaining a personal problem
9 He Said, She Said pp. 84–93	■ Reporting verbs ■ Communication methods	■ Quoted speech vs. reported speech ■ Reported questions Grammar reference p. 114	■ Short conversations	■ Comparing different accounts of a story
10 Don't Give Up! pp. 94–103	■ Goals and achievements ■ Emotions related to accomplishments	■ Reflexive pronouns ■ Reflexive pronouns with *by* ■ Causative *have/get* Grammar reference p. 115	■ Challenging situations	■ Reassuring someone

Unit 6–10 Review Game pp. 104–105

Writing	Reading	Video	Accuracy and fluency	Speaking outcomes
An article about online safety	*A School with a Difference* Reading to write: *How to Be Safe Online!* Culture: *Punishment or Rehabilitation?*	*Working Together* *Who would you talk to if you needed advice?* *Watch Your Identity*	Pronunciation of /ʊ/ and /u/ Using the simple past after *if* in the second conditional	I can . . . talk about school life. talk about good and bad behavior at school and home. discuss difficult situations. ask for and give advice. discuss different systems for dealing with crime.
A newspaper article about an event	*Houses Made of Garbage* Reading to write: *Volunteers Clean Valley Nature Reserve* Culture: *Under the Australian Sun*	*Where Does it All Go?* *What kind of volunteer work can you do in your school or town?* *Build It Better* *Driving into the Future* (CLIL Project p. 119)	Including *is* or *are* in passive sentences	I can . . . identify materials. talk about how people recycle and reuse materials. talk about eco-construction. apologize. discuss solar energy and sun safety.
A story about a personal experience	*Krakatoa* Reading to write: *Story Source* Culture: *It isn't just a hobby.*	*Land of Volcanoes* *Do you often lose things?* *Storm Chasers*	Pronunciation of /æ/ and /ɒ/ Using the past perfect for events completed before another past moment	I can . . . discuss natural disasters. ask and answer questions about past experiences. discuss past events. ask about and discuss personal problems. discuss tornadoes and people who chase tornadoes.
An essay about social networking sites	*Communication Changes* Reading to write: *Are Cell Phones Good for Teenagers?* Culture: *The World Speaks One Language*	*Social Networks* *What do you think about celebrity gossip?* *The Language of the Future?* *Pictures with Meaning* (CLIL Project p. 120)	Pronunciation of final consonants /d/, /l/, /m/, and /n/ Not using *do* in reported questions	I can . . . talk about different ways of speaking. discuss social networking. talk about different communication methods. compare stories. discuss language use throughout the world.
A personal action plan	*Make Your Dreams Come True* Reading to write: *Achieving My Goal* Culture: *Olympics for the Brain*	*Lifeguard and Athlete* *Have you ever given a class presentation?* *Circus Star*	The sound /iː/ in words with the letters *ie* and *ei* Consonant clusters Getting/having something done	I can . . . talk about goals and accomplishments. discuss emotions related to accomplishments. discuss steps toward achieving goals. reassure someone. discuss an academic competition.

Irregular verbs p. 121

1 Life on the Edge

Discovery EDUCATION

BE CURIOUS

The Long Winter

Which do you prefer – towns and cities or the country?

An Island Flood

Life in the Desert

1. What do you see in this picture?

2. Where do you think this kind of weather takes place? What other places have "extreme" weather?

3. What might be different about life in places with extreme weather?

UNIT CONTENTS
Vocabulary Extreme weather; basic needs
Grammar Simple present and present continuous review; simple past and past continuous review
Listening Biking the Pan-American Highway

Vocabulary: Extreme weather

1. Match the words and phrases with the correct pictures.

1. _g_ high winds
2. ___ blizzard
3. ___ hail
4. ___ heat wave
5. ___ thunder and lightning
6. ___ heavy rain
7. ___ fog

 2. Listen, check, and repeat.

3. Which of the words and phrases in Exercise 1 do you associate with a) very hot weather, b) very cold weather, c) hot or cold weather?

4. Think about where you live. When do you experience extreme weather? Write the words and phrases from Exercise 1 in the following categories.

> **Get it RIGHT!**
> Don't use the article *a* to talk about weather.
> Yakutsk has **very cold** weather.
> NOT: ~~Yakutsk has **a very cold** weather.~~

Sometimes in the summer	Sometimes in the winter	At least once a month	Only once or twice a year	Never

Speaking: What's it like outside?

5. **YOUR TURN** Work with a partner. Ask and answer the questions.

1. What other words do you know to describe weather?
2. What's the weather like today where you live?
3. What weather stories are in the news right now?

6. Talk to your partner about the weather where you live.

> We're having a bad heat wave this week. Right now it's 35°C!

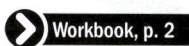 Workbook, p. 2

Reading Freezing in Siberia!; A fun vacation; Tristan da Cunha
Conversation Agreeing and disagreeing
Writing A persuasive email

The COLDEST TOWN on EARTH

Freezing in Siberia!

Yakutsk – the coldest town on Earth. From November to March, it's only light for three or four hours a day, and the temperature is hardly ever above freezing. The average daytime temperature is –30°C, and at night, it sometimes falls as low as –60°C. Now that's cold!

Right now, I'm writing on my computer in the library. It's warm inside, but outside, people are wearing heavy pants, tall boots, hats, scarves, and heavy coats. It often takes me half an hour to get ready to leave the house. When I get home, it takes me another half an hour to take off all those clothes!

Life in the extreme cold is difficult. At –20°C, the air freezes inside your nose. At –40°C, you can't stay outdoors for more than 10 minutes or your skin freezes. At –45°C, the metal on your glasses sticks to your face! I don't go out very much. People only walk short distances from one warm place to another. All activities happen indoors – from shopping to sports. A popular local sport that lots of boys do is wrestling. I don't wrestle. I like to jump rope, and I try to do it three or four times a week. Both jumping rope and wrestling use a lot of energy, and they keep you warm and strong. That's important when you live in subzero conditions!

In the summer, Yakutsk is a different city. In June and July, it's the season of "white nights," when the sky never gets dark, not even at midnight. The snow melts, and the temperature rises to 30°C and higher. Most people are happy to have a heat wave after 10 months of winter. Camping and barbecues are the favorite summer activities, with parties all night long. I'm thinking about summer weather a lot these days because there are still four more months of winter. I can't wait for summer!

DID YOU KNOW...? The lowest ever recorded temperature in Yakutsk, Siberia, northeast Russia, was –64°C.

Reading: A blog

1. Look at the title of the blog. What is special about the town of Yakutsk?

 2. Read and listen to Meg's blog. Check your answer in Exercise 1.

3. Read the blog again. Answer the questions.

   1. What are the average temperatures in Yakutsk in winter?
   2. What kinds of clothes do people wear outside in the winter?
   3. Why does it take a lot of time to get ready to go out in the winter?
   4. What is the season of "white nights"?
   5. What do people do in the summer in Yakutsk?

4. **YOUR TURN** Work with a partner. Ask and answer the questions.

   1. Would you like to live in Yakutsk? What are the good things about living there? What are the bad things?
   2. Are there any places in your country that are similar to Yakutsk?
   3. Which is the coldest region in your country? What's the hottest?
   4. How is life in your town different in summer and in winter? In what way?

   I wouldn't want to live in Yakutsk. It's too cold there!

Grammar: Simple present and present continuous review

5. Complete the chart.

Use the simple present to describe what normally happens. This includes routines and facts.	
The metal on your glasses **sticks** to your face.	I **don't like** hot weather.
I _____ cold weather. Winter **is** my favorite season.	We _____ **go out** a lot in the winter. It's too cold!
Use the present continuous to describe something happening right now or these days.	
I'**m wearing** a hat.	My friend **isn't studying** for tomorrow's test right now.
We'**re** _____ a lot of hot food like soup these days because it's cold outside.	I'**m not** _____ boots because it's too hot outside for them.

> Check your answers: Grammar reference, p. 106

6. Circle the correct answers.

1. **I'm trying** / **I try** to stay inside the house these days.
2. When the weather is bad, most activities **happen** / **are happening** indoors.
3. My friends **love** / **are loving** cold weather.
4. **We watch** / **We're watching** the weather report on TV right now.
5. In my town, the snow **melts** / **is melting** only in April or May.
6. Matthew **plans** / **is planning** his vacation in the Bahamas right now.
7. My cousin moved to Costa Rica because she **doesn't like** / **isn't liking** cold winters.
8. Right now, Daniel and Elizabeth **put** / **are putting** their boots on to walk to school.

7. Complete the text with the simple present or present continuous forms of the verbs. Listen and check.

Mark and his family ¹ *love* (love) the place they live: Costa Rica. But this week, they ² _____ (live) a different life. They ³ _____ (visit) their cousins in Barrow, Alaska. Costa Rica is a warm, tropical country. The temperature ⁴ _____ (not change) much there. It's around 27°C all year round. The average temperature in Barrow is 11°C, and the temperature ⁵ _____ (stay) below 0°C for 160 days of the year. Mark's in Barrow right now. He says, "I ⁶ _____ (have) fun with my cousins this week, but we ⁷ _____ (not go) outside much. I ⁸ _____ (not have) the right clothes!" In Costa Rica, Mark usually ⁹ _____ (play) soccer outside after school, but this week, he ¹⁰ _____ (play) video games indoors. In Costa Rica, he ¹¹ _____ (go) to the beach on Saturday or Sunday. In Barrow, he ¹² _____ (go) to hockey games. He says, "I can't wait to get back to hot weather!"

Speaking: It's too hot!

8. YOUR TURN Make notes about how hot weather and cold weather affect you. Then ask and answer the questions with a partner.

- What do you eat?
- How well do you sleep?
- Where do you exercise?
- What do you do for fun?

> In really cold weather, I eat a lot of bread and soup. In really hot weather, I don't eat anything. I'm not hungry!

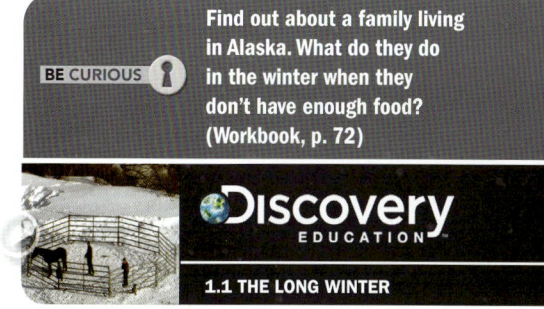

BE CURIOUS Find out about a family living in Alaska. What do they do in the winter when they don't have enough food? (Workbook, p. 72)

Discovery EDUCATION

1.1 THE LONG WINTER

On the ROAD

Listening: Biking the Pan-American Highway

1. Look at the map of the Pan-American Highway. How many kilometers do you imagine the highway is? How long do you think it would take to travel the entire highway by bike?

2. Listen to a radio program about a family's experience on the Pan-American Highway. How does Diane, the mother, feel now that the trip is finished?

3. Listen again. Circle the correct answers.

   1. How long is the Pan-American Highway?
      a. 28,000 kilometers   b. 100 kilometers   c. 13,000 kilometers

   2. In what country did the Miller family take a plane?
      a. Ecuador   b. Argentina   c. Panama

   3. How far did the family ride each day?
      a. between 11 and 13 kilometers   b. between 14 and 16 kilometers   c. between 50 and 100 kilometers

   4. How did the Miller family communicate with family members?
      a. They read blogs.
      b. They wrote a blog post every week.
      c. They talked on the phone.

   5. What did Robert miss the most while he was traveling?
      a. having a home
      b. free entertainment
      c. going to a different place every night

   6. How can listeners find out more about the Millers' trip?
      a. They can send an email to Robert and Diane.
      b. They can read the blog or Diane's book.
      c. They can read Diane's book or call her on the phone.

Vocabulary: Basic needs

4. Match the words and phrases with the words associated with them. Then listen and check your answers.

   1. ___ food and drink
   2. ___ clothes
   3. ___ entertainment
   4. ___ health care
   5. ___ transportation
   6. ___ communication
   7. ___ a home
   8. ___ education
   9. ___ money

   a. house, apartment
   b. movies, games, sports
   c. high school, college, homeschooling
   d. email, text messages, phone calls
   e. hospitals, laboratories, clinics
   f. spaghetti, salad, juice
   g. cash, credit cards, coins
   h. buses, trucks, bikes
   i. boots, jackets, hats

5. Look again at the words in Exercise 4. Write them in order of importance to you. Then discuss your list with your partner.

Grammar: Simple past and past continuous review

6. Complete the chart.

Use the simple past to describe actions and events in the past.	
We **took** a plane over part of Panama.	They **didn't have** to stop for food.
We _____ our own food.	He **didn't** _____ his arm, but it hurt a lot.
What _____ you **miss** the most?	
Use the past continuous to describe actions and events in progress in the past.	
I _____ **spending** the night in Quito when I heard that the road was closed.	He **wasn't wearing** a helmet when he fell.
They _____ **eating** their lunch by the road when the storm started.	You **weren't talking** to me when I dropped my phone.
What **were** you _____ last night when the electricity went out?	

> Check your answers: Grammar reference, p. 106

7. Circle the correct answers.
1. My bike **broke / was breaking** down while I **rode / was riding** through Mexico.
2. When she **studied / was studying** in Greece, Evelyn **bought / was buying** food from local markets.
3. I **sat / was sitting** in the park when I **heard / was hearing** the news.
4. When the hail **began / was beginning**, I **talked / was talking** on the phone.
5. You **called / were calling** while I **watched / was watching** the football game.
6. Neil and Austin **drove / were driving** through the blizzard when they **ran / were running** out of gas.

8. Complete the sentences with the correct form of *used to* and the verbs in parentheses.
1. I _____ (think) everyone in South America spoke Spanish, but now I know that people in Brazil speak Portuguese.
2. Steve _____ (not ride) his bike much, but now he rides it every day.
3. My grandparents _____ (not come) to see us often, but now they visit every month.
4. Public transportation _____ (be) terrible in this town, but now we have a great subway system.
5. We _____ (not cook) a lot of meals at home, but now we only go to restaurants on special occasions.

used to

Use **used to** when something happened over a period of time but doesn't happen anymore.

I **used to be** a swimmer, but now I play soccer.

We **didn't use to ride** our bikes a lot, but now we ride every day.

Did you **use to live** in Boston?

Speaking: Last night and long ago

9. YOUR TURN Use the phrases below to write five questions. You can use the simple past or past continuous.

what	do	last night
when	go	when you were younger
where	eat	
	live	

10. Work in pairs. Ask and answer your questions.

> What were you doing last night?

> I was doing my homework. What about you?

 Say it **RIGHT!**

In statements, *used to* often sounds like /justə/. Listen and repeat the sentences.
I **used to** spend a lot of money on public transportation, but now I ride my bike.
He **used to** like living in Canada, but he doesn't anymore. It's too cold!

REAL TALK — 1.2 WHICH DO YOU PREFER – TOWNS AND CITIES OR THE COUNTRY?

A Great Place TO LIVE

Conversation: City, town, or country?

1. **REAL TALK** Watch or listen to the teenagers. Check (✓) the things that the teenagers like about living in the city.

☐ bike riding	☐ fresh air	☐ looking at animals
☐ concerts	☐ hiking	☐ different neighborhoods
☐ shopping	☐ museums	☐ parks

2. **YOUR TURN** Which do you prefer – small towns, cities, or the country? Tell your partner.

3. Listen to Kate talking to Mark about Greenville. Complete the conversation.

   USEFUL LANGUAGE: Agreeing and disagreeing
   don't you think?   ✓ Don't you agree?   I don't think so.   See what I mean?   I disagree.

   Kate: Do you live near school, Mark?
   Mark: No, I live in Greenville. Have you been there?
   Kate: Yes, I live there, too. It's a great place to live. ¹ _Don't you agree?_
   Mark: Well, it's really quiet. Actually, nothing ever happens, and there's nothing to do. It's boring.
   Kate: Well, ² _____ There are lots of things to do. What about the new mall and the community center?
   Mark: Maybe, but all my friends live here, in the city, and I can't go out with them in the evening.
   Kate: Yeah, but Greenville is healthier, ³ _____
   Mark: The air, you mean? ⁴ _____ It's close to the city, so I don't think living in Greenville makes a difference. And there's so much heavy rain.
   Kate: Well, if there's heavy rain in Greenville, there's heavy rain in the city, too. They both have the same weather.
   Mark: That's true. I like taking my dog for walks. Greenville is good for that.
   Kate: ⁵ _____ It's not all bad.
   Mark: That's true. Maybe you're right. Small towns are OK, but I still wish I lived in the city.

4. Practice the conversation with a partner.

5. **YOUR TURN** Work with a partner. Take turns giving your opinion. Then agree and disagree.

Situation 1	Situation 2
Living in a city.	Going to a big school.
Good: lots to do, easy to travel around	Good: lots of facilities, clubs, variety of different subjects to study
Bad: noisy, stressful, unhealthy	Bad: noisy, impersonal, more bullying

   There's a lot to do in the city, and that's good, don't you think?

   Well, I like small towns. They're not as noisy as big cities. . . .

Hi Laura!

I'd like you to come visit me this summer. I miss you! You live in a big city, but I live in a cabin by a lake and that's cool, too. Ask your parents if you can spend a week with me and my family this summer. Here's what you can tell them:

First of all, we can do lots of fun stuff. For example, we can go swimming all day, every day. My family also has a boat, and we can go water skiing or visit other places on the lake. There's an island in the middle of the lake, and we can have a barbecue there.

Second, it's healthy to be out here by the lake. You'll get a lot of exercise. For instance, we can go hiking in the woods (and we can go swimming again when we come back!). We can shop for organic food at the farmers' market. And there's no pollution, and this part of the state is really clean and nice.

The best part is that we can be together! I haven't seen you in six months. That's a long time.

I really hope you can visit us this summer! Talk to your mom and dad. If they have any questions, they can talk to my parents.

Love,
Addison

Reading to write: A persuasive email

6. Look at the pictures and read Addison's email to Laura. What does she want Laura to do?

◉ Focus on CONTENT

When you write a persuasive email, you can follow this format:
- Start with a topic sentence that states your position on something.
- Explain why you think your readers should do what you're suggesting. Start your sentences with phrases such as *First of all*, *Second*, and *The best part*.
- Close your email by stating your position again. Try to say it in a different way this time.

7. Find examples of each of the points in Focus on Content in Addison's email.

◉ Focus on LANGUAGE
Introducing details
For example and *for instance* are similar in meaning.
- *There's a lot to do in the city.* **For instance** / **For example**, *you can visit art museums.*

Writing: A persuasive email

☐ **PLAN**
Think of something you'd like to persuade someone else to do. Use the list in the Focus on Content box and make notes.

☐ **WRITE**
Write your email. Use your notes from above to help you. Write about 150 words.

☐ **CHECK**
Check your writing. Can you say "yes" to these questions?

- Have you followed the instructions in the Focus on Content box?
- Did you use *for example* or *for instance*?

8. Match the sentences.

1. There are lots of fun things to do in the mountains. For example, ___
2. We have lots of different kinds of weather here. For instance, ___
3. There are lots of great restaurants in my town. For instance, ___
4. Mary eats an unhealthy amount of sugar every day. For example, ___

a. today she had doughnuts and soda for breakfast, an ice-cream sundae for dessert at lunch, and a big piece of cake at dinner.

b. we have Greek ones, Italian ones, and my favorite, a place that only serves pancakes.

c. you can ride horses, hike, or go camping.

d. we have blizzards in the winter, heavy rains in the spring, and heat waves in the summer.

Tristan da Cunha

The most remote inhabited island on Earth!

Tristan da Cunha, the most remote inhabited island on the planet, is in the middle of the Atlantic Ocean. It's over 2,800 kilometers from the nearest land, and to get there, you need to fly to Cape Town, in South Africa. Then, because there's no airport on the island, you have to travel by ship for seven days.

Tristan da Cunha was named after the Portuguese discoverer who first saw the island. Although it is almost 10,000 kilometers from London, it's part of a British territory. The official language is English, but the people who live there also speak a local dialect. The British monarch is the head of state, and they use British pounds as their currency.

The island is very small – only 11 kilometers long. Queen Mary Peak, a volcano in the middle of the island, is 2,000 meters high, and it's active, too! The weather doesn't get too hot or too cold, but there are times of heavy rain.

The island is home to 80 families, about 260 people in total, and they have only eight last names. These are the last names of some of the first people to settle on the island. There is only one town and one school, and that's the only place with an Internet connection.

In October 1961, the island's volcano erupted, and the whole population went to live in the UK. They got jobs and new homes, but they didn't like living so far from their island. They weren't used to the noise, the traffic, and the cold winter. So, in November 1962, 200 islanders returned to Tristan da Cunha and their old lives there. They were happier without television, cars, and the stress of modern life!

DID YOU KNOW…?

Many of the original settlers of the island had asthma. Over 50 percent of the people on Tristan da Cunha have asthma now. Scientists have learned a lot about the disease by studying the people of the island.

Culture: A remote island

1. Look at the picture. Where do you think this place is? What is special about it?

2. Read and listen to the article. Check your answers in Exercise 1.

3. Read the article again. Complete the table.

Approximate distance from the nearest land:	2,800 kilometers
Official language:	
Approximate distance from London:	
Length of island:	
Number of families:	
Number of schools:	
Month and year that the volcano erupted:	
Number of people who returned to Tristan da Cunha in 1962:	

4. **YOUR TURN** Work with a partner. Ask and answer the questions.

   1. Would you like to visit Tristan da Cunha? Why? / Why not?

   2. What do you think are the good things about living on the island? What are the bad things?

BE CURIOUS Find out about the people in Bali, India. What are their two main foods? (Workbook, p. 73)

1.3 AN ISLAND FLOOD

UNIT 1 REVIEW

Vocabulary

1. Write the extreme weather word for each picture.

1. _____fog_____ 2. _____

3. _____ 4. _____

5. _____ 6. _____

Grammar

2. Complete the sentences.
   1. You can't go outside right now. It _'s raining_ (rain) really hard!
   2. I _____ (work) after school and on the weekends to make extra money.
   3. My teacher _____ (not talk) right now. She's writing a report at her desk.
   4. We _____ (not like) cold weather. That's why we live in Florida.
   5. My little brother _____ (cry) when there is thunder and lightning.
   6. The chef is in the restaurant kitchen. He _____ (make) a special soup.

3. Circle the correct answers.
   1. The surfer **swam / was swimming** in the ocean when she saw the shark.
   2. When I was younger, I **watched / used to watch** a lot of TV. I don't anymore.
   3. It **rained / used to rain** about 10 centimeters last night.
   4. What **did you do / were you doing** at 9:00 p.m. last night?
   5. My sister **wasn't thinking / didn't use to think** that education was important. Now she studies really hard.
   6. I **did / was doing** all my homework. Do you want to play a video game?

Useful language

4. Complete the conversation.

| you agree | think |
| See what I | disagree |

John: Hey, Dylan. My family is taking a vacation abroad this summer. We might go to Canada.

Dylan: Canada? There are blizzards there! The weather is pretty harsh, don't you ¹_____?

John: Actually, it's nice in the summer. What about you? What are your plans?

Dylan: I want to learn Spanish. My friend Mike is visiting his grandma in Colombia, and he invited me to come. I can learn a lot of Spanish. Don't ²_____?

John: No. Mike's American. You won't learn Spanish.

Dylan: I ³_____. I can learn from his grandma!

John: Well, maybe you're right. It'll be fun, even if you don't learn a lot of Spanish.

Dylan: ⁴_____ mean? It's a great idea!

PROGRESS CHECK: Now I can . . .
- ☐ talk about extreme weather.
- ☐ discuss how my environment affects my life.
- ☐ talk about past incidents and habits.
- ☐ ask for agreement.
- ☐ write a persuasive email.
- ☐ discuss a faraway place.

CLIL PROJECT

1.4 LIFE IN THE DESERT, p. 116

2 First Things FIRST!

Discovery EDUCATION

BE CURIOUS

- Get Up and Go!
- What do you think makes a good friend?
- Irish Dancing

1. What do you see in this photo?

2. How busy are you? Do you have lots of different things going on in your life?

3. How do you feel about all your different activities?

UNIT CONTENTS

Vocabulary Priorities; emotions
Grammar have to/don't have to; must; Modals of obligation – should, ought to, had better; It's + adjective + infinitive
Listening Take it easy!

Vocabulary: Priorities

1. **Match the photos (a–h) with the phrases.**

1. _b_ shopping for clothes
2. ___ working out
3. ___ hanging out with friends
4. ___ doing something creative
5. ___ getting enough sleep
6. ___ having time for yourself
7. ___ helping around the house
8. ___ chatting with friends online
9. ___ staying out late on the weekend

2. **Listen, check, and repeat.**

3. **What activities are the words below associated with? Write phrases from Exercise 1 in the correct place below.**

   1. making a cake or writing a song   _____
   2. going to parties or movies at night   _____
   3. lifting weights or doing exercises   _____
   4. washing the dishes, cleaning your room   _____
   5. taking a walk, reading a book   _____
   6. watching TV, playing games, talking   _____

Speaking: What matters most?

4. **YOUR TURN Work with a partner. Ask and answer the questions.**

   1. Which thing in the list in Exercise 1 is most important to you? Why?
   2. Which things do you argue about with your parents?
   3. Which thing stresses you the most? Why?

   > Let's see. I think the most important thing for me is having time for myself – so I can just relax and do what I want to do!

Workbook, p. 8

Reading Getting Some Shut-Eye; Stories of Stress; Ten Things I Bet You Didn't Know About . . . Cheerleading
Conversation Helping someone to do something
Writing A blog post about solving a problem

Time for BED

Getting Some Shut-Eye

Did You Know?
Teenagers who sleep enough:
> usually have better skin than those who don't sleep enough.
> eat less junk food than teens who don't.
> are less likely to experience depression than those who don't.

Teenagers have to get more sleep! According to researchers, teenagers need to sleep a lot more than adults: eight to 10 hours every night. Sadly, only 15 percent of teenagers sleep eight hours on a school night, and that's just not enough.

Here are three reasons to get more sleep:

Your body needs sleep.
Your body is still growing, and your brain is still developing. Teenagers shouldn't forget how much their bodies need that extra sleep.

Sleep helps you do better in school.
When you're tired, you can't concentrate very well. And when you can't concentrate, it's difficult to learn.

Sleep keeps you healthy.
Without enough sleep, your body gets weak, and it's easy for you to catch colds and other illnesses. Tired people often eat food with more sugar in it, and that isn't good for you.

What can you do to get more sleep?
> Don't drink anything with caffeine at night, including soda.
> If you're hungry, have a light snack. That sometimes helps people sleep.
> One hour before you go to bed, turn off the TV and shut down your computer.
> Don't take your cell phone to bed with you!

Reading: A magazine article

1. Look at the picture. How many hours of sleep do you think teenagers need?

2. Read and listen to the article about teenagers and sleep. What's the main aim of the article?

   a. to tell parents what to do about teenagers who sleep a lot

   b. to offer advice to teenagers about how to get up earlier in the morning

   c. to tell teenagers why sleep is important and how to get more of it

3. Read the article again and answer the questions.

   1. What is one reason teenagers may feel depressed or sad?
   2. How many hours of sleep do most teenagers need?
   3. What percentage of teenagers sleep eight hours on school nights?
   4. What can happen at school if you don't get enough sleep?
   5. What kind of food do tired people usually eat more of?
   6. What should you do one hour before you go to bed?

 Say it RIGHT!

Notice the different sounds of the letter *c*. Can you find another example of each in the article?

/s/ — ne**c**essary
/k/ — **c**affeine

4. **YOUR TURN** Work with a partner. Ask and answer the questions.

   1. What time do you usually go to bed during the week? Do you find it difficult to get to sleep? Why? / Why not?
   2. Do you think you get enough sleep? What kinds of things keep you from getting a good night's sleep? What happens if you don't sleep enough?

> What time do you usually go to bed during the week?

> I usually go to bed around 11:00. What about you?

14 | Unit 2

Grammar: *have to/don't have to*

5. Complete the chart.

Use have/has to *to say that it is necessary to do something.*
Use don't/doesn't have to *to say that it is not necessary to do something, but you can do it if you want to.*

Affirmative	Negative
I _____ **get** more sleep.	I _____ **get up** early on Saturdays.
My brother _____ **get up** early on Saturdays. He works in a restaurant.	My little sister _____ **help** with the housework. She's only two.

> Check your answers: Grammar reference, p. 107

6. Complete the sentences with the correct form of *have to*.

1. A professional tennis player _____ train for four or five hours every day.
2. I _____ study math three or four hours every night. It's really difficult for me!
3. My mom is a piano teacher, so I _____ pay for my piano lessons.
4. My brother is really lucky. He _____ do any homework. He's only three years old.
5. My parents _____ work on weekends, so we usually do something fun together.
6. My best friend _____ get up early on Saturday. His baseball practice starts at 8:00 a.m.

7. Use the words to write sentences. Use *must* or *must not*.

must	
Use must/must not *to talk about rules, laws, or prohibited actions.*	
You **must** be quiet in the library.	You **must not** touch the art in a museum.
She **must** return her books on time.	He **must not** use his cell phone here.

1. You / eat in the classroom
   _____
2. You / wear your seat belt in the car
   _____
3. You / leave trash on the beach
   _____
4. You / come to school on time
   _____
5. You / clean up your trash when you go camping
   _____
6. You / take scissors on a plane
   _____

Speaking: *Do you have to . . . ?*

8. **YOUR TURN** Work with a partner. Ask and answer questions using *Do you have to . . .* and the phrases.

clean your room
get up early on Saturday or Sunday
go to bed at a specific time
help cook meals
practice a musical instrument
study English over the weekend
take care of your younger brother or sister
wash the dishes

> Do you have to take care of your younger sister?

> Yes, sometimes I do, when my parents have to work late.

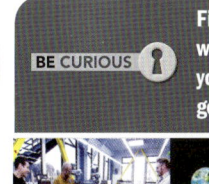

BE CURIOUS Find out about a new way to wake up in the morning. Do you think the machine is a good idea? (Workbook, p. 74)

2.1 GET UP AND GO!

Unit 2 | 15

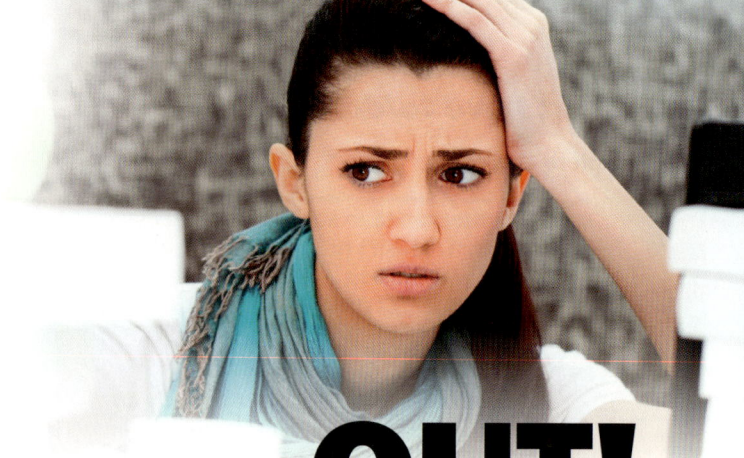

Stressed OUT!

Listening: Take it easy!

1. Look at the girl in the picture above. How does she feel? What are some reasons she might feel that way?

2. Listen to a radio interview with a psychologist, Dr. Hilary Jamieson, talking about teenage stress. What are the three essential tips Dr. Jamieson gives?

3. Listen again. Circle the things Dr. Jamieson suggests.
   1. Make a schedule and keep to it.
   2. Go out with your friends and have a good time.
   3. Participate in a sport.
   4. Listen to music or watch TV.
   5. Talk to someone.
   6. Breathe deeply and try to relax.

Vocabulary: Emotions

4. Match the words with the correct pictures. Then listen and check your answers.
   1. ___ embarrassed
   2. ___ awful
   3. ___ proud
   4. ___ terrified
   5. ___ stressed out
   6. ___ exhausted
   7. ___ wonderful

5. Think of a time when you or someone you know felt one of the emotions in Exercise 4. Tell your partner about it.

> I felt stressed out last week. I had a lot of homework, and my mother was mad at me, too.

> Really? I felt wonderful last week. This week I feel exhausted because . . .

Grammar: Modals of obligation – *should*, *ought to*, *had better*

6. Complete the chart.

Should, ought to, *and* had better *have similar meanings. Use them to say what is a good or right thing to do.*		
Use should *and* shouldn't *for a personal opinion.*	Use ought to *and* ought not *to when you're talking about duty or the law.*	Use had better *and* had better not *to give very strong advice.*
You **should try** to work out more.	I _____ **call** the police about the car accident.	You **had better start** studying for your test now.
He _____ **get** so stressed out.	You **ought not to enter** that part of the airport.	You _____ **be** late for the test.

> Check your answers: Grammar reference, p. 107

7. Choose the correct answers.

1. If you're sick, you **had better / had better not** see a doctor.
2. My brother doesn't know what he **should / shouldn't** do about college.
3. You **ought / ought not** to park your car here. It's illegal.
4. We **should / shouldn't** go see a movie when we have so much work to do.
5. She **ought / ought not** to be more careful when she's cooking. She always burns herself.
6. I **had better / had better not** bother my father right now. He's really busy.

8. Use the words in parentheses to write + (affirmative) or – (negative) sentences.

1. It's <u>not easy to find</u> enough time to study sometimes. (– / easy / to find)
2. It's _____ some exercise every day. (+ / important / to get)
3. It's _____ with friends on the weekend. (+ / relaxing / to hang out)
4. It's _____ too many after-school activities. (– / smart / to do)
5. It's _____ all your time studying. (– / fun / to spend)
6. It's _____ your arms and legs when you're taking a test. (+ / helpful / to stretch)

> **It's + adjective + infinitive**
> Use It's + adjective + infinitive to give your opinion.
> **It's important to talk** to others when you're stressed.
> **It's not helpful to think** negative thoughts.

> **Get it RIGHT!**
> Use *to* after *ought*.
> You **ought to call** the police.
>
> Don't use *to* after *should* or *had better*.
> You **should drink** less coffee.
> You **had better leave** for school now.

Speaking: Do I have to?

9. Read the situations below. Check (✓) the ones you have experienced.

- ☐ I'm really tired, but I have so much homework to do!
- ☐ I really want to get on the school team this year, but I need to practice hard!
- ☐ My parents got mad at me last night because I came home really late.
- ☐ I argued with my best friend, and now he/she won't respond to my texts.

10. YOUR TURN Work with a partner. Take turns reading each of the situations in Exercise 9 and giving advice.

> *My parents got mad at me last night because I came home really late.*

> *You should call them next time and tell them where you are.*

> Workbook, pp. 10–11

Best Friends FOREVER

Conversation: What makes a good friend?

 1. **REAL TALK** Watch or listen to the teenagers. Check (✓) the things they say.

☐ buys good birthday presents	☐ is kind and helpful	☐ likes to go out on the weekend
☐ does all the same activities	☐ helps with decisions	☐ likes to talk on the phone
☐ just has to be there	☐ helps with homework	☐ listens
		☐ is honest

2. What do you think makes a good friend? What would you add to the list above?

 3. Listen to Olivia ask Laura about a school project. Complete the conversation.

USEFUL LANGUAGE: Helping someone to do something

- I'm not very good at things like that.
- It's really pretty simple.
- ✓ I'm not sure how to do it.
- Let me show you.
- I'll give you a hand if you like.

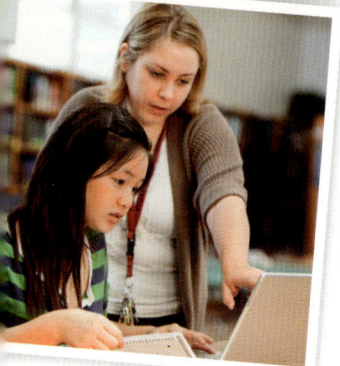

Olivia: Hey, Laura. Can I ask you something?
Laura: Yeah, sure. What's up?
Olivia: It's this science project. 1 _I'm not sure how to do it._
Laura: Mr. Brown's really strict about it. He put instructions on the school intranet.
Olivia: Oh! I should look, then. Do you know how to get access to the intranet?
Laura: Yes, you have to type in your password. 2 _____ See? Type it like this, and click "Submit."
Olivia: Thanks. That's really nice of you!
Laura: 3 _____ You shouldn't have any problems with it. Just make sure you format it correctly.
Olivia: Oh, no! 4 _____
Laura: Don't worry. 5 _____
Olivia: Great! Thanks a lot.

4. Practice the conversation with a partner.

5. **YOUR TURN** Work with a partner. Take turns asking for and giving help. Use the following ideas or your own ideas.

Situation 1: You want to download a video, but you don't know how.
Possible steps: Find the video; click on the "Download" button; name the video and click "Save."

Situation 2: You can't find any material for a school project.
Possible steps: Find online sources; go to the library; find people to interview.

Stories of STRESS

STUDYING HARD?
STRESSED OUT?
TOO MUCH TO DO?

Tell us your story. What was the problem and how did you feel? How did you solve it and what's your advice to students with similar problems? We publish the best stories on our website!

MIKE, SAN DIEGO, CA: I have a story to tell about a time last month when I had too much to do. And I think I have some great advice. The problem was that I had a big history test and besides that, I had a lot of other projects to do, too. I was super stressed out. I was studying hard one Saturday afternoon, for about three hours straight. Then a friend came over. He helped me solve the problem. He said, "Take a little time off!" We had a snack, and then we took my dog for a walk. Then I started studying again. What happened? I was relaxed, I had more energy, and I was able to study for the rest of the day. Best of all, I got an A on the test! My advice: You have to take a break sometimes.

Reading to write: Solving a problem

○ *Focus on* **CONTENT**
When you're writing about a solution to a problem, it's necessary to tell the reader what the problem is. Then tell the reader your solution to the problem in clear steps. You can write these steps in order of their importance. Start with the most important step.

6. Read Mike's blog post. Answer the questions.

1. What was the problem?
2. How did Mike feel?
3. How did he solve it?
4. What is Mike's advice to other students?

○ *Focus on* **LANGUAGE**
Quantifiers: *a few, a little, too many, too much*
- Use *a few* and *a little* to talk about a small amount or number. Use *a few* with plural countable nouns, and *a little* with uncountable nouns.
  - We played a video game for **a few** minutes.
  - I decided to take **a little** time off.
- Use *too many* and *too much* to talk about things that are "more than is good for the situation."
  - I had **too many** other projects to do.
  - He said I was studying **too much**.

Writing: A blog post

◻ **PLAN**
Think about a time you were stressed out or had too much to do. What was the problem? How did you feel and how did you solve it? What's your advice to other students who have the same problem?

◻ **WRITE**
Write your blog post. Use your notes from Exercise 6 and Mike's story to help you. Write 80–100 words.

◻ **CHECK**
Check your writing. Can you answer "yes" to these questions?
- Did you say what the problem is?
- Did you give a solution in clear steps?
- Did you state the steps to the solution in order of importance?

7. Complete the sentences with *a few, a little, too many,* and *too much*.

1. David only has _____ books in his backpack. It isn't heavy.
2. I brought _____ food for lunch today. Would you like half of this sandwich?
3. There were _____ people in line for the movie, so we left without seeing it.
4. I can go to bed early because I only have _____ homework today.

Ten Things I Bet You Didn't Know About...
CHEERLEADING

1. Cheerleading is more than 100 years old! The first cheerleading team came out to support the University of Minnesota football team in November 1889.

2. Today, more than 97 percent of all cheerleaders are female, but 100 years ago they were all male.

3. Now, on college or university cheerleading squads in the United States, half of the members are male.

4. Cheerleading is very competitive, and it's difficult to make most squads. The successful candidates often have to spend their summers training together for the next season.

5. Football is the main sport associated with cheerleading, but there are also cheerleaders for basketball, soccer, baseball, and even wrestling!

6. Cheerleading is a great way to fight stress. It also helps you feel good and make friends!

7. Cheerleading won't hurt your grades! It's important to have discipline – as an athlete and as a student. Cheerleading helps with this.

8. Cheerleading is hard physical work. Cheerleaders train hard – as hard as the football players they support – and they have to be very fit. Ninety-eight percent of female cheerleaders are also gymnasts.

9. Cheerleading can be dangerous. Many cheerleaders injure their arms and legs. Some also injure their backs and heads.

10. Cheerleading started in the United States and is still very much an American activity, but there are organized cheerleaders in more than 31 countries around the world.

Culture: Cheerleading

1. **Look at the photos and answer the questions.**
   1. Where are the people? What are they doing?
   2. What do you know about cheerleading? Make a list.

 2. **Read and listen to the article. Does it mention any of the facts you wrote in Exercise 1?**

3. **Read the article again. Are the sentences below true (*T*) or false (*F*)?**
   1. All cheerleaders are girls. ___
   2. Cheerleaders only support football teams. ___
   3. Most cheerleaders don't do well in school. ___
   4. Cheerleading is hard work. ___
   5. Cheerleading is a very safe activity. ___
   6. Cheerleaders only exist in the United States. ___

4. **YOUR TURN Work with a partner. Ask and answer the questions.**
   1. Would you like to be a cheerleader? Why? / Why not?
   2. Why do you think cheerleading helps students' grades?
   3. What are the most popular school sports and activities in your country? Do you think these sports can help you do better in school? Why? / Why not?

DID YOU KNOW...?
There are more than 4 million cheerleaders in the world.

BE CURIOUS Find out about an Irish dance champion. How is Irish dance different from dance in your country? (Workbook, p. 75)

Discovery EDUCATION
2.3 IRISH DANCING

UNIT 2 REVIEW

Vocabulary

1. Complete the sentences.

| get enough sleep | do something creative |
| time for myself | help around the house |

1. I need to be alone sometimes. I need _____.
2. My mom sometimes asks me to _____. I hate cleaning the bathroom!
3. I'm always tired because I don't _____.
4. I want to be a designer or an artist because I want to _____.

2. Match the sentences.

1. I just fell down in the hall outside of class. ___
2. I just ran five kilometers! ___
3. I have four big tests this week. ___
4. My sister's volleyball team just won a big game. ___

a. I'm proud of them.
b. I'm really stressed out.
c. I'm exhausted.
d. I'm so embarrassed!

Grammar

3. Write sentences with should (✓) or shouldn't (✗).

1. You / play computer games in the evening (✗)
   You shouldn't play computer games in the evening.
2. Teenagers / help their families on the weekends (✓)
   _____
3. You / use your cell phone before bed (✗)
   _____
4. My sister is stressed out. She / talk to a friend (✓)
   _____
5. Teenagers / eat healthy food whenever they can (✓)
   _____
6. I / watch TV right now (✗)
   _____

4. Fill in the blanks with the correct form of *have to*.

1. You *have to* be quiet in the library.
2. The basketball game is free. We _____ pay for tickets.
3. Julio wears jeans and T-shirts to school. He _____ wear a uniform.
4. Students _____ eat in the cafeteria. They are allowed to leave the school for lunch.
5. Mike _____ study for his math test tonight. He can't go out.

Useful language

5. Complete the conversation.

| Let me show you. | I'm not very good at things like that. | I'm not sure how to do it. |

Kate: Oh, no.
Pete: Are you OK? What do you need?
Kate: I'm just stressed out about my science homework. ¹_____ I need some coffee, I think.
Pete: Don't drink coffee now. Make some herbal tea.
Kate: Make herbal tea? ²_____
Pete: Look. ³_____ It's easy.
Kate: It is?
Pete: Yes. Boil some water and pour it over a tea bag. Like this.
Kate: That *was* easy. Hey, this tea is good!

PROGRESS CHECK: Now I can . . .

☐ discuss my priorities.
☐ express obligation and prohibition.
☐ write a blog post to help someone solve a problem.
☐ make strong recommendations.
☐ offer help to someone.
☐ discuss a sport or cultural activity.

3 ART All Around Us

BE CURIOUS

- Original Art
- Have you ever been to a concert?
- A World of Music
- Art in Perspective

1. Describe what you see in this picture.
2. What is your opinion of this kind of art?
3. In what ways is this kind of art different from art you see in museums?

UNIT CONTENTS

Vocabulary Visual arts; musical instruments
Grammar Verb + -ing form (gerund) review; -ing forms (gerunds) as subjects; verbs + prepositions + -ing forms
Listening Leo the one-man band

Vocabulary: Visual arts

1. Match the people, places, and things with the correct pictures.

1. _g_ comics
2. ___ living statue
3. ___ digital art
4. ___ sculpture
5. ___ drawing
6. ___ mural
7. ___ exhibition
8. ___ pottery
9. ___ graffiti
10. ___ portrait painter

 2. Listen, check, and repeat.

3. Put the words from Exercise 1 in the correct categories.

   a. Works of art: _____

   b. Place to see art: _____

   c. A performer or an artist: _____

Speaking: Look again

4. **YOUR TURN** Put the words from Exercise 1 in new categories.

Cool	Educational	Strange

5. Work with a partner. Share your opinions about kinds of art.

   I like looking at comics. They're really cool.

 Workbook, p. 16

Reading Everyone's an Artist; Fantastic Free Concert; A Temporary Desert City
Conversation Inviting a friend and arranging to meet
Writing A blog post about a concert

Unit 3 | 23

WHAT is ART?

EVERYONE'S AN ARTIST

You draw, you paint portraits, you do sculptures, or you're a living statue. It doesn't matter — everyone's an artist!

THE CASE FOR We look at the *Mona Lisa* or a Picasso painting, and we say, "That's art." But what about the amazing graffiti on your street? What about photographs posted online by our friends? What about your school art exhibition? You worked hard, and it's great. So, is that art? To me, art is anything that's creative. Of course, I like going to famous museums. But I also like drawing portraits of my friends. I'm not very good, but I'm creative. I'm passionate about it, and my friends like it. Most of all, I like it!

Josh, age 15, San Diego, California

THE CASE AGAINST I like visiting art museums, too. Why? Because I like looking at good art. Art is not the drawings of four-year-old children. It isn't painting your body crazy colors and standing in the street. And it certainly isn't graffiti. Some people say, "If it's creative and cool, it's art." I don't agree. Art is the result of hard work and study. My aunt is an artist. She went to art school for six years. She doesn't make much money, but sometimes her sculptures are in exhibitions. Her art is great. Art is very hard, and not many people can do it well.

Kayla, age 16, Charlotte, North Carolina

WHAT IS ART? WHAT'S YOUR OPINION?

DID YOU KNOW...?
The British graffiti artist Banksy sold a piece of graffiti for $1.8 million.

Reading: An online debate

1. **Work with a partner. Ask and answer the questions.**
   1. Do you ever see art that you think is terrible? Why do you think it's bad?
   2. What makes a person an artist?
   3. Do you have friends or family members who are artists?

2. **Read and listen to the debate. How do Josh and Kayla define "art"?**

3. **Read the debate again. Are the statements true (*T*) or false (*F*)?**
   1. Josh thinks that graffiti is art. ___
   2. Kayla enjoys going to art museums. ___
   3. To Josh, photographs posted online aren't examples of art. ___
   4. Kayla believes that art is anything that is creative and fun. ___
   5. Josh and his friends like the portraits he draws. ___
   6. Kayla thinks that good art is easy. ___

4. **YOUR TURN** **Work with a partner. Ask and answer the questions.**
   1. What's your opinion in the art debate? Is everyone an artist?
   2. What kind of background or education do you think an artist should have?
   3. Is graffiti art? If so, is all graffiti art or only some graffiti?
   4. Are pictures you take with your cell phone and then post online art? Why or why not?

   > I think graffiti is sometimes good art. There's an artist in my neighborhood who . . .

Grammar: Verb + -ing form (gerund) review

5. Complete the chart.

We can use the -ing form of a verb after some verbs to talk about things we like or don't like.

Common verbs followed by -ing forms: like, love, hate, enjoy, (not) mind

	-ing form		
I **love**	_drawing_	(draw)	pictures in my free time.
Mark **enjoys**	_____	(look)	at sculptures.
My sister **hates**	_____	(help)	around the house.
Some people **don't like**	_____	(go)	to museums.

> Check your answers: Grammar reference, p. 108

Get it RIGHT!
Use the -ing form after *enjoy*.
I **enjoy going** to art exhibitions. NOT:
I **enjoy to go** to art exhibitions.

Say it RIGHT!
When you like or don't like something strongly, use *love* or *hate* and put extra stress on that verb. Listen and repeat the sentences.
I **love** painting. I **hate** shopping.

6. Complete the sentences with the correct forms of the verbs.

1. My friends ___love going___ (love / go) to the movies on the weekends.
2. I _____ (not mind / spend) time at art exhibits, but not more than two hours at a time.
3. Oscar _____ (enjoy / paint) murals, but not portraits.
4. My father _____ (not like / shop) for clothes. He never goes to the mall.
5. Some of my friends _____ (hate / read) comics, but I enjoy it a lot.
6. I _____ (like / study) in the library, not alone at home.

7. Circle the correct answers. Then complete the sentences.

| get up | ✓ live | paint | take |
| go | meet | sleep | work out |

My name is Jill, and I'm a professional artist. I live in Los Angeles. I ¹**like / don't like** ___living___ here because Los Angeles is full of open-minded, creative people. Mornings are my favorite time of the day, and I ²**love / hate** _____ early. Because it's sunny but not hot outside, I really ³**hate / like** _____ a long walk before I start work. It's great exercise. I usually paint for a few hours, maybe from 9:00 to 12:00, and then I have lunch. I ⁴**don't enjoy / enjoy** _____ friends for lunch. We usually make lunch together. After lunch, I ⁵**like / don't mind** _____ for about 30 minutes. Then I go back to work. I ⁶**finish / keep** _____ in the evening, about 7:00 or 8:00 p.m. I ⁷**love / don't love** _____ at the gym or going running on the beach. And, I ⁸**like / hate** _____ to bed late. I'm usually asleep by 9:00 or 10:00. It's a busy life, but I'm happy.

Speaking: I love shopping!

8. YOUR TURN Work with a partner. Tell your partner about the things you like and don't like doing.

Like	Don't like
don't mind, enjoy, like, love	don't enjoy, don't like, hate

> *I like staying up late at night. I don't enjoy getting up early!*

BE CURIOUS — Find out about Aboriginal paintings in Australia. Do they represent the land, water, or air? (Workbook, p. 76)

3.1 ORIGINAL ART

Workbook, pp. 16–17

Unit 3 | 25

MUSIC Everywhere!

Listening: Leo the one-man band

1. What do you imagine a one-man band is? Where do you think he performs?

2. Listen to Marcia, a journalist, interviewing Leo. Check your answers in Exercise 1.

3. Listen again. Answer the questions.
   1. Where are Marcia and Leo?
   2. Where are two places that Leo plays music?
   3. Which of Leo's instruments is new?
   4. How long did Leo play on the day of the interview?
   5. What types of music does he like playing?
   6. Which instruments does he not know how to play?

Vocabulary: Musical instruments

4. Match the words with the correct pictures. Then listen and check your answers.

   1. ___ guitar
   2. ___ drums
   3. ___ flute
   4. ___ saxophone
   5. ___ violin
   6. ___ keyboard
   7. ___ harmonica
   8. ___ piano
   9. ___ trumpet
   10. ___ cello

5. **YOUR TURN** Work with a partner. Ask and answer the questions.
   1. What instruments can you play? How long did it take to learn to play them?
   2. What kind of music do you enjoy listening to?
   3. Where can you go in your town to listen to musicians playing in the street?

Grammar: -ing forms (gerunds) as subjects

6. Complete the chart.

> You can use the -ing form as the subject of a sentence.
>
> _Playing_ (play) several instruments at once takes a lot of energy.
> _____ (sing) at the same time I play instruments is hard.
> _____ (be) here at the festival is really special to me.
>
> For the negative, use not before the -ing form.
>
> **Not enjoying** some kinds of music is normal. You don't have to like everything.

> Check your answers: Grammar reference, p. 108

7. Match the phrases to make sentences.

1. Learning ___
2. Running ___
3. Singing ___
4. Reading ___
5. Drinking ___
6. Eating ___

a. in a heavy metal band can be hard on your voice.
b. lots of books is a good way to improve your writing skills.
c. a new instrument takes a lot of practice.
d. a lot of fresh fruit and vegetables is good for you.
e. in a marathon requires a lot of athletic ability.
f. soda every day is bad for your teeth.

8. Rewrite the sentences.

1. It's difficult to play three instruments at the same time.

    Playing three instruments at the same time is difficult.

2. It's important to practice for at least an hour a day.

    _____

3. It's not a good idea to take a test on an empty stomach.

    _____

4. It's exciting to have your art in an exhibit.

    _____

5. It isn't cheap to take private music lessons every week.

    _____

6. It's fun to be able to play an instrument well.

    _____

> ➔ *Spell it* **RIGHT!**
>
> **Spelling the -ing forms:**
> fix – fix**ing**   work – work**ing**
> If the verb ends in a silent -e, remove the -e and add -ing.
> live – liv**ing**   dance – danc**ing**
> If a verb ends in a vowel + a consonant, double the consonant.
> hug – hu**gg**ing   run – ru**nn**ing

Speaking: Are you open-minded about music?

9. YOUR TURN Do you agree or disagree with the statements below?

1. I enjoy listening to all kinds of music.
2. Calling some kinds of music "bad" isn't right. If people like it, it's good music for them.
3. Listening to my friends' music is fun, even if it's not my style.
4. I like discovering new bands or singers.

> **Verbs + prepositions + -ing forms (gerunds)**
>
> You can use the -ing form after some verbs and prepositions.
>
> I want to **apologize for missing** your art exhibition.
>
> Do you **feel like going** to a movie tonight?
>
> This year, Allison needs to **concentrate on studying**, not **hanging out** with her friends.

10. Discuss your answers to Exercise 9 with a partner. Do you agree on everything? Then tell another pair about your partner's answers.

> *Kim likes finding new bands, but she doesn't like all kinds of music. Her sister listens to pop music, and Kim hates that!*

REAL TALK 3.2 HAVE YOU EVER BEEN TO A CONCERT?

Ready to ROCK?

Conversation: Have you ever been to a concert?

1. **REAL TALK** Watch or listen to the teenagers. Check (✓) the sentences you hear.

   ☐ I've played in some.
   ☐ I prefer going to the cinema (movies).
   ☐ Concert tickets are cheaper than movie tickets.
   ☐ I've been to seven or eight concerts.
   ☐ I love listening to music with a lot of people around.
   ☐ Live music is the best!

2. **YOUR TURN** Have you ever been to a concert? Who did you see? What were the good things and the bad things about the concert?

3. Listen to Mia and Austin talking about a concert. Complete the conversation.

   USEFUL LANGUAGE: Inviting a friend and arranging to meet

   ✓ How about going . . . ?   That's a good idea.   Should I ask . . . to take us?
   Sounds good.   What time should we meet?

   Mia: Hey Austin! ¹ _How about going_ to a concert tomorrow?
   Austin: Yeah, why not? Who's playing?
   Mia: A pop rock band called The Sweets. They're a new band. I got free tickets.
   Austin: Sure. ² _____ Where are they playing?
   Mia: The Apollo Club, on Washington Street.
   Austin: OK. ³ _____
   Mia: It starts at 8:30. I think we should go together. How about meeting at my house at 7:30?
   Austin: OK. ⁴ _____
   Mia: Yeah! ⁵ _____ Then maybe my mom could pick us up when it's finished.
   Austin: OK. See you tomorrow, then.

4. Practice the conversation with a partner.

5. **YOUR TURN** Work with a partner. Take turns inviting your friend and arranging to meet. Use the ideas below or your own ideas. Use the conversation in Exercise 3 as a model.

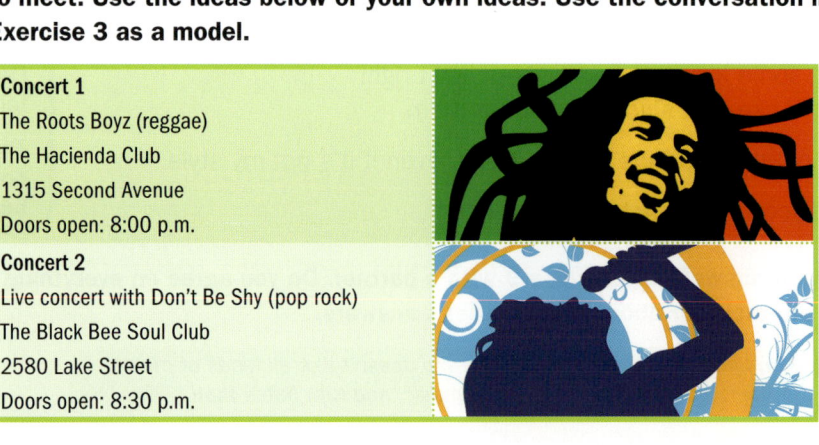

Concert 1
The Roots Boyz (reggae)
The Hacienda Club
1315 Second Avenue
Doors open: 8:00 p.m.

Concert 2
Live concert with Don't Be Shy (pop rock)
The Black Bee Soul Club
2580 Lake Street
Doors open: 8:30 p.m.

FANTASTIC FREE CONCERT

I just came back from a fantastic free concert. It was in a park about three kilometers from my house, and there was a great atmosphere. There were hundreds of young people there, dancing and enjoying themselves. There were about five bands, but the best one was Hurricane. They're from Cleveland, Ohio, and they play a mixture of lots of different styles, from folk and rock to reggae and blues. I loved listening to the singer (Layla Smith). She has a really amazing voice, and the guitarists and drummer played together really well. They just recorded a CD, and I want to get it! Seeing them play live was great. If you get the chance to see them, go for it! ☺

–Alba

Reading to write: A blog post about a concert

6. **Look at the picture and read Alba's blog about a concert. Did she enjoy it?**

    Focus on **CONTENT**
   When you write about a concert, you can include this information:
   - Where it was
   - The audience
   - Who played
   - The styles of music
   - Information about the band(s)
   - Why you liked or didn't like the music

7. **Read Alba's blog again. Make notes on the items in the Focus on Content box.**

   Focus on **LANGUAGE**
   Singular and plural forms of *be*
   There **was** a great atmosphere. The best band **was** Hurricane. They (the band members) **are** from Cleveland, Ohio.

8. **Find more examples of singular and plural forms of *be* in the blog post.**

9. **Complete the sentences with the present or past form of the verb *be*.**

   1. In my opinion, they ___are___ the best rock band on the planet!
   2. There _____ a lot of people at the concert last night, from age 15 to 50.
   3. Most of the people here at the concert tonight _____ obviously big fans of the group, singing every song!
   4. The audience at last night's show _____ tiny, so there _____ (not) a very good atmosphere.
   5. The band _____ (not) famous right now, but I think they will be soon.
   6. All the musicians _____ very professional, but the music _____ (not) usually very exciting.

Writing: A blog post about a concert

PLAN
Plan a blog post about a concert you've been to. Use the list in the Focus on Content box and make notes.

WRITE
Write your blog post. Use your notes from Exercise 7 to help you. Write about 120 words.

CHECK
Can you say "yes" to these questions?
- Is the information from the Focus on Content box in your writing?
- Did you get all the verbs in the correct singular or plural forms?

A Temporary DESERT CITY

So, some friends have just given you tickets to the Burning Man festival, but you're not sure what to expect. Read these frequently asked questions to find out more:

1 _____ It's a community arts festival. It takes place every year for a week at the end of August in the Black Rock Desert in Nevada, in the US. More than 60,000 people went last year. Volunteers create a community in the desert called Black Rock City. They build everything themselves. The city is in the shape of a giant semi-circle.

2 _____ No, it started in San Francisco, California, in 1986, next to the Golden Gate Bridge. It moved to the desert five years later.

3 _____ Because fire is an important theme of the festival. People build an enormous wooden statue of a person, more than 30 meters tall, and burn it during the festival. They also build and burn lots of other things. Last year, they had an enormous mechanical octopus!

4 _____ They dress up in crazy costumes. They also wear goggles and masks, which protect them from breathing the desert's dust. Besides that, there are a lot of other fun activities. There is usually a balloon chain of 450 different balloons. The chain is one kilometer long and it lights up the sky.

5 _____ When the festival ends, people must take everything away with them and leave the desert exactly as it was before the festival started. The organizers worry about damaging the environment.

6 _____ It's unusual because there aren't any famous bands or celebrities. Hanging out together as a community is what it's all about – everyone is on the same level.

Culture: The Burning Man festival

1. **Look at the picture of a festival in the US. What do you think people do there?**

2. **Read and listen to the article. Check your answer in Exercise 1.**

3. **Read the article again. Match the questions (a–f) to the answers (1–6) in the article.**

   a. What else do people do at the festival?
   b. Has the festival always taken place there?
   c. What happens after the festival?
   d. What is the Burning Man festival?
   e. How is it different from other festivals?
   f. Why is it called the Burning Man festival?

4. **YOUR TURN Work with a partner. Ask and answer the questions.**

   1. Would you like to go to a festival like Burning Man? Why? / Why not?
   2. Does your school or town have its own festival? What type of festival is it? What can you do there?

DID YOU KNOW...?
Every August, Black Rock City becomes the third largest city in Nevada – but then it disappears in September!

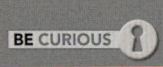

Find out about three different kinds of music. What three countries do the kinds of music come from? (Workbook, p. 77)

3.3 A WORLD OF MUSIC

UNIT 3 REVIEW

Vocabulary

1. **Complete the sentences.**

comics	exhibition	living statue
✓ graffiti	sculptures	mural

   1. There's some new ____graffiti____ on the wall outside the library.
   2. I love _____ that are made of stone or metal.
   3. There's an amazing _____ in the cafeteria at school. It covers one long wall.
   4. My brother is a big fan of superhero _____. He buys a lot of them.
   5. I went to an _____ of modern paintings last weekend.
   6. One of my friends makes a little money on weekends as a _____. He paints his body silver and wears all silver clothes.

Grammar

2. **Write sentences with the simple present and the -ing form of the verb.**

   1. my aunt / like / play / the guitar
      _____My aunt likes playing the guitar._____
   2. Mark and David / hate / sing / in music class
      _____
   3. the president of the company / not mind / walk / to work
      _____
   4. I / love / practice / the piano
      _____
   5. the artist / enjoy / paint / by the river
      _____
   6. the festival's participants / not like / sit / in the rain
      _____

3. **Complete the sentences.**

   1. My friends and I talk about ____making____ a music video, but we never do it. (make)
   2. _____ a lot is important if you want to become a good musician. (practice)
   3. _____ in big festivals is fun, but not everyone likes it. (participate)
   4. Did you decide against _____ to play the saxophone? (learn)
   5. In my opinion, _____ graffiti on walls is a terrible thing to do. (paint)
   6. My father isn't thinking about _____ abroad this year. (travel)

Useful language

4. **Complete the conversation.**

What time	✓ going	Should I	good idea	Sure

   Kyle: Hey Jenna. How about ¹ ____going____ to a street festival with me?

   Jenna: A street festival? Where?

   Kyle: Downtown. There will be lots of people playing music on the street for free. There's going to be lots of food there, too. I really want to go.

   Jenna: ² _____. Sounds great! ³ _____ should we meet?

   Kyle: It's from 12:00 p.m. to midnight. How about going for lunch, around 1:00?

   Jenna: That's good. ⁴ _____ ask my mom to take us?

   Kyle: That's a ⁵ _____ ! She doesn't mind taking us, does she?

   Jenna: No, I don't think so. She might want to see the festival, too.

   Kyle: Perfect. See you at 1:00, then?

   Jenna: Yes. See you then!

PROGRESS CHECK: Now I can . . .

- ☐ talk about visual arts.
- ☐ express my likes and dislikes.
- ☐ discuss music.
- ☐ make invitations and arrangements.
- ☐ write about a concert that I've been to.
- ☐ discuss a cultural event.

CLIL PROJECT

3.4 ART IN PERSPECTIVE, p. 117

4 Sign Me UP!

Discovery EDUCATION

BE CURIOUS

- The Age of Discovery
- What's the most exciting thing you've ever done?
- Fun in Australia

1. Describe what you see in this picture.
2. How does this picture make you feel?
3. Do you think this kind of sport would be fun?

UNIT CONTENTS

Vocabulary Adventure travel; phrasal verbs related to travel
Grammar Present perfect with *already*, *yet*, *just*, and *yes/no* questions; present perfect with *for*, *since*, and *How long . . . ?*
Listening Adventure travel experiences

Vocabulary: Adventure travel

1. **Match the phrases with the correct pictures.**

   1. _c_ go backpacking
   2. ___ go on a cruise
   3. ___ go ballooning
   4. ___ go mountain biking
   5. ___ go rafting
   6. ___ go on a safari
   7. ___ go sailing
   8. ___ go to summer camp
   9. ___ go rock climbing

2. **Listen, check, and repeat.**

3. **Which of the activities in Exercise 1 involve:**
   a. participating in a sport?
   b. sleeping away from home?
   c. using some kind of transportation?

> **Get it RIGHT!**
> We use *go* before activities that end in *-ing*.
> You can **go rafting** near here. NOT:
> You can **do rafting** around here.

Speaking: I'm in!

4. **YOUR TURN** Work in groups of three or four. Ask and answer the questions and write the results.

   How many students . . .
   a. would like to go rafting?
   b. have gone to a summer camp?
   c. would definitely not want to go rock climbing?
   d. have been on a cruise?
   e. are afraid of going ballooning?
   f. have sailed in a small sailboat?

5. **Tell your results to the class. Make a class chart.**

   > Twelve people in the class would enjoy going on a cruise.

   > Twelve? I have fifteen. Fifteen people would enjoy going on a cruise.

Workbook, p. 22

Reading Anchors Aweigh!; Tipping help!; Five Good Reasons to Visit New Zealand
Conversation Signing up for an adventure activity
Writing An email comparing different customs

Unit 4 | 33

Take to THE WAVES

ANCHORS AWEIGH!

"I've never sailed before. This is my first time, and it's an amazing feeling." Sandra, 16, is on the *Stavros S. Niarchos*, a 70-meter sailing ship, with 40 other young sailors. The *Stavros* is an exact copy of the ships that pirates sailed two or three hundred years ago. It belongs to the Tall Ships Youth Trust. The Trust offers sailing trips at realistic prices for teenagers and young adults. Every year, thousands of young people get their first taste of the sea thanks to the Trust. Up to 70 percent of them are disabled or disadvantaged. For everyone, it's a once-in-a-lifetime experience.

Sandra is on a trip from the Azores, in the North Atlantic, to Spain. The trip lasts a week, and they have already been at sea for three days. "We do everything," she explained. "We sail the ship, we cook, we clean, and we take turns keeping watch at night. I never knew there was so much work on a ship!"

Her friend, Emma, 15, has never been on a boat before either. "I haven't adjusted to life at sea yet. It's very different from life on land!"

"We've done some cool stuff," says James, 17. "My favorite part is climbing the mast. It's 30 meters tall! The views are incredible," said James. "We've just seen dolphins and turtles for the first time. We haven't seen any whales yet, but the captain says there are whales near the Spanish coast. This is definitely the best thing I've ever done!"

If you want to know more about the Tall Ships Youth Trust, visit their website at tallships.org.

Reading: An online article

1. Look at the title and the pictures. What kind of trip is it? Are the teenagers working, having fun, or both?

2. Read and listen to the article. Check your answers in Exercise 1.

3. Read the article again. What does each of the numbers refer to?

   1. 70: _____length of the ship in meters_____ ; _____

   2. 40: _____

   3. two or three hundred: _____

   4. thousands: _____

   5. 15: _____

   6. 30: _____

DID YOU KNOW...?
Over 95,000 people have sailed 1.8 million nautical miles with the Tall Ships Youth Trust.

4. **YOUR TURN** Work with a partner. Ask and answer the questions.

   1. What do you think you can learn on a sailing trip like this?

   2. What are two reasons you would enjoy sailing on a boat like this? What are two reasons you wouldn't enjoy it?

   > *I think you can learn about yourself on a trip like this.*

   > *What do you mean?*

Grammar: Present perfect with *already*, *yet*, and *just*

5. Complete the chart.

We can use *already* in affirmative sentences in the present perfect.	
I**'ve already been** at sea for four days.	He _____ _____ **cooked** three meals for the others on the ship.
We can use *yet* in negative sentences in the present perfect.	
They **haven't found** turtles **yet**.	My sister _____ **visited** the ship _____.
Use *just* with the present perfect to say that something happened very recently.	
We**'ve just seen** dolphins.	I _____ _____ **boarded** the ship.

> Check your answers: Grammar reference, p. 109

6. Look at the chart. Complete the sentences with *already*, *yet*, or *just*.

1. I'm sorry, but the ship has ___already___ left. It left about three hours ago.
2. We haven't sailed alone _____.
3. I've _____ seen a whale! Look! Over there!
4. The boat hasn't left the port _____.
5. She's _____ been on three trips this year.
6. I've _____ finished lunch. It was delicious.

Present perfect questions

We can use *yet* in present perfect questions to ask if something has happened before now.

Have you seen any whales **yet**?	Yes, I have. / No, I haven't.
Has the ship arrived in Spain **yet**?	Yes, it has. / No, it hasn't.

7. Complete the conversation with the present perfect. Then listen and check.

A: Are you ready for the trip?

B: Well, sort of. ¹ _I haven't packed everything yet_ (I / not pack / everything / yet), but I know what I want to take.

A: Did you print your tickets?

B: No, not yet. ² _____ (Sam / not send / them / yet).

A: ³ _____ (you / do / anything / yet)?

B: Yes! ⁴ _____ (I / already / pack / my clothes).

A: What about your cell phone?

B: ⁵ _____ (I / just / put / my charger / in my bag), but I'm not going to take my tablet. There's no Internet connection on the ship.

A: And your passport?

B: Yes, don't worry, Mom! ⁶ _____ (I / already / check / that). It's in my purse.

Speaking: New experiences

8. YOUR TURN Work with a partner. Look at the activities, and interview each other. Ask your partner five questions using *already*, *yet*, and *just* about what he or she has done so far this year.

burn any food	send a text message to the wrong person
climb in a window	stay up all night
hurt yourself or break a bone	take a hike
lose your keys	wear socks that don't match

> Have you lost your keys yet this year?
>
> Yes, I have. / No, I haven't.

BE CURIOUS Find out about Ferdinand Magellan. Why were Europeans interested in traveling to Asia? (Workbook, p. 78)

Discovery EDUCATION

4.1 THE AGE OF DISCOVERY

Fun? It was INCREDIBLE!

Listening: Adventure travel experiences

1. **Look at the pictures of teenagers on vacation in Rocky Mountain National Park, in Colorado. Do their activities look like fun to you?**

2. **Listen to three short conversations with some of the teenagers in the pictures. Which sentence best summarizes how they feel about the trip?**
   a. They all love everything about their trips.
   b. They think Rocky Mountain National Park is really boring.
   c. They like some of the things they're doing more than other things.

3. **Listen again. Answer the questions.**
   1. How long has Lily been at the national park? What has she just finished doing?
   2. Does Evan love backpacking? Where did he go yesterday afternoon?
   3. How long has Katie been a rock climber? Which of Katie's family members is with her?

Vocabulary: Phrasal verbs related to travel

4. **Complete the sentences with the correct phrasal verbs. Then listen and check your answers.**

✓ come back	look around	make sure
find out	look forward to	take off
give up	look out	

   1. I really, really want to _____come back_____ here!
   2. _____ – that wall is going to fall down any minute!
   3. You played a good game, and I can't possibly beat you. I _____.
   4. Fasten your seat belts. The plane is about to _____.
   5. I _____ going on vacation this year.
   6. I like to _____ about new trails.
   7. You need to _____ to check your equipment.
   8. Let's have lunch up there and _____ a little.

5. **YOUR TURN Work with a partner. Ask and answer the questions.**
   1. What is something you look forward to doing in the next year?
   2. What are two things you make sure to do before you go to school every day?
   3. After tourists visit your city, what is something that they want to come back and do again?
   4. Before you visit a new place, do you like to find out all about it first?
   5. When you feel tired or you want to give up, what do you do?
   6. When you go to the mall with your friends, do you know exactly what you want, or do you prefer to just go and look around for a while?

   > I look forward to going rafting. It sounds super fun!

Grammar: Present perfect with *for* and *since*

6. Complete the chart.

Use the present perfect with *for* or *since* for past actions and events continuing into the present.	
Use *for* with a period of time such as *a week, two months,* or *five years.*	
I've been here for three days.	He _____ worked at the rafting company _____ a month.
Use *since* with a specific date or time.	
They _____ been here _____ last Wednesday.	She's lived in Colorado since 2010.

> Check your answers: Grammar reference, p. 109

7. Complete the sentences with *for* or *since*.

1. She's led safari tours every month _____ last November.
2. We've been backpacking in the park _____ Friday.
3. He hasn't gone on a cruise _____ three years, but he loves them.
4. We've played football together _____ 2011.
5. I've lived in Colorado _____ four years.
6. They've looked forward to this vacation _____ a long time.

8. Complete the conversation with the correct words.

ballooning	for	✓ How	since
been	have	long	yet

Riley: ¹ _How_ long have you lived in Turkey?

Noah: Since 2008. I moved here with my family. How ² _____ have you been here?

Riley: Only ³ _____ three weeks. I'm on vacation with my aunt and uncle.

Noah: Cool. How long ⁴ _____ you been in Istanbul?

Riley: Only a few days.

Noah: Have you been to Cappadocia ⁵ _____?

Riley: No, but we're going to go there tomorrow. Have you ⁶ _____ there?

Noah: Yeah, it's fantastic. You can go ⁷ _____.

Riley: Really? That's cool!

Noah: Yeah. My family has done it once a year ⁸ _____ we moved here. I love it.

How long . . . ? and the present perfect

Use *How long* and the present perfect to ask about the duration of an action or event.

How long have you lived in San Diego? (since 2008 / for 12 years)

How long has she been on the ship? (since July / for three months)

Say it RIGHT!

When you answer questions with *How long . . . ?*, say the time words with more emphasis than the rest of the sentence. Listen and repeat the question and answer.

How long have you lived in Buenos Aires?
I've lived here for **three years**.

Speaking: I can't wait to do it again!

9. YOUR TURN Work with a partner. Choose three activities, and ask if your partner has ever done them. Then ask additional questions to continue the conversation.

fly in an airplane	go rock climbing	go to summer camp	travel to Africa
go ballooning	go sailing	travel by ship	travel to the US

> Have you ever traveled to the US?
>
> Yes, I have.
>
> How long were you there?

> Workbook, pp. 24–25

REAL TALK 4.2 WHAT'S THE MOST EXCITING THING YOU'VE EVER DONE?

No experience NEEDED!

Conversation: No experience needed!

1. **REAL TALK** Watch or listen to the teenagers. Check (✔) the things you hear.

   ☐ been on a roller coaster
   ☐ gone camping in the snow
   ☐ jumped off a tall rock
   ☐ skied on a black ski run
   ☐ gone ballooning in the desert
   ☐ gone canyoning
   ☐ played in a concert
   ☐ walked behind a waterfall

2. **YOUR TURN** What's the most exciting thing you've ever done? Tell your partner.

3. Listen to Abigail talking to Dave about a rafting trip. Complete the conversation.

   USEFUL LANGUAGE: Signing up for an adventure activity

   What do I need to bring? | How long is | ✔ Can I ask you a few things about | Is it only for
   Does the price include | Where can I sign up? | What about

   Abigail: ¹ *Can I ask you a few things about* the rafting trip?
   Dave: The Blue River one? Sure. What would you like to know?
   Abigail: Just a few things. ² _____ people who have gone rafting before?
   Dave: No, it's not. You don't need any experience. It's really easy, and we have qualified guides in each boat.
   Abigail: Great! ³ _____
   Dave: Well, you can go just the way you are now. You already have on good shoes that won't fall off, and we provide life jackets and helmets for everyone.
   Abigail: ⁴ _____ the trip down the Blue River?
   Dave: It's all day, from 9:00 to 6:00.
   Abigail: OK. ⁵ _____ food?
   Dave: Food is included in the price.
   Abigail: ⁶ _____ transportation?
   Dave: Yes. We take you to the river and drop you off back here when the trip is finished. We handle everything, so you can just enjoy the adventure.
   Abigail: It sounds really fun. ⁷ _____
   Dave: Right here!

4. Practice the conversation with a partner.

5. **YOUR TURN** Work with a partner. Take turns asking about the activities below.

Activity 1	Activity 2
Sailing in the ocean with qualified instructors.	Rock climbing on Red Mountain with qualified instructors.
We provide: life jacket, hot drinks on Belle Island	We provide: rock-climbing equipment, helmets, transportation to Red Mountain
You bring: swimsuit and towel, warm clothes	You bring: appropriate clothing for weather, good tennis shoes or rock-climbing shoes
Transportation from hotel to beach not included.	All day 10:00 to 5:00
Morning (9:00–12:00) or afternoon (3:00–6:00)	

38 | Unit 4

To: audrey@net.cup.org
From: jean-claude@net.cup.org
Subject: Tipping help!

Dear Audrey,

How are you doing? I wonder if you could help me with something. I was recently on a mountain biking trip in Europe with some Americans. When we ate in restaurants, I did what we do in France: I either left a small tip, or I didn't leave a tip at all. Not only did the Americans leave a big tip (sometimes 20 percent or more of the bill!), but they also thought I was rude because I didn't. I can't believe Americans give the waiter that much money each time they eat out. Next month, I'm going to visit these friends in California for a biking trip there. You're American, but you've lived in France. What is the correct thing to do when we eat out?

Sincerely,
Jean-Claude

Dear Jean-Claude,

Wow! I'm not surprised you're confused. Although people tip waiters in both France and in the United States, tipping practices are different. In France, the tip – a service fee – is included in the bill. When I've been in France, I've sometimes left a few coins, or I've left as much as a euro for a meal. In the United States, however, waiters make very small salaries, and service is not included in the bill. Waiters depend on tips to survive, so Americans always leave a tip. Be prepared to add 15 to 20 percent to everything you order in a restaurant in the United States. And have fun biking!

Sincerely,
Audrey

Reading to write: An email comparing different customs

6. Look at the picture. Do you know what the money we leave a server in a restaurant is called? Read the emails and find out.

Focus on CONTENT
Comparing
When you're comparing two different customs, be sure to compare the same topic for both places. Choose one topic at a time and compare how each place deals with the topic.

7. Look at the emails again. Answer the questions.

1. What topic is Jean-Claude writing about?
2. What is the custom in France?
3. What is the custom in the United States?

Focus on LANGUAGE
Conjunctions
Use conjunctions to show relationships between ideas.
both . . . and
either . . . or
not only . . . but also
however
although

8. Find one example of each conjunction in the emails.

Writing: An email comparing different customs

PLAN
Think of something from your country that might be confusing to someone from a different country. This could be greeting people, hand gestures, things people do (or don't do) in public, the things people do to have fun, or unique foods.

WRITE
Write an email to an imaginary friend from another country. Use the email above to help you. Write about 120 words.

CHECK
Can you say "yes" to these questions?

- Is the information from the Focus on Content box in your writing? Are you comparing the same thing in both cultures?
- Did you use conjunctions to show relationships between ideas?

Five Good Reasons to Visit NEW ZEALAND

1. **The volcanoes.** The islands of New Zealand appeared 23 million years ago as a result of a series of volcanic eruptions. The eruptions created dramatic mountains and more than 3,800 lakes! The largest lake, Lake Taupo, lies in the crater of one of the biggest volcanoes on Earth. There are at least 12 active volcanoes, and tourists can go on special volcano tours – an unforgettable experience. With five months of snow in winter, skiing and other winter sports are very popular. You can even ski on a volcano if you want!

2. **The forests.** More than 30 percent of New Zealand is forest. Some of the forests have remained unchanged for millions of years. They're old, beautiful, and mysterious! They have made New Zealand a perfect choice for film directors. Did you know that the forests, lakes, and mountains were the settings for several important Hollywood movies like *The Hobbit*, *The Lord of the Rings*, and *The Chronicles of Narnia*?

3. **The beaches.** New Zealand has more than 6,000 kilometers of coastline. The beaches are long and sandy, and the conditions are perfect for water sports. Kayaking, diving, surfing, and sailing are all popular sports with locals and visitors. You can't visit New Zealand without visiting at least one of its fantastic beaches!

4. **The whales and dolphins.** Half of the world's whale and dolphin population lives in the seas around New Zealand. Kaikoura, on the South Island, is one of the best whale-watching spots in the world. If you've never seen a whale up close, this is your chance, and you shouldn't miss it.

5. **The culture.** Humans have only lived on the islands for about 1,000 years. The first people to arrive were islanders from Eastern Polynesia, called Maori. Today, about 15 percent of the population of New Zealand is Maori. Their culture and their customs developed into the Maori way of life. Maori language, literature, music, dance, sports, and even TV are all important in New Zealand. If you're in New Zealand, you should visit a *marae* – a Maori community facility – or even learn to speak the language.

Culture: New Zealand

1. **Look at the pictures of different outdoor activities that you can see or do in New Zealand. Answer the questions.**
    1. Have you ever done any of the activities?
    2. Which of the activities would you like to try?

2. **Read and listen to the article. Match the photos from Exercise 1 to the reasons for visiting New Zealand.**
    1. ____ 2. ____ 3. ____ 4. ____ 5. ____

3. **Read the article again. Find the numbers in the box in the article and explain what they refer to.**

23 million years ago	30 percent	1,000 years
3,800	millions of years	15 percent
12	6,000 kilometers	
five months	half	

4. **YOUR TURN** Work with a partner. Ask and answer the questions.
    1. Would you like to go to New Zealand? Why? / Why not?
    2. What outdoor activities can you do in and around your town or city?
    3. Do you have a favorite outdoor activity? If so, what is it? Why do you like it?

DID YOU KNOW…?
The human population of New Zealand is four million. The sheep population is 36 million!

BE CURIOUS Find out about some of the things that make Australia unusual. What unusual sport happens in Alice Springs? (Workbook, p. 79)

Discovery EDUCATION
4.3 FUN IN AUSTRALIA

UNIT 4 REVIEW

Vocabulary

1. **Complete the sentences with the activities.**

go backpacking	go on a cruise	go sailing
go ballooning	go on a safari	✓ go to summer camp

   1. If you _go to summer camp,_ you'll make friends and learn new skills with kids your own age.
   2. Let's _____! My father bought a new boat and he wants to go out on the lake.
   3. We're going to _____ while we're in South Africa. I hope we see lions.
   4. I'd love to _____. It must be fun to be on a big ship with swimming pools!
   5. My brother wants to _____ for four days. I don't understand why because he hates walking. He won't even walk our dog!
   6. I'm going to _____ in New Mexico again next week. I love floating along in the air, quietly looking down at the ground.

Grammar

2. **Seth and Mary are planning a weekend trip to the mountains. Write sentences or questions using the present perfect.**

   1. Seth and Mary / buy a guidebook / already
      Seth and Mary have already bought a guidebook.
   2. Mary / not reserve a place to camp / yet
      _____
   3. Seth / pack his backpack / yet ?
      _____
   4. Mary / check the weather report / just
      _____
   5. They / not fill the car with gas / yet
      _____

3. **Write *for* or *since* to complete the phrases.**

   1. _for_ a long time
   2. _____ a year
   3. _____ January 10
   4. _____ Monday
   5. _____ 10 days
   6. _____ two weeks

Useful language

4. **Complete the conversation.**

about transportation	do I	include	Where
✓ Can I		how	Is it only

   Nick: Hi! ¹_Can I_ ask you a few things about the mountain biking trip?
   Gabriella: Yeah. What would you like to know?
   Nick: I've done a lot of biking, but I haven't gone mountain biking yet. ²_____ for people who have already done it?
   Gabriella: No, this is on beginner trails. It's easy.
   Nick: OK. What ³_____ need to bring?
   Gabriella: Nothing. Just wear tennis shoes and comfortable clothes. We supply the helmets and the bikes.
   Nick: Cool. What ⁴_____ to the start of the trail? Do you drive us there?
   Gabriella: No, but there's a parking lot right there. You can drive and park your car there and meet us. Or you can walk. It isn't far at all.
   Nick: OK. And ⁵_____ long is the trip?
   Gabriella: All day, from 9:00 a.m. to 4:00 p.m.
   Nick: Does the price ⁶_____ lunch?
   Gabriella: Yes, and two snacks.
   Nick: Cool! ⁷_____ can I sign up?

PROGRESS CHECK: Now I can . . .

- ☐ talk about adventure travel.
- ☐ ask and answer questions about personal experiences.
- ☐ ask and answer questions about the duration of activities.
- ☐ talk about signing up for an adventure activity.
- ☐ write about different customs.
- ☐ discuss reasons to visit a place.

▶ UNITS 3–4 REVIEW, Workbook, pp. 28–29

5 Yikes!

Discovery EDUCATION

BE CURIOUS

- Creepy Creatures
- What are you afraid of?
- Calendars of the Ancient Maya
- City or Country?

1. Describe what you see in this picture.

2. How does this picture make you feel?

3. What kinds of things make you feel afraid?

UNIT CONTENTS

Vocabulary Fears; -ed and -ing adjective endings
Grammar Future review; first conditional; modals of probability – must, can't, may, might, could
Listening Conversations at an amusement park

Vocabulary: Fears

1. **Match the photos (a–h) with the words.**

   1. __e__ flying
   2. ____ heights
   3. ____ the dark
   4. ____ elevators
   5. ____ insects
   6. ____ birds
   7. ____ clowns
   8. ____ snakes

2. **Listen, check, and repeat.**

3. **Match the comments about fears to the words in Exercise 1.**
   1. "I'm worried they might fly in through an open window and scratch me, or they might get into my hair!" _____
   2. "I can't look out the windows of tall buildings. I get dizzy and have to sit down!" _____
   3. "They're supposed to be funny, but their faces are really scary!" _____
   4. "I always take the stairs." _____
   5. "I sleep with a light on every night." _____
   6. "I prefer to travel by train or car than by plane." _____
   7. "I hate it when one flies into my face! I don't care how small it is, I always jump." _____
   8. "I'm terrified when I'm out in the woods. I carry a stick and watch the grass for them." _____

Speaking: Reactions to fear

4. **YOUR TURN** Talk to three people in your class. Answer the questions below.
   1. Do you know anyone who has any of these fears or other common ones?
   2. How does the fear change his or her behavior?

Person	Fear	Behavior changes
Anna	flying	drives long distances to avoid planes

5. **Tell your partner about the people you know and their fears.**

   My mother has a fear of flying. She drives really long distances to avoid going on a plane!

> Workbook, p. 30

Reading Ask Maria; Afraid to fly!; Superstitions? Who Needs Them?!
Conversation Expressing disbelief
Writing An email to a friend about plans and problems

HELP!

Ask MARIA

Today we're going to look at fears and phobias. Everybody's afraid of something – elevators, insects, snakes – and famous people have fears, too. Did you know that Daniel Radcliffe is scared of clowns, Orlando Bloom is scared of pigs, and Nicole Kidman is scared of butterflies? For Justin Timberlake, it's spiders, and for Matt Damon, snakes. For most people, these fears aren't very important. However, when a fear becomes a phobia – an extreme and uncontrollable fear – it can cause serious problems.

Carlos, 14 (California)

"I can't sleep at night without a light, and sometimes it can be embarrassing. Next week, I'm traveling to New York on a school trip, and I'm going to share a room with other students. I don't want them to think I'm a baby! Please help. I'm really worried!"

Don't be embarrassed. Did you know that Keanu Reeves is afraid of the dark? And no one says he's a baby! Don't worry about what other people will think of you. Just tell your roommates that you want the light on at night like it's the most normal thing in the world.

Isabella, 13 (Florida)

My uncle is getting married next month, and my mom, my dad, and I are going to the wedding – in Las Vegas! The problem is that I'm terrified of flying, and the flight to Las Vegas takes four and a half hours. What am I going to do?"

Lots of people are afraid of flying. Jennifer Aniston, for example, hates planes, so you're in good company! Try to relax before the flight. If you get some exercise, you'll feel tired, and then maybe you can sleep. Listen to your favorite music. When you feel nervous, close your eyes, and take long, deep breaths. If you do just one or two of these things, you'll be fine!

Reading: An advice column

1. Look at the famous people in the pictures. What do you think they're afraid of?

2. Read and listen to the online advice column and check your answers to the question in Exercise 1.

3. Read the advice column again and answer the questions.
    1. What is the difference between a fear and a phobia?
    2. Why does Isabella have to travel?
    3. What is Maria's advice to Isabella?
    4. Why does Carlos have to travel?
    5. What is Carlos worried about?
    6. What is Maria's advice to Carlos?

4. **YOUR TURN** Work with a partner. Ask and answer the questions.
    1. Do you think Maria gave good advice?
    2. Do you know of any other famous people who have fears or phobias? What are their fears?
    3. Do you think it's easy to help people with phobias? Why or why not?

DID YOU KNOW...?

Arachnophobia – fear of spiders – is the most common phobia. Fifty percent of all women suffer from arachnophobia.

Grammar: Future review – *will*, *be going to*, present continuous

5. Complete the chart.

> *Use* will, be going to, *and the present continuous to talk about the future.*
> *Use* will *for actions and events that we decide to do in the moment of speaking.*
> Are you going running now? I _____ (go) with you.
> *Use* going to *for planned actions and events. They may be in the near future or in a more distant future time.*
> My brother and his friends are _____ (be) in different schools next year.
> *Use the present continuous for planned actions and events, usually in the very near future.*
> Lauren _____ (have) dinner with her mother tonight.
> *Be going to is used much more than* will *in conversation.*

> Check your answers: Grammar reference, p. 110

6. Choose the best option.

1. Your bag looks heavy. Give it to me. I **will / am going to** help you carry it.
2. What **are you doing / will you do** this weekend? Do you have plans?
3. My friends can't go out tonight. They **will / are going to** study for the big math test.
4. What **are we having / will we have** for dinner tonight?
5. If all of you are going dancing now, I think I **will / am going to** go to bed. I'm tired.
6. Dave and Julianne **will / are going to** take a trip to Chile next year.

7. Complete the sentences with a verb from the box. Use *will* for first conditional sentences. For other sentences, use *be going to*.

go	see	study
get	stay	✓ take

1. I _am going to take_ an English course in New York next summer.
2. If my brother doesn't go to college, he _____ a job.
3. My best friend _____ harder next semester. Her grades are just terrible now.
4. If I don't have any plans this weekend, I _____ home and watch TV.
5. We _____ Julie tonight.
6. Your friends _____ to camp this summer.

> **First conditional**
> *Use first conditional sentences to talk about things that may happen in the future.*
> If you don't go to bed soon, you **will** be tired tomorrow.
> If you hurry up, we **will** have time to see a movie tonight.
> If you wear your boots, your feet **won't** get wet in the rain.

Speaking: *I'm going to . . .*

8. YOUR TURN Work with a partner. Ask and answer the questions.

1. What are you going to do when you finish high school?
2. What are you doing this weekend?

> What are you going to do when you finish high school?

> I think I'm going to go to college. But maybe I'll travel for a few months first.

BE CURIOUS Find out about king cobras. Are you scared of snakes? Why or why not? (Workbook, p. 80)

Discovery EDUCATION

5.1 CREEPY CREATURES

Scared? I was TERRIFIED!

Listening: Conversations at an amusement park

1. Work with a partner. Look at the picture on the left. How do you think the people on the roller coaster feel? Do you like roller coasters? Why? / Why not?

2. Listen to two conversations between a group of friends at an amusement park. How do Alyssa and Bruno feel (a) at the beginning of the day, and (b) at the end of the day?

3. Listen again. Choose the correct answer to each question.

Conversation 1:

1. Which ride is Alyssa scared of?
   a. The Scream Machine   b. The Colossus   c. The Tidal Wave

2. Why doesn't Bruno like the Tidal Wave?
   a. The line is short.   b. He doesn't like the water.   c. He wants to swim.

3. Why does Colin suggest starting with The Scream Machine?
   a. The line is short.   b. It's very scary.   c. It's a lot of fun.

Conversation 2:

4. What was Colin's favorite ride?
   a. The Colossus   b. The Tidal Wave   c. The Scream Machine

5. What was the problem at the end of the day?
   a. They missed the bus.   b. They spent a lot of money.   c. There's nothing to eat.

Vocabulary: -ed and -ing adjective endings

4. Look at the pictures and read the Notice it box. Circle the correct adjectives. Then listen and check your answers.

   1. The movie we saw last night was **terrified / terrifying**!
   2. Yesterday, we looked at the physics of roller coasters in class. It was very **interested / interesting**.
   3. I was completely **surprised / surprising** when I got the present you sent me.
   4. We went on a 20-kilometer walk in the country last weekend. It was **exhausted / exhausting**!
   5. I'm **confused / confusing**. Do we have a test tomorrow or not?
   6. My brother fell down in the cafeteria yesterday. Everyone saw him, and he felt really **embarrassed / embarrassing**.
   7. After a three-week vacation at the beach, I felt really **relaxed / relaxing**.
   8. Some reality shows on TV are really **disgusted / disgusting**.

5. **YOUR TURN** Write six true sentences about your feelings and beliefs using the cues below. Then tell your partner.

interested in	_____	is / are disgusting
embarrassed by	_____	is / are exhausting
terrified of	_____	is / are confusing

NOTICE IT
Use -ed adjective endings to say how you feel. Use -ing adjective endings to talk about something or someone that causes that feeling.

I was terrified.

The ride was terrifying.

Grammar: Modals of probability – *must, can't, may, might, could*

6. Complete the chart.

Use *must* for something you're almost certain of.	Use *can't* for something you believe is impossible.	Use *may*, *might*, and *could* for something that you believe is possible.
You have to be 14 or older to go on that ride. It _____ **be** really terrifying.	Ralph doesn't speak French, so he _____ **be** from France.	I don't know where your sister is, but she _____ **be** upstairs. I _____ **not go** to the barbecue because I haven't finished my homework. My dog doesn't want to eat. He _____ **be** sick.

> Check your answers: Grammar reference, p. 110

7. Choose the correct answers.

1. The roller coaster **must / can't** be fun. There are lots of people in line.
2. You **must / can't** expect to win the lottery. Millions of people play it every week.
3. You **must / can't** be really tired. You fell asleep twice during the movie.
4. My neighbor **must / can't** make a lot of money. He's always taking expensive trips.
5. She **must / can't** be a good student. She misses school at least once a week.
6. I **must / can't** be late. I left an hour early!

8. Complete the sentences with *must*, *can't*, or *could*.

1. You haven't eaten all day? Let me make you a snack. You _____ be hungry!
2. My mom _____ be at work or at the mall. She's not here.
3. We _____ fail the test. The teacher said we could look at our books.
4. Your brother _____ get hurt if he's not careful.
5. That guy over there is speaking French. He _____ be the new student from Canada.
6. You drank three glasses of water 15 minutes ago. You _____ be thirsty again.

> **Get it RIGHT!**
> Don't use *must* to discuss probability in the future.
> *If you don't go to bed now, you **will** be tired tomorrow.* NOT: *If you don't go to bed now, you **must** be tired tomorrow.*

Speaking: Surprising situations

9. YOUR TURN Read the situations below. Why do you think they're happening? Discuss with a partner. Be creative, and use *must*, *can't*, *might*, *may*, and *could*.

Situation 1: John bought a new bike last week, but he isn't using it. He's walking to school this morning.

Situation 2: Sean is a great athlete. He loves to play basketball, baseball, and football, but he isn't playing any sports at school this year.

Situation 3: Alicia has an important test in school tomorrow, but right now she's on a plane, going to Japan.

> *John's bike must be broken.*
>
> *It can't be broken. It's new.*
>
> *Well, it could have a flat tire. Maybe . . .*

REAL TALK 5.2 WHAT ARE YOU AFRAID OF?

NO way!

Conversation: What are you afraid of?

1. **REAL TALK** Watch or listen to the teenagers. Can you remember three of the fears the teenagers mention?

2. **YOUR TURN** Answer the question from the video about yourself. Tell your classmates about your biggest fear.

3. Listen to Rosa and Jack talking about their friend Mike. Complete the conversation.

> **USEFUL LANGUAGE: Expressing disbelief**
> I don't believe it! That's impossible! No way! Are you serious? Come on!

Rosa: Is Mike going to come sailing with us tomorrow?
Jack: ¹_____ He's terrified of deep water.
Rosa: What? ²_____ He's a really good swimmer!
Jack: I know, he's a *great* swimmer. He's competing in the 50-meter freestyle at the pool next week. But he's scared of going out in open water. I think it's because you can't see down to the bottom.
Rosa: ³_____ I didn't think Mike was scared of anything.
Jack: Well, he's afraid of the ocean. It's actually a really common phobia.
Rosa: ⁴_____ I've never heard of it.
Jack: Mike told me himself.
Rosa: ⁵_____ I'm going to call Mike and ask him.

4. Practice the conversation with a partner.

5. **YOUR TURN** Work with a partner. Take turns starting the conversation and expressing disbelief. Use the situations below or your own ideas.

Situation A
You're going camping with some friends. Your friend Julie has arachnophobia, a fear of spiders. She goes walking a lot and loves outdoor sports.

Situation B
You're going to go to an amusement park with your class. Your friend Luke is a BMX champion, but he has veloxrotaphobia. He has a fear of roller coasters.

Say it RIGHT!
Remember that in everyday conversation, *going to* often sounds like gənə. Listen and repeat the sentences.
We're going to learn about phobias in science class tomorrow.
Daniel isn't going to see the new movie about birds.

To: Pete
From: Stefan
Subject: Afraid to fly!

Hi Pete,

Thanks for the email with your news. Now here's my news. Check this out: I'm going to stay with my cousins in Colorado this summer. I'm going with my parents, and the idea is that we'll all go camping together. It's really exciting, but the problem is that we're flying there ☹! I've never been on a plane before, and the truth is, I'm really worried about flying. I don't know what to do! When I think about getting on a plane, I feel tense and start sweating. It's embarrassing. Listen to this: I had to tell my mom, and she said it's just like going on a bus. She told me not to worry. Not very helpful! I want to go by car, but that will take four days. And so, the fact is, I might not go at all because I'm terrified of planes. What do you think I should do?

Sincerely,

Stefan

Reading to write: An email to a friend

6. Read Stefan's email. What is he worried about?

> ● *Focus on* **CONTENT**
> When you write an email about a problem, you can include this information:
> - A greeting *(Hi Mike! Dear Sandra,)*
> - Some personal news
> - What the problem is
> - How you feel about it and why
> - What you have / haven't done about it
> - A question to ask what your friend thinks

7. Read Stefan's email again. What information does he include for each category from the Focus on Content box?

> ● *Focus on* **LANGUAGE**
> **Introducing something**
> *Listen to this:*
> *The idea is (that) . . .*

8. Find examples of the items in the Focus on Language box in Stefan's email. Can you find two other ways of introducing information?

9. Rewrite the sentences using the words given.

1. We're going to Argentina next month. (listen to this)

   Listen to this: We're going to Argentina next month.

2. I'm going to get a dog. (check this out)

   _____

3. A lot of people have phobias about roller coasters. (the fact)

   _____

4. She doesn't want to go. (the truth)

   _____

Writing: An email to a friend about plans and problems

◯ **PLAN**

Think about a problem or worry you've had recently. It can be about anything: school, homework, your family, fears, phobias, or the future. Then think of someone you could send an email to for help with that problem. Look at the Focus on Content box and make notes about what you'll write.

◯ **WRITE**

Write your email. Use your notes and the language below to help you. Write about 120 words.

Thanks for your email / letter.

The idea is that . . .

It's really exciting / surprising / embarrassing . . .

I feel terrible / confused because . . .

What can I do? / What do you think I should do?

◯ **CHECK**

Check your writing. Can you answer "yes" to these questions?

- Is the information from the Focus on Content box in your email?
- Have you used expressions like *The problem is that . . .* in your email?

Superstitions? Who Needs Them?!

Many superstitions have been around for thousands of years. For example, some people believe that walking under ladders brings bad luck or finding a horseshoe brings good luck. Some superstitions began recently – for example, many soccer players don't change their socks or underwear while their team is winning.

Lots of people, however, believe strongly that superstitions are silly. They say that believing in superstitions is a way of trying to control things we can't control. They say that superstitions are based on old habits, old customs, and old beliefs. How is it possible that you could have bad luck by opening an umbrella inside a house? Why is the number 13 more dangerous than other numbers?

To prove their point, they have "Anti-Superstition Parties." These are usually held on a Friday the Thirteenth, a date that many people think brings bad luck. At these parties, people break mirrors, walk under ladders, and dance with open umbrellas. And nothing bad happens!

Alan Moore, a Chicago dentist, has gone to several anti-superstition parties. He said, "People must be crazy to believe that the number 7 is lucky or that they could be more successful by putting a horseshoe outside their house." Chelsea Evans, a chef from Dallas, agrees. "I love the parties. I've broken lots of mirrors and my life is going great!"

Culture: Anti-superstition parties

1. **Read the title of the article and look at the picture. What do you think the article is about?**

2. **Read and listen to the article. Check (✓) the things you read and hear about.**

   - ☐ breaking mirrors
   - ☐ black cats
   - ☐ blowing out birthday candles
   - ☐ opening umbrellas
   - ☐ walking under ladders
   - ☐ throwing rice

3. **Read the article again. Are the sentences below true (*T*) or false (*F*)?**

   1. All superstitions have a recent origin. ____
   2. Some soccer players are superstitious. ____
   3. Lots of superstitions come from old habits and beliefs. ____
   4. At anti-superstition parties, people are careful to follow old superstitions. ____
   5. Alan and Chelsea are scared to go to anti-superstition parties. ____
   6. Chelsea's life is fine even though she has broken a lot of mirrors. ____

4. **YOUR TURN Work with a partner. Ask and answer the questions.**

   1. What superstitions exist in your country? Do you believe in any of them?
   2. Are there logical or scientific explanations for superstitions?
   3. Have you ever heard of anti-superstition parties? Would you like to go to one?

DID YOU KNOW...?
Fear of the number 13 is called **triskaidekaphobia.**

BE CURIOUS Find out about ancient Mayan calendars. What happened on Mayan "good days" and "bad days"? (Workbook, p. 81)

Discovery EDUCATION
5.3 CALENDARS OF THE ANCIENT MAYA

UNIT 5 REVIEW

Vocabulary

1. **Write the common fears next to the words they are related to. There are two extra words.**

birds	elevators	heights	snakes
clowns	✓ flying	insects	the dark

   1. airplanes ___flying___
   2. tall buildings _____
   3. small spaces _____
   4. poisonous animals _____
   5. no light _____
   6. spiders, beetles, butterflies _____

Grammar

2. **Write sentences or questions with *be going to*. Use contracted forms if possible.**

   1. We / fly / to Japan / tomorrow
      We're going to fly to Japan tomorrow.
   2. Jim / learn / the guitar / next semester
      _____
   3. They / order / pizza / tonight
      _____
   4. She / not use / her computer / this weekend
      _____
   5. I / go to college / when I finish high school
      _____
   6. Danielle / look for / a new job / next year
      _____

3. **Complete the sentences with *must*, *can't*, or *might*.**

   1. Whose suitcase is that? It _____ belong to Erin, but I'm not sure.
   2. I had my wallet just a second ago. It _____ be here somewhere.
   3. Anna _____ be home sick. I saw her at school five minutes ago.
   4. It's so cold outside that it _____ snow tonight.
   5. You _____ be tired yet. We only started walking a few minutes ago.
   6. Daniel isn't answering his phone. It _____ be turned off because he always answers it.

Useful language

4. **Complete the conversation.**

believe it	on
impossible	serious

   Grace: We're going to an amusement park next weekend. Want to come?

   Ryan: No, I'd better not. I always have bad luck when I go to amusement parks.

   Grace: What do you mean?

   Ryan: Every time I go, something bad happens. Last time, I was at the top of a roller coaster and the electricity went out. I sat in the car for 45 minutes.

   Grace: Are you [1]_____?

   Ryan: I'm not joking. And another time, I was on the Spinning Hat ride and the person next to me got sick. It was disgusting!

   Grace: Come [2]_____. Just because you had a few bad things happen doesn't mean something bad will happen every time. That's [3]_____.

   Ryan: No it isn't! And then, last summer, I went with my friends and fell down – I was just walking along – and had to go to the hospital!

   Grace: I don't [4]_____!

   Ryan: It's true! Sorry, but I think I'll just stay home.

PROGRESS CHECK: Now I can . . .

- ☐ identify and discuss common fears.
- ☐ talk about future events.
- ☐ talk about things that are possible and not possible.
- ☐ express disbelief.
- ☐ discuss superstitions.
- ☐ write an email to a friend about plans and problems.

CLIL PROJECT

5.4 CITY OR COUNTRY?, p. 118

Uncover Your Knowledge
UNITS 1–5 Review Game

TEAM 1 START

- Share an opinion with your teammate and ask him or her to agree with you. Your teammate disagrees with you and explains why.
- Tell your teammate about a time you felt embarrassed, stressed out, or wonderful.
- Say three future actions: one you've just decided to do, one for this weekend, and one for next year.
- Use each of these words in a unique sentence: terrified, interesting, confused, relaxing.
- Have your teammate tell you two things that are very surprising. Express your disbelief in two ways.
- Name the top three priorities you have in life, and explain why they are important to you.
- What do you have to do to get a good grade in English? Tell your teammate, using have to/don't have to.
- Give examples of three adventure travel activities you want to try.
- Role-play a conversation with your teammate. Invite him or her to an art exhibit and plan to meet.
- Say how long you've studied English. Then use a negative statement to tell your teammate the last time you saw a movie in a theater.
- Describe something you're looking forward to, something you want to find out about, and someplace you want to come back to.

■ GRAMMAR
■ VOCABULARY
■ USEFUL LANGUAGE

52 | Units 1–5 Review

TEAM 2
START

- Use the verbs *learn*, *play*, and *make* as the subjects of three different sentences.
- Name six basic needs that people have.
- Think about a few things you wanted to do last week. Use *already* to talk about something you did, and *yet* to talk about something you haven't done.
- How can you ask someone for information? Give three examples.
- Say two things you did yesterday and two things you used to do in the past but don't do anymore.
- In 30 seconds, name five things people are often afraid of.
- Say one thing you're almost sure about, one thing you think is possible, and one thing you believe is impossible. Use modals of probability.
- Give examples of five types of extreme weather.
- Tell your teammate something you hate doing, something you love doing, and something you don't mind doing.
- Name one type of artwork, one place to see art, and one type of artist.
- Role-play a conversation with your teammate. Ask him or her to help you with something.
- Tell your teammate that studying more would be a good thing for you to do. Say it three different ways, using modals of obligation.
- Imagine you are in a band. What instrument do you play? What other instruments do you have in the band? Give four examples.
- Tell your teammate two things you do every day and two things you are doing right now.

INSTRUCTIONS:

- Make teams and choose game pieces.
- Put your game pieces on your team's START.
- Flip a coin to see who goes first.
- Read the first challenge. Can you do it correctly?

   Yes ➔ Continue to the next challenge.

   No ➔ Lose your turn.

The first team to do all of the challenges wins!

Units 1–5 Review | 53

6 DIFFICULT *Decisions*

Discovery EDUCATION

BE CURIOUS

- Working Together
- Who would you talk to if you needed advice?
- Watch Your Identity

1. Describe what you see in this picture.

2. How do you imagine the student in the back feels? Why do you imagine she feels this way?

3. Have you ever felt confused or scared about something that happened at school? Why?

UNIT CONTENTS

Vocabulary School life; expressions with *make* and *do*
Grammar Second conditional; second conditional *Wh-* questions
Listening Would you tell the teacher?

Vocabulary: School life

1. Read the phrases related to school life. Then circle the correct answers.

being assigned to detention	cheating	wearing a uniform
being punctual	following the dress code	winning a prize
being rude	getting sent to the principal's office	
bullying	getting extra credit	

1. You can ____ in English if you read two books over the vacation.
   a. get sent to the principal's office   **b. get extra credit** (circled)

2. I'm sorry, but you can't wear those boots to school. You need to ____.
   a. follow the dress code   b. win a prize

3. Emily ____ because she was rude to Mr. Moore.
   a. cheated   b. got sent to the principal's office

4. If you're late to class three times in a semester, you will ____.
   a. wear a uniform   b. be assigned to detention

5. Don't use your cell phone during a test. That's ____.
   a. cheating   b. getting extra credit

6. All students must treat each other with respect. We don't tolerate ____ in our school.
   a. bullying   b. being punctual

7. I think you should join the Math Challenge team. You might ____.
   a. win a prize   b. be rude

8. Mike is never late to class. It's important to him to ____.
   a. follow the dress code   b. be punctual

9. A lot of students don't like ____, but I do. It saves me money on clothes.
   a. wearing a uniform   b. being assigned to detention

10. Christine ____ to the Spanish teacher yesterday. Usually, she's very polite.
    a. was assigned to detention   b. was rude

> **Say it RIGHT!**
> 6.02
> Notice the way these words are pronounced. Then add one more word for each sound.
> /ʊ/ would, could, bullying, _____
> /u/ do, rude, you, _____

2. 🔊 6.01 Listen, check, and repeat.

3. Put the phrases from Exercise 1 in the correct categories.

Rewards	Punishments	Good behavior	Bad behavior

Speaking: Actions and consequences

4. YOUR TURN Work with a partner. Ask and answer the questions.

1. What rewards and punishments do students get at your school?
2. Do you think your school is strict? Why? / Why not?

> Teachers sometimes play a game after we've done good work.

Workbook, p. 36

Reading A School with a Difference; How to Be Safe Online!; Punishment or Rehabilitation?
Conversation Asking for and giving advice
Writing An article about online safety

YOU make the RULES!

A SCHOOL WITH A DIFFERENCE
This week's student reporter, Jodi White, visits the Brooklyn Free School in New York.

It's Wednesday morning, and it's time for the weekly school meeting. This week's topic is "wheels." One student proposes a new rule that students can bring skateboards, skates, and bicycles to school. A teacher suggests that they do this one day a week, and the whole school votes on a "wheels" day for next Friday. As simple as that! Would I be able to change the rules in my school if I wanted to? No, if I wanted to change the rules, it would be really hard!

But the Brooklyn Free School is different. Here the students make the decisions – about everything! They can decide to go to class or they can decide to watch TV or play a computer game, but most students choose to go to class – it's more interesting! When they don't like a class, they just walk out. If I didn't stay until the end of a class at my school, I'd be assigned to detention!

At the Free School, the teachers don't assign students to detention, and no one gets sent to the principal's office. The students choose what they want to study and how. If you were at the school and you wanted to study car mechanics, for example, or cooking, would the school let you do it? Yes. If you wanted to start a new school magazine, you would suggest it, and together the school would find a way to do it.

That's how the Free School works. The ideas come from the students, and everyone works together to make them happen. I'd love to go to the Free School!

DID YOU KNOW...?
There are more than 90 schools like the Brooklyn Free School in the United States. They're sometimes called "anarchistic free schools" or "free skools."

Reading: An article from a school newspaper

1. Look at the title of the article and the name of the school. What kind of school is it? Why do they describe it as "free"?

2. Read and listen to the article about a school in New York. What are two ways that this school is different from your school?

3. Read the article again. Are these sentences true (*T*) or false (*F*)?

    1. The school has meetings every month. ___
    2. The students make suggestions, and the teachers vote on their suggestions. ___
    3. There are no rules. ___
    4. The students choose their own subjects. ___
    5. The teachers don't tell the students what to do. ___
    6. The reporter doesn't want to study at the Free School. ___

4. **YOUR TURN** Work with a partner. Ask and answer the questions.

    1. Would you like to go to a school like the Brooklyn Free School? Why? / Why not?
    2. How much can students change the rules or classes at your school?
    3. What kinds of classes would you like to take that your school doesn't offer? Where could you learn those things outside of school?

    > I think I'd like that school. If you want, you can watch TV!

    > I'd like it because I could choose what I wanted to study. . . .

Grammar: Second conditional

5. Complete the chart.

Use the second conditional to describe imaginary situations and possible consequences.	
Imaginary situation	**Possible consequences**
if + simple past **If** I **changed** the school rules,	*would (not)* + base form of the verb students **wouldn't wear** uniforms.
If you **missed** class, **If** she **didn't like** the class,	you _____ **be** assigned to detention. she _____ **go**.
Many American English speakers use *were* rather than *was* after **I, he, she,** and **it**, especially in a more formal style.	
Formal style	**Informal style**
If I _____ rude to my teacher, my parents would be very mad at me.	If I _____ always punctual, I wouldn't be assigned to detention so much.

> Check your answers: Grammar reference, p. 111

6. Circle the correct answers.

1. If I **was** / **would be** rude to a teacher, I **got** / **would be** assigned to detention.
2. If I **didn't** / **wouldn't** pass my finals, my parents **didn't** / **wouldn't** be very happy.
3. If a teacher **sent** / **would send** me to the principal's office, I **felt** / **would feel** embarrassed.
4. My teacher **called** / **would call** my parents if I **didn't** / **wouldn't** go to school.
5. My friends **did** / **would like** to go to the Free School if they **opened** / **would open** one in our town.
6. I **didn't** / **wouldn't** study math if I **went** / **would go** to the Free School.

7. Complete the sentences with the correct form of the verbs.

1. If I _____ (come) home late one night, . . .
   a. my parents _____ (be) very angry. I _____ (get) some kind of punishment.
   b. my parents _____ (talk) to me about the issue.
   c. my parents _____ (not say) anything.

2. If I _____ (say) something rude to my parents, . . .
   a. I _____ (feel) bad, and I _____ (say) sorry immediately.
   b. they _____ (ask) me what I was upset about.
   c. they _____ (punish) me with no TV or computer for a week.

3. If I _____ (borrow) something from my friend without asking, . . .
   a. it _____ (not be) a problem. My friend does it to me all the time!
   b. my friend probably _____ (not talk) to me for a week!
   c. I _____ (put) it back before they noticed.

> **Second conditional yes/no questions**
>
> Use *if* to ask yes/no questions in the second conditional.
>
> **If** your teacher **got** angry with you in class, **would** you **feel** embarrassed?
>
> **Would** you **say** anything **if** your teacher **forgot** to give you homework?
> Yes, I **would**.
> No, I **wouldn't**.

Speaking: If I did that, . . .

8. YOUR TURN Circle the answers in Exercise 7 that are true for you. Then compare your answers with a partner.

If I came home late one night, I'd get some kind of punishment for sure!

> Workbook, p. 37

BE CURIOUS Find out about the women in a small town in Mexico. How is the business they started different from most businesses? (Workbook, p. 82)

Discovery EDUCATION
6.1 WORKING TOGETHER

Unit 6 | 57

What would YOU DO?

Listening: Would you tell the teacher?

1. Work with a partner. What would you do if you saw one of your classmates cheating on a test? What if you found a wallet full of money in the street?

2. Listen to a conversation between two teenagers, Rachel and Luke. What are they discussing?

3. Listen again. Circle the correct answers.

   1. If Rachel saw a classmate cheating on a test, she would . . .
      a. say nothing and continue with her work.
      b. tell a teacher.
      c. try to cheat as well.

   2. If Luke found a wallet full of money on the street near his school, he would . . .
      a. take it to the nearest police station.
      b. give it to a teacher at school.
      c. keep it.

   3. If Rachel borrowed something from a friend and then lost it, she would . . .
      a. tell her friend.
      b. buy a new one.
      c. say nothing and hope the friend doesn't notice.

Vocabulary: Expressions with *make* and *do*

4. Complete the email with *make* or *do*. Then listen and check your answers.

To dan@cup.org
From eric@cup.org
Subject Advice

Hi Dan,
I need your advice. We have to give presentations in science class tomorrow, and I have a problem. One of my classmates, Jeremy, asked me to ¹ _do_ **him a favor**: He wanted me to help him with his presentation. Jeremy doesn't like science, and he doesn't like to ² _____ **homework**, but I agreed to help him. We started to ³ _____ **research** together, but he was bored. "Let's hurry up so we can ⁴ _____ **something fun**!" he said. He started to copy whole paragraphs from the Internet and paste them into his presentation. I explained that you can use the Internet for research, but you shouldn't copy like that. "It won't ⁵ _____ **a difference**," he said. "Mrs. Lewis won't find out." Then he looked at my presentation and copied from me! I didn't want to ⁶ _____ **him mad**, so I didn't say anything else. I'm new to this school, and I want to ⁷ _____ **friends**, but I also want to ⁸ _____ **the right thing**. What should I do?
Eric

---

5. **YOUR TURN** Work with a partner. Ask and answer the questions.

   1. How often do you do homework with your friends?

   2. Is doing homework with someone a good way to make new friends? Why or why not?

   3. Eric wants to do the right thing. What do you think he should do in this situation?

Grammar: Second conditional *Wh-* questions

6. Complete the chart.

Use Wh- questions in the second conditional to ask about imaginary situations and possible consequences.

What	would your teacher do	if	one of your classmates _____ on a test?
Who	would you talk to	if	you _____ a serious problem with a friend?
When	would you go to school	if	you _____ the days you went?
If	you wanted to do something fun this weekend,	where	would you _____?
If	you got a new pet,	why	would you _____ one kind of pet over another?

> Check your answers: Grammar reference, p. 111

7. Circle the correct answers.

1. What **did** / **would** you do if you **were** / **would be** the principal at your school?
2. If you **needed** / **would need** to find a quiet place to study at your school, where **would you go** / **did you go**?
3. Who would you **do** / **did** research on if you **have** / **had** to give a presentation on someone famous?
4. If you **get** / **got** perfect grades, what would your parents **say** / **said**?
5. When would you **apologize** / **apologized** if you **make** / **made** your best friend mad – at that moment, or a few days later?
6. If you **have** / **had** to make a difficult decision, who **will** / **would** you ask to help you?

8. Complete the conversation.

A: What ¹_____ you _____ (do) if another kid in your school ²_____ (bully) you?

B: I don't know. Maybe I ³_____ (hide).

A: Really? Where ⁴_____ you _____ (hide)?

B: I don't know. But, hiding isn't a good idea. I know! I ⁵_____ (fight) the bully.

A: Really? Where ⁶_____ you _____ (have) the fight?

B: Maybe outside? But, no. A fight ⁷_____ (be) stupid. I ⁸_____ (talk) to someone about the problem.

A: Who ⁹_____ you _____ (tell)?

B: My parents, probably. Let me ask you a question: Why ¹⁰_____ you _____ (ask) me crazy questions like this?

A: It's for the school newspaper. I'm talking to a lot of people about bullying.

> **Get it RIGHT!**
>
> Use the simple past after *if* with the second conditional.
> If our teacher **gave** extra credit, my grades would be better. NOT: ~~If our teacher **gives** extra credit, my grades would be better.~~

Speaking: In this situation, I would . . .

9. YOUR TURN Work with a partner. Ask and answer the questions.

1. If you were home alone and someone knocked on the door, what would you do?
2. What would you do if you found out your best friend lied to you about lots of things?
3. If you were 18, what would you do that you can't do now?
4. What would you do if you decided to stay home from school one day?

> *If I were home alone and someone knocked on the door, I would make sure I knew the person before I opened the door.*

> Workbook, pp. 38–39

REAL TALK 6.2 WHO WOULD YOU TALK TO IF YOU NEEDED ADVICE?

I need your ADVICE.

Conversation: I don't know what to do!

1. **REAL TALK** Watch or listen to the teenagers. Check (✓) the three people that are <u>not</u> mentioned.

☐ aunt	☐ cousin	☐ mother
☐ best friend	☐ father	☐ neighbor
☐ brother	☐ grandmother	☐ sister

2. **YOUR TURN** Who would you talk to if you needed advice? Tell your partner.

3. Listen to Hayley talking to her friend Josh about a problem. Complete the conversation.

   USEFUL LANGUAGE: Asking for and giving advice
   - If I were you
   - ✓ What's going on?
   - I need some advice.
   - Sure. What's up?
   - What should I do?
   - Have you tried

   Hayley: Josh, can I talk to you?
   Josh: Yes, of course. ¹ _What's going on?_
   Hayley: ² _____ I don't know what to do.
   Josh: ³ _____
   Hayley: Well, there's a girl in my class who is saying nasty things about me.
   Josh: Really? What sort of things?
   Hayley: Oh, that I copy her homework and cheat on tests. It's awful! ⁴ _____
   Josh: ⁵ _____, I wouldn't listen to her. What do your other friends say?
   Hayley: They say the same thing. But I can't help it.
   Josh: Hmm. ⁶ _____ talking to her about it?
   Hayley: Yeah, but it doesn't change anything. She keeps doing it.
   Josh: Let's talk to her together. Maybe that will help.
   Hayley: That's a good idea. Thanks, Josh!

4. Practice the conversation with a partner.

5. **YOUR TURN** Work with a partner. Take turns asking for and giving advice. Use the problems below or your own ideas.

   Problem 1
   Someone in your class has taken your backpack. No one knows who took it.

   Problem 2
   You can't find some books you left in the classroom yesterday.

HOW TO BE SAFE ONLINE!

It's easy to bully someone online, and many teenagers suffer from this. So how can you make sure it doesn't happen to you? Follow our essential advice.

- Don't post contact information (address, email, cell phone number) online.
- Check your privacy settings on social networking sites. Make sure you know how to keep your personal information private.
- Don't share your online passwords, not even with your best friends.
- Never respond or retaliate if someone bullies you. This can make things worse.
- You should block any users who send you nasty messages, even if they're your friends.
- Think carefully about posting photos of yourself online. Once your picture is online, anyone can download, share, or even change it.
- Don't ignore cyberbullying or keep it secret. You should ALWAYS tell someone.

Reading to write: An advice article

6. Look at the picture and read the article. What is it about?

Focus on CONTENT
When you write an article to help people solve a problem, you can include this information:
- a title
- the problem you will give advice about
- who the problem affects
- a question that the article will try to answer
- a list of short, clear pieces of advice

7. Read the article again. Does it include all of the things from the Focus on Content box? How many pieces of advice are there?

Focus on LANGUAGE
Giving advice in writing
Use the imperative to give advice in writing.
Affirmative: base form
Block *people who are rude to you.*
Negative: *Don't* + base form
Don't forget *to check your privacy settings.*

8. Find one other way to give advice in the article.

9. Complete the sentences.

✓ Don't   Make   Never   should   think

1. *Don't* forward cyberbullying videos or messages about other people.
2. You _____ never give anyone your passwords.
3. If someone bullies you, _____ carefully about changing your user ID and profile.
4. _____ sure you report anything abusive you see online.
5. _____ agree to keep chats with people you don't know "secret."

Writing: An advice article

PLAN
Think of a problem that you think might affect your classmates, friends, or people in your town. Use the guidelines in the Focus on Content box, and make a list of six pieces of advice you would give to solve the problem.

WRITE
Write your article. Use your notes and the online safety article above to help you. Write about 120 words.

CHECK
Can you say "yes" to these questions?

- Is the information from the Focus on Content box in your article?
- Have you given advice using the imperative, both affirmative and negative?

PUNISHMENT OR REHABILITATION?

If a teenager committed a crime in your neighborhood, what do you think should happen?

The case for punishment:
It's all about consequences. If I didn't study for a test, I wouldn't pass it. If I put my hand in a fire, I would be burned. Simple. So if you commit a crime, you should face the consequences, and that's prison. I heard about a program in Switzerland where teenagers who commit crimes get free school, sports, psychological help, and even a place to live. Are you kidding? That's expensive – more expensive than prison. Our tax money should help society, not people who break the rules of society.
Ellie, 15, Portland, Maine

The case for rehabilitation:
What teenagers need when they're in trouble is help – and we need to spend our tax money to help them. The program in Switzerland was expensive, but it helped teenagers stop committing crimes. Teenagers need to learn that there are alternatives to crime. They need to learn skills so that they can get a job. They need to believe that they are valuable members of society. If you throw them in prison and forget about them, they learn to become better criminals, not better citizens.
Collin, 16, Boise, Idaho

? What should we do with teenagers who commit crimes? Lock them up, or help them change their lives?

Culture: Juvenile justice

1. **Look at the photo. What do you think society should do with teenagers who commit crimes? Why?**

2. **Read and listen to the debate. How does Ellie answer the question in Exercise 1? How does Collin answer it?** (6.08)

3. **Read the debate again. Answer the questions.**
   1. According to Ellie, what should the consequences of committing a crime be?
   2. What did the program in Switzerland give teenagers who committed a crime?
   3. How does Ellie think tax money should be spent?
   4. What does Collin think teenagers in trouble need?
   5. What is the purpose of teaching skills to teenagers who commit a crime?
   6. What does Collin believe happens when you put teenagers in prison?

4. **YOUR TURN Work with a partner. Ask and answer the questions.**
   1. Do you agree with Ellie or Collin? Why?
   2. Is there a program in your country like the program in Switzerland? Do you think it's a good idea?
   3. Can you think of one or two solutions to teenage crime that don't involve prison or expensive programs?

BE CURIOUS Find out about staying safe online. Who does the video say are the number-one victims of identity theft? (Workbook, p. 83)

Discovery EDUCATION
6.3 WATCH YOUR IDENTITY

UNIT 6 REVIEW

Vocabulary

1. **Match the words with the definitions.**

   1. uniform ___
   2. detention ___
   3. dress code ___
   4. punctual ___
   5. bullying ___
   6. cheating ___

   a. on time, not late
   b. rules about what clothes to wear
   c. copying another student's work
   d. special clothes for school
   e. a type of punishment
   f. being aggressive to another person

Grammar

2. **Complete the sentences with the second conditional forms of the verbs.**

   1. If you _____ (be) more confident, you _____ (make) more friends.
   2. If he _____ (not go) to school, he _____ (be) bored.
   3. If they _____ (wear) uniforms, they _____ (look) the same.
   4. We _____ (have) more free time if we _____ (not have) so much homework.
   5. You _____ (not be) so tired if you _____ (not stay) up late.
   6. If she _____ (study) harder, she _____ (get) better grades at school.

3. **Write questions using the second conditional.**

   1. What / you / do / if / you / see someone cheating on a test?

   _____

   2. Where / you live / if / you / can go anywhere in the world?

   _____

   3. If / you / win / $5,000 / what / you / do?

   _____

   4. If / your friend / not answer / your email / what / you / say?

   _____

   5. If / you / not pass / your next test / you / feel upset?

   _____

   6. What / you / do / if / you / can live forever?

   _____

Useful language

4. **Complete the conversation.**

going on	I were	What should
Have you	some advice	

   Bryce: Hey, Kelly, I really need ¹_____.
   Kelly: You do? OK. What's ²_____?
   Bryce: I was assigned to detention because I've been late for my history class three times this semester.
   Kelly: That's not so terrible.
   Bryce: Yes, it is. My parents get really mad about that kind of thing. ³_____ I do?
   Kelly: If ⁴_____ you, I would be totally honest and tell them the truth.
   Bryce: No, they never listen. They just get mad and stay mad.
   Kelly: ⁵_____ tried talking to them? You never know.
   Bryce: That's true. I'm not a little kid anymore. Maybe they'll really listen.
   Kelly: Give it a try. You never know.

PROGRESS CHECK: Now I can . . .

- ☐ talk about school life.
- ☐ talk about good and bad behavior at school and home.
- ☐ discuss difficult situations.
- ☐ ask for and give advice.
- ☐ write about school rules.
- ☐ discuss different systems for dealing with crime.

7 Smart PLANET

Discovery EDUCATION
BE CURIOUS

- Where Does It All Go?
- What kind of volunteer work do you do?
- Build It Better
- Driving into the Future

1. Describe what you see in this picture.
2. How does this picture make you feel?
3. Which things in the picture are natural and which are man-made?

UNIT CONTENTS

Vocabulary Materials; eco-construction verbs
Grammar Simple present passive; infinitives of purpose; simple past passive
Listening Tour of a museum EcoHouse

Vocabulary: Materials

1. Match the words with the correct pictures.

1. _g_ bricks
2. ___ plastic
3. ___ metal
4. ___ glass
5. ___ water
6. ___ cotton
7. ___ paper
8. ___ cement
9. ___ rubber
10. ___ wood
11. ___ plants

2. Listen, check, and repeat.

3. Write the materials.

   1. We often use this material to make furniture like chairs and tables. _____
   2. This material is very common for making T-shirts. _____
   3. We make tires for cars with this material. _____
   4. We use this material to make books and magazines. _____
   5. We usually use this material to make knives, forks, and spoons. _____
   6. This material is often gray, and we use it to build bridges and buildings. _____

Speaking: What's in your house?

4. **YOUR TURN** Think about your house or apartment. Write as many objects as you can think of for each material below.

Cotton	Glass	Wood	Paper	Rubber	Plastic	Metal

5. Work with a partner. Talk about the things in your house.

   My family has a beautiful glass vase in the living room and . . .

> Workbook, p. 44

Reading Houses Made of Garbage; Volunteers Clean Valley Nature Reserve; Under the Australian Sun
Conversation Apologizing
Writing A newspaper article about an event

Unit 7 | 65

A WAR Against WASTE

HOUSES Made of GARBAGE

Mike Reynolds builds houses from recycled materials. These houses are a symbol of his war against waste. Mike's houses are built using the things that other people throw away. His Earthships (as his houses are called) are beautiful buildings. They are shaped and colored to reflect the landscape around them. He uses bottles to create beautiful walls full of light. There are plants everywhere, inside and out. But the plants and the bottles, like everything else in the Earthships, are not only there for decoration.

Every single material in an Earthship is carefully chosen. Old car tires are used to build strong external walls. The rubber protects the houses from the cold northern winds in winter. These walls are built at the back of the house. The external walls at the front of the house are built from metal cans or glass bottles, instead of bricks. They're held together with earth from the ground around them. No cement is used at all.

The beautiful bottle walls are built to the south to give light during the day. The larger front windows heat the house. They also create perfect conditions for growing all kinds of fruits and vegetables because the plants are protected against the bad weather. When you live in an Earthship, you don't need anything from the outside world. You grow your own food, you get electricity from the sun and wind, and you get water from the rain and snow.

Mike and the Earthship organization use their ability and experience to help people all over the world. In 2010, they visited victims of the earthquake in Haiti. They taught them how to build safe, new homes quickly and cheaply from materials that they could find around them. Mike points out that trash only exists because we humans create it – but we can also learn to recycle it.

DID YOU KNOW...?
Recycled car tires are used to build roads and sidewalks.

Reading: A magazine article

1. **Look at the picture. Work with a partner. Ask and answer the questions.**
   1. What are the people building?
   2. What materials are they using?
   3. Why are they using them?

2. **Read and listen to an article about Mike Reynolds. What kind of houses does he build?**

3. **Read the article again. Answer the questions.**
   1. How does Mike protect his Earthships from the cold?
   2. How does he provide light during the day?
   3. Why does he grow his plants in the front of the house?
   4. How does he get energy and water?
   5. How did he and his organization help other people?
   6. What is Mike's main message to the world?

4. **YOUR TURN Work with a partner. Ask and answer the questions.**
   1. Are the materials that Mike Reynolds uses for his Earthships available where you live? What other recycled materials from your area could be used for an Earthship?
   2. Are Earthships practical or possible where you live?
   3. What is your opinion of Earthships? Would you like to live in an Earthship? What would your ideal Earthship look like?

Grammar: Simple present passive

5. Complete the chart.

Use the passive when it is not important who does the action, or when you don't know who does it.
To form the simple present passive, use is/are + past participle.

Active	Passive
Affirmative	
They **make** this wall of bottles.	This wall _____ **made** of bottles.
People **use** car tires to build strong walls.	Car tires **are** _____ to build strong walls.
Negative	
They **don't make** that bottle of plastic.	That bottle **isn't** _____ of plastic.
People **don't build** the houses with bricks.	The houses _____ **built** with bricks.

> Check your answers: Grammar reference, p. 112

6. Complete the sentences with the simple present passive forms of the verbs.

1. The house _____is made_____ (make) of bottles and cans.
2. Rubber tires _____ (not recycle) in some areas.
3. The water from the kitchen _____ (reuse) in the yard.
4. The recycling bins _____ (not clean) every week.
5. A lot of energy _____ (consume) in most houses.
6. This wall _____ (not decorate) with colored bottles.

7. Write simple present passive sentences. Use infinitives of purpose.

1. wood / use / build / houses in this neighborhood / .
   Wood is used to build houses in this neighborhood.
2. these plants / grow / provide / people with food / .
   _____
3. walls / design / protect / people from extreme temperatures / .
   _____
4. heat from the sun / use / give / power to the house / .
   _____
5. cans / recycle / create / walls / .
   _____

Infinitives of purpose

Use infinitives of purpose to say why something is done.

*I recycle my bottles **to help the environment**.*

*Plants are used **to prevent flooding**.*

Speaking: Plan a building!

8. **YOUR TURN** Work with a partner. Plan a new building that is made from recycled materials. What can you do with the materials below? Write your ideas and add other materials and uses. Be creative!

Glass bottles	Car or bike tires	Newspapers	Soda cans	Old clothes
beautiful chandeliers				

9. Join another pair. Tell them about your new building.

In our building, glass bottles are used to make beautiful chandeliers and lamps.

And newspapers are used . . .

BE CURIOUS Find out about the trash in our oceans. How many kilos of trash do we throw in the oceans every day? (Workbook, p. 84)

Discovery EDUCATION

7.1 WHERE DOES IT ALL GO?

New Challenges, NEW SOLUTIONS

Listening: Tour of a museum EcoHouse

1. Look at the picture. How is the room similar to and different from the living room in your home?

2. Listen to a guide explaining the living room. It's part of an exhibit. What kind of living room is it?
   a. A historical living room
   b. A living room of the future
   c. A typical modern living room

3. Listen again. Answer the questions.
   1. How long has the EcoHouse been open?
   2. How many appliances are there in the living room?
   3. What does the museum use the EcoHouse for?
   4. Which appliances use the most energy?
   5. What did the experiment show?
   6. What does one student want to do at school?

Vocabulary: Eco-construction verbs

4. Match the words with the definitions. Then listen and check your answers.

   1. _d_ install
   2. ___ build
   3. ___ design
   4. ___ reduce
   5. ___ discover
   6. ___ change
   7. ___ save
   8. ___ consume

   a. to make something by putting bricks or other materials together
   b. to stop someone or something from being killed or destroyed
   c. to find information, especially for the first time
   d. to put a piece of equipment somewhere and make it ready to use
   e. to use something such as a product, energy, or fuel
   f. to make something less
   g. to make or become different
   h. to draw or plan something, like clothes or buildings

5. **YOUR TURN** Work with a partner. Ask and answer the questions.
   1. What is one thing you could do to reduce trash at school and in your home?
   2. What do you think is going to be important when architects design new buildings in the future?
   3. Are architects the only ones who can discover new building techniques? Who else can participate in the process?

Grammar: Simple past passive

6. Complete the chart.

Use the passive when it is not important who did the action, or when you don't know who did it.
To form the simple past passive, use was/were + past participle.

Active	Passive
Affirmative	
We **built** the EcoHouse in 1985.	The EcoHouse **was built** in 1985.
We **updated** the appliances two months ago.	The appliances _____ **updated** two months ago.
Negative	
We **didn't install** a recycling bin until last year.	A recycling bin **wasn't** _____ until last year.
They **didn't install** solar panels 60 years ago.	Solar panels _____ **installed** 60 years ago.
Use by with the passive to show who did the action.	
The EcoHouse **was designed by** the museum.	
The most energy **was consumed by** the heater.	
Questions and answers with the passive	
When **was** the EcoHouse **built**?	It **was built** in 1985.
_____ the EcoHouse **built** in 1985?	Yes, it **was**.
Were the old apartments **destroyed** this year?	No, they **weren't**.

> Check your answers: Grammar reference, p. 112

7. Complete the paragraph with the simple past passive forms of the verbs.

The building ¹ *was completed* (complete) in 1985. It ² _____ (build) on a large piece of land outside the city. The air conditioners ³ _____ (install) 10 years ago. They ⁴ _____ (not put) in the bedrooms. The kitchen ⁵ _____ (redesign) two years ago.

8. Rewrite the sentences using the simple past passive and *by*.

1. The Spanish soccer team won the World Cup for the first time in 2010.

   The World Cup was won by the Spanish soccer team for the first time in 2010.

2. The Chinese found dinosaur bones over 2,000 years ago in Sichuan.

   _____

3. Ray Tomlinson sent the first email in 1971.

   _____

Speaking: Test your knowledge!

9. Put the words in the correct order to make questions.

1. by J. K. Rowling / written / *Romeo and Juliet* / Was / ?

   _____

2. the first *The Hunger Games* movie / was / When / released / ?

   _____

Get it RIGHT!

Remember to include *was* or *were* in past passive sentences.
The building **was built** in 1985.
NOT: ~~The building built in 1985.~~
People **were taught** to build homes quickly. NOT: ~~People taught to build homes quickly.~~

10. YOUR TURN Write four more questions of your own. Use the simple past passive. Then work with a partner. Ask and answer the questions in Exercise 9 and your own questions. Who knows the most answers?

> When was the first cell phone call made?

REAL TALK 7.2 WHAT KIND OF VOLUNTEER WORK CAN YOU DO IN YOUR SCHOOL OR TOWN?

Be part of the SOLUTION.

Conversation: What kind of volunteer work can you do in your school or town?

1. **REAL TALK** Watch or listen to the teenagers. Which ideas for volunteer work would you like to do? Write 1–6 next to them; 1 is your favorite idea, and 6 is your least favorite idea.

    ___ join after-school clubs   ___ clean up trash
    ___ read to older people   ___ babysit
    ___ help older people with   ___ help in the school garden
          their animals

2. **YOUR TURN** Do you do volunteer work? What do you do, and why do you do it? If not, why not? Tell your partner.

3. Listen to James talking to Natalie. Complete the conversation.

USEFUL LANGUAGE: Apologizing

| I didn't mean to | I'm really sorry. | It was my fault. | ✓ My apologies. |

James: Hey, Natalie. What happened to you yesterday?
Natalie: Yesterday? What do you mean?
James: Don't you remember? We agreed to go to the park and clean up trash? A whole bunch of us were there. You said you wanted to do it.
Natalie: Oh, no! ¹ _My apologies._ I forgot about that.
James: Natalie, I sent you a text to remind you!
Natalie: I know. ² _____ I didn't set my alarm clock.
James: You were supposed to bring trash bags. We were counting on you.
Natalie: ³ _____ What did you do?
James: I had to call my dad and ask him to bring us trash bags. He was pretty mad because he was busy with something else.
Natalie: ⁴ _____ forget. I feel really bad about that.
James: It's OK. We're doing it again next month. Can we count on you?
Natalie: Yes! I'll be there. I promise.

4. Practice the conversation with a partner.

5. **YOUR TURN** Work with a partner. Take turns apologizing to a friend and explaining what the problem was. Use the situations below.

Situation A
You forgot to help your friend read books to children at a library. Your friend had to do it alone.

Situation B
You didn't help your friend prepare a presentation for class about recycling. Your friend was up really late working on it.

Say it RIGHT!

To make adjectives stronger, you can use words like *really*, *very*, and *extremely*. Put extra stress on these words. Listen and repeat the sentences.
I'm **really** sorry.
They were **very** noisy.
We're **extremely** excited!

Volunteers Clean Valley Nature Reserve by Chris Davies

Last Sunday, about 100 people went to the Valley Nature Reserve to clean up the river. The event was organized by the Valley Conservation Society, which helps to protect the environment. Every year, local volunteers clean up trash that is thrown in the river. This year, I was one of them. We picked up hundreds of plastic bottles, plastic bags, and metal cans. That stuff was disgusting! The Society also removes non-native plants from the land near the river. These plants kill off native species and affect biodiversity. At the Valley Nature Reserve, we cut down kudzu, a pretty, but dangerous, plant. The cleanup was hard work, but it was fun. And the river looked great! Why not join us next time? We're already planning next year's event. It'll be in April. For more information, go to the Valley Nature Reserve website. ■

Reading to write: Cleaning up a river

6. Look at the photo. What kind of trash did the volunteers find? Read the article and check.

> ◉ *Focus on* **CONTENT**
> When you write a newspaper article, ask yourself these questions before you begin:
> - What was the event?
> - When was it?
> - Where was it?
> - Who was involved?
> - What did they do?
> - What were the results?
> - What will happen next?

7. Underline the answers to the Focus on Context box questions in the article.

> ◉ *Focus on* **LANGUAGE**
> Don't repeat the same word or words too much when you write. Use different words to refer to something you wrote about before.
> *The event* = the Valley Nature Reserve cleanup
> *I was one of them* = one of the volunteers

8. Write what the words from the article refer to.

1. *These plants* kill off native species: *non-native plants*
2. *That stuff* was disgusting: _____
3. . . . but *it* was fun: _____
4. *It'll* be in April: _____
5. *a pretty but dangerous plant*: _____

Writing: A newspaper article about an event

☐ **PLAN**
Plan your newspaper article about an event. Use the list in the Focus on Content box and make notes.

☐ **WRITE**
Write your article. Use your notes to help you. Write about 120 words.

☐ **CHECK**
Can you say "yes" to these questions?

- Is the information from the Focus on Content box in your article?
- Did you answer the questions from the Focus on Content box?

Workbook, pp. 48–49

UNDER THE AUSTRALIAN SUN

Australia is one of the sunniest countries on the planet, and sun is an important part of Australia's traditional outdoor lifestyle. Barbecues are held in sunny backyards 12 months a year. People spend days on end surfing at beautiful golden beaches. One in four homes has a swimming pool in the yard. You don't believe me? Look out the airplane window when you land at Sydney Airport. But there's more to sun than fun!

Australia gets more than 3,500 hours of sunlight a year – that's 10 hours a day – and solar energy is big business. Australia has invested enormously in solar energy. Solar panels provide energy to houses, schools, businesses, and factories all over the country. They have reduced the country's energy bills and had a very positive environmental impact.

However, there's a price to pay for so much sunshine. Rays from the sun can be very dangerous. The risk of skin cancer is high, so ads everywhere tell people to *Slip! Slop! Slap!* This very successful three-step approach was invented by experts to remind us what to use to protect our skin.

- **First,** *slip* on some special clothing. Clothes with special sun filters were invented by Australians and are really popular.

- **Next,** *slop* on some powerful sunscreen – even if you're only going out for 10 minutes. Use sunscreens with a sun protection factor (SPF) of at least 30+.

- **Finally,** *slap* on a big hat. Find a big hat that is designed so the sun doesn't hit your head or neck.

So remember, it's great to have fun in the sun, but wherever you are, and whatever you're doing – having a barbecue, chilling out at the pool, or surfing at the beach – don't forget to SLIP, SLOP, SLAP!

Culture: Good sunshine, bad sunshine

1. Look at photos *a* and *b*. What can you see in each photo? What connects the two photos?

2. Read and listen to the article. Is the Australian attitude toward the sun mainly positive or mainly negative?

3. Read the article again. Answer the questions.
   1. How does the sun influence the Australian way of life?
   2. Why are solar panels successful in Australia?
   3. Why is the sun a problem in Australia?
   4. What are the three things you should slip on, slop on, and slap on?

4. **YOUR TURN** Work with a partner. Ask and answer the questions.
   1. Would you like to visit Australia? Why? / Why not?
   2. What's the sunniest place in your country?
   3. Is solar energy common in your country?
   4. How do you protect yourself from the sun?

DID YOU KNOW...?
Eighty percent of Australians live within 50 kilometers of the coast.

BE CURIOUS Find out about a natural disaster in a town in Kansas, in the United States. How was the town different after it was rebuilt? (Workbook, p. 85)

Discovery EDUCATION
7.3 BUILD IT BETTER

UNIT 7 REVIEW

Vocabulary

1. Write the name of each material.

1. G _L_ _A_ _S_ _S_
2. B _ _ _ _ _
3. W _ _ _ _
4. P _ _ _ _ _ _
5. P _ _ _ _
6. M _ _ _

Grammar

2. Rewrite the sentences. Use the simple present passive.

1. They recycle these metal cans.
   These metal cans are recycled.

2. They make these sweaters from plastic bottles.
   _____

3. They use corn to make heating oil.
   _____

4. They produce electricity from this water.
   _____

5. They build these houses from organic materials.
   _____

3. Complete the questions and answers with the simple past passive forms of the verbs.

| build | discover | ✓ make |
| destroy | grow | |

1. When __was__ the first talking movie __made__?
   It __was made__ in 1927.

2. When _____ tea first _____ in China?
   Tea _____ 4,000 years ago.

3. Where _____ gold _____ in the 1800s?
   Gold _____ in California in the 1800s.

4. When _____ Pompeii _____ by a volcanic eruption?
   Pompeii _____ by a volcanic eruption in 79 CE.

5. Where _____ the first public railways _____?
   The first public railways _____ in England in the 1800s.

Useful language

4. Complete the conversation.

| really sorry | I didn't mean to | apologies | was my fault |

Mom: Kevin, don't throw out the soda cans and newspapers with the trash! We recycle those.

Kevin: Oh, yeah. I'm [1]_____. I totally forgot.

Mom: But we talked about this last month. Everyone in the house was going to help recycle. Remember?

Kevin: Yeah. My [2]_____. I'll try to do better.

Mom: Thank you. Also, you have to clean the kitchen after you make snacks. Last night, it was a mess!

Kevin: Yeah, that [3]_____. I made a snack and then went to bed. I was too tired to clean it up.

Mom: Kevin, come on.

Kevin: Sorry, Mom. [4]_____ make you mad. It won't happen again.

PROGRESS CHECK: Now I can . . .

☐ identify materials.
☐ talk about how people recycle and reuse materials.
☐ talk about eco-construction.
☐ apologize.
☐ write a newspaper article.
☐ discuss solar energy and sun safety.

CLIL PROJECT

7.4 DRIVING INTO THE FUTURE, p. 119

8 Run for Cover!

Discovery EDUCATION
BE CURIOUS

- Land of Volcanoes
- Do you often lose things?
- Storm Chasers

1. Describe what you see in this picture.

2. Tornadoes sometimes appear in movies or TV shows. Have you ever seen a tornado on screen? What was happening?

3. Have you ever seen a tornado in real life? How would you react if you did?

UNIT CONTENTS

Vocabulary Natural disasters; survival essentials
Grammar Past perfect; past perfect yes/no questions; past perfect and simple past
Listening Survival story

Vocabulary: Natural disasters

1. Match the words with the correct pictures.

1. _b_ tsunami
2. ___ volcanic eruption
3. ___ earthquake
4. ___ flood
5. ___ forest fire
6. ___ tornado
7. ___ hurricane
8. ___ landslide
9. ___ avalanche

2. Listen, check, and repeat.

3. Match the news reports with disasters (a–i) from Exercise 1.
1. "The wave is enormous. It's like a wall of water." ___
2. "The mountain is very dangerous. Rocks can fall at any time." ___
3. "The flames are now covering the hills, but people's homes are not in danger." ___
4. "The building is shaking. It's really frightening." ___
5. "I can see smoke and hot lava coming down the mountain." ___
6. "The funnel of wind pulled the roof off of a house, and it landed three kilometers away." ___

> **Say it RIGHT!**
>
> Pay attention to the pronunciation of these vowel sounds:
> /æ/ dis**a**ster, l**a**ndslide, n**a**tural
> /ɒ/ r**o**ck, imp**o**ssible, n**o**t
> Find one more example of each sound in Exercise 3.
> _____ _____

Speaking: Terror or excitement?

4. YOUR TURN Work with a partner. Ask and answer the questions.
1. Which of the disasters from Exercise 1 are possible in your country?
2. What's the worst type of natural disaster, in your opinion? Why?
3. Do you know anyone who's experienced any of these disasters?
4. What's one more natural disaster not listed here?

> Where we live, lots of these natural disasters are possible: earthquakes, floods, hurricanes, and landslides.

> Workbook, p. 50

Reading Krakatoa; Story Source; Chasing the Storms
Conversation Asking about and talking about personal problems
Writing A story about a personal experience

The Loudest Sound in
MODERN HISTORY

KRAKATOA

What's the loudest noise you can imagine? Double it and that might be close to the noise that the volcanoes on Krakatoa island made when they erupted in 1883. Scientific experts say that it was the loudest sound in modern history. People heard it in Australia, more than 3,000 kilometers away.

Krakatoa is a volcanic island between the islands of Java and Sumatra in Indonesia. When the volcanoes erupted, the explosions created a tsunami with waves more than 40 meters high. In fact, the tsunami caused more deaths than the volcanoes themselves. It killed 34,000 people and destroyed 165 towns and villages.

A huge cloud of dust traveled around the planet. As a result, the temperature of the world dropped one degree. The weather didn't return to normal until five years later, in 1888. People who saw the event said that the cloud had caused fantastic colors in the sky.

Terrible eruptions continued for weeks. Any survivors on other islands who hadn't escaped yet found out that they couldn't escape. They watched the explosions from a distance and organized festivals to celebrate the volcano. What had caused the eruptions? They didn't know. They also didn't know that the eruptions were so serious.

The Krakatoa volcano didn't erupt again until 1927. This eruption created a new island at the same location. There were more eruptions between 2009 and 2012, but they weren't dangerous.

Today, Indonesia has 130 active volcanoes – more than any other country in the world. So a new eruption is possible at any time!

Reading: A magazine article

1. Look at the title and the picture. What do you think the article is about?

2. Read and listen to the article. What was the loudest sound in history?

3. Read the article again. Are the sentences true (*T*) or false (*F*)?

   1. The volcanoes on Krakatoa island erupted in 1883. ___
   2. More people died because of the tsunami than the volcanic eruptions. ___
   3. After the volcanic eruptions, the weather quickly returned to normal. ___
   4. People living on nearby islands knew exactly what caused the eruptions. ___
   5. Krakatoa had several dangerous eruptions between 2009 and 2012. ___
   6. No other countries have as many volcanoes as Indonesia. ___

4. **YOUR TURN** Work with a partner. Ask and answer the questions.

   1. Why do you think there were climatic differences for five years after the volcano?
   2. Are there any areas with volcanoes in or near your country? Where are they? Are they still active?
   3. Have you heard about any recent volcanic eruptions or tsunamis? What do you remember about them?

DID YOU KNOW...?
There are over 500 active volcanoes in the world. A large horseshoe-shaped area around the Pacific Ocean is called the "Ring of Fire." Over half the world's active volcanoes can be found there.

Grammar: Past perfect

5. Complete the chart.

Use the past perfect to refer to something that happened before a specific time in the past. To form the past perfect, use had + past participle.

Affirmative	Negative
I was interested in Krakatoa because I **had read** a book about it.	I just read about Krakatoa. I **hadn't heard** about it before then.
The volcano _____ **been** fairly quiet for several years before the eruption.	I visited Indonesia last year. I _____ **been** there before, so it was new to me.
What _____ you **heard** about volcanoes before you visited one? Why _____**n't** you **researched** anything about Indonesia before you went there?	
Contractions had = **'d** had not = **hadn't**	

> Check your answers: Grammar reference, p. 113

6. Complete the sentences with the past perfect forms of the verbs.

1. I _____ (read) about the volcanic eruption at Pompeii, but I didn't know much about Krakatoa.

2. Alan was surprised when he heard the thunder. When _____ the storm _____ (begin)?

3. We _____ (not have) an earthquake before 2004. Since then, we've had three!

4. There were two floods in our town last summer. Before that, I _____ (see) only one flood in 10 years.

5. Sadie went to Europe for the first time last summer. She _____ (not be) there before that.

6. I heard students laughing, and then I heard a loud noise. What _____ they _____ (do)?

7. Put the words in the correct order to make questions.

1. you / about Krakatoa / heard / today / before / had

   Had you heard about Krakatoa before today?

2. before the day of the show / had / bought the tickets / he

   _____

3. her teacher / Julie / had / met / before class started

   _____

4. had / before your parents came home / cleaned / you / your room

   _____

Past perfect yes/no questions	
Had you ever **seen** a tornado before you moved here?	Yes, I **had**. / No, I **hadn't**.
Had Amber **known** about the volcano on the next island?	Yes, she **had**. / No, she **hadn't**.

Speaking: Before the disaster, . . .

8. Imagine a volcano erupted 30 kilometers from your home. You and your family survived because you were prepared. Write three things you had done to prepare for the disaster.

1. *Before the eruption, I had bought extra water.*
2. _____
3. _____

BE CURIOUS Find out about volcanoes in Russia. What is Sasha's job? (Workbook, p. 86)

9. YOUR TURN Work in pairs. Talk about your preparations. Who was better prepared?

> Before the eruption, I had bought extra water.

> That's good. I had forgotten that. But I had asked my mother to fill the gas tank of the car.

8.1 LAND OF VOLCANOES

Survival by ALL MEANS!

Listening: Survival story

1. **Work with a partner. Ask and answer the questions.**
   1. Do you enjoy exercising outdoors or walking in nature? Where have you done that and what was it like?
   2. What kinds of things would you take with you if you were on a long hike or walking a long distance?

2. **Listen to two friends discussing a news story about a hiker. Is it a happy or a sad story?**

3. **Listen again. Answer the questions.**
   1. What's the climate in Queensland like?
      _____
   2. What happened when the hiker was out running?
      _____
   3. What was the weather like?
      _____
   4. What had Sam brought with him?
      a bottle of _____, _____, _____, packs of _____
   5. How did the contact lenses save him?
      _____
   6. How did they find him in the end?
      _____
   7. How long was he lost?
      _____

Vocabulary: Survival essentials

4. **Match the words and phrases with the correct pictures. Then listen and check your answers.**

   1. ___ sunscreen
   2. ___ water bottle
   3. ___ sunglasses
   4. ___ compass
   5. ___ map
   6. ___ sleeping bag
   7. ___ penknife
   8. ___ flashlight
   9. ___ first-aid kit

5. **YOUR TURN Work with a partner. What's the most important survival equipment if you get lost in the following situations? Give reasons.**

   a. In the mountains in the winter
   b. In a forest at night
   c. In the middle of a city

Grammar: Past perfect and simple past

6. Read the sentences. Then circle the correct answer to complete the rules.

> The young man's parents **called** the police after he **had been** gone for three days.
> The boy **had drunk** the liquid from all the contact lens cases when they **found** him.
> The boy **didn't tell** his story until he **had drunk** a lot of water.
>
> 1. We **can / can't** use the past perfect and the simple past in the same sentence.
> 2. We use the **simple past / past perfect** for the action that was completed first.

> Check your answers: Grammar reference, p. 113

7. Circle the correct answers.

1. Kent _____ about the weather until he _____ outside for a few minutes.
   a. didn't think / had been   (circled)
   b. had thought / had been

2. After Jen _____ her map for a long time, she _____ to turn left.
   a. studied / had decided
   b. had studied / decided

3. The skier's family _____ worried only after the avalanche _____.
   a. had gotten / had happened
   b. got / had happened

4. By the time my father _____, I _____ the party.
   a. had called / left
   b. called / had left

8. Complete the text with the simple past or past perfect forms of the verbs. Then listen and check your answers.

I ¹___saw___ (see) an interesting movie last night. It was the true story of a guy named Aron Ralston. He was alone in a canyon in a national park. A large rock ²_____ (fall) on his right hand, and his hand was stuck between the rock and a wall. Unfortunately, before he ³_____ (leave) home, he ⁴_____ (not tell) his friends or family where he was going. They didn't know he was lost. He was in the canyon for five days. He ⁵_____ (drink) all his water already, and he ⁶_____ (eat) all his food, when he had an idea. He ⁷_____ (bring) along a small, cheap penknife, so he ⁸_____ (use) it to cut off his arm. It was terrible, but he did it. He was free. He started walking and found a family in the park. After they ⁹_____ (give) him some water, they ¹⁰_____ (call) emergency services. He survived! It was a very exciting story.

> **Get it RIGHT!**
>
> Use the past perfect, not the present perfect, for referring to events completed before another past moment.
> After I **had read** three books about forest fires, I decided to become a firefighter. NOT: ~~After I have read three books about forest fires, I decided to become a firefighter.~~

Speaking: I hadn't done my homework yet!

9. Think about what you did yesterday. Write down one thing you had done, and one thing you hadn't done, by the time you did each thing in the box.

| had breakfast | ate lunch | went to bed |
| got to school | had dinner | |

> By the time I had breakfast, I had taken a shower.

10. YOUR TURN Work with a partner. Ask and answer questions about the things you did.

> Had you taken a shower by the time you had breakfast?

> Yes, I had. What about you?

> No, I hadn't. But I had made my bed.

REAL TALK 8.2 DO YOU OFTEN LOSE THINGS?

Don't PANIC!

Conversation: Do you often lose things?

1. **REAL TALK** Watch or listen to the teenagers. Check (✓) the things that are mentioned.

   ☐ cell phone ☐ sunglasses ☐ bike
   ☐ pencil ☐ remote control ☐ keys

2. **YOUR TURN** Do you often lose things? Tell your partner about things you have lost, what happened, and how you felt.

3. Listen to Adam and Daniela talking about a problem. Complete the conversation.

> **USEFUL LANGUAGE:** Asking about and talking about personal problems
>
> I don't know what to do!   ✓ What's the matter?   Don't panic!   Oh, no!   Let me think.

Adam: Hi, Daniela! ¹ _What's the matter?_

Daniela: I can't find my backpack! It has all my books in it!

Adam: ² _____ When did you last see it?

Daniela: I remember I put it in my locker before gym class.

Adam: Did you get it after gym?

Daniela: I don't remember. I went to the varsity basketball game right after that.

Adam: Did you have it at the game?

Daniela: I don't know. Maybe. I went to the mall with Emily. The game had finished, and we were hungry. And then we went to the park.

Adam: Did you leave it in the park?

Daniela: I'm not sure. I know Emily remembered her backpack. I asked her where she had bought it. But then I came home and when I realized I didn't have it, I went back. It wasn't there!

Adam: OK. ³ _____ Maybe you left it in the mall, in one of the stores.

Daniela: No, I don't think so. For one thing, no one has called me.

Adam: Had you written your name or phone number on your backpack?

Daniela: Yes. Now what? ⁴ _____

Adam: OK, hang on. ⁵ _____ OK, I have an idea. Let's go to the park and see if it's there. Then we'll go to the mall and ask for it at the Lost and Found. Then we'll go to school. Who knows? Maybe you left it in class.

4. Practice the conversation with a partner.

5. **YOUR TURN** Work with a partner. Describe a personal problem. Have your partner try to help you.

Problem 1	Problem 2
You're at school. Your cell phone isn't in your bag. It's new, and it was expensive. It has all your friends' phone numbers in it and hundreds of pictures and songs. You had it this morning at home.	You're at a friend's house. You can't find your flash drive. It has all the work you did for a group presentation on it. You need it tomorrow. You had it earlier today at school.

Home | STORIES | Music | Movies

STORY SOURCE
Do you have a scary or difficult story to tell? Did you have a scary or difficult experience? Write and tell us what happened.

One afternoon last April, I was at home. I had turned the TV on and was about to watch my favorite show when suddenly, the electricity went off. Then my mom called to say that a tornado was in the area. Where I live, there are tornadoes every year, so, naturally, we had learned what to do at school.

We went down to the basement and hid in a closet. We could hear the storm, louder and louder, and then the walls started to shake. I had been a little scared the time before, but this time I was terrified. After about three minutes, when everything had become quiet again, we went to the kitchen to look outside. I saw that our house was OK, but unfortunately, the house next door was destroyed.

I called my mom immediately. My parents were safe, too. It was a horrible experience, but fortunately, we all survived.

Reading to write: A blog about an experience

6. Look at the picture. What experience is the writer describing? What do you think your reaction to this experience would be?

> *Focus on* **CONTENT**
> When you write about an experience, you can include this information:
> - When it happened
> - Where you were
> - What happened
> - How you felt
> - The end of the story

7. Read the blog again. Underline the five pieces of information from the Focus on Content box.

> *Focus on* **LANGUAGE**
> **Adverbs**
> Use adverbs to link ideas together and make the story more dramatic and interesting.
> . . . when **suddenly**, the electricity went off.

8. Find four more examples of adverbs in the blog.

suddenly _____ _____ _____ _____

9. Complete the sentences with the adverbs in Exercise 8.

1. I had always lived in a place where there were hurricanes, so _naturally_ I knew what to do when we heard the warning.

2. We didn't wait for the authorities to tell us to leave when the floods started. We left _____.

3. The earthquake was strong, but _____, there was no tsunami afterwards.

4. _____ for our neighbors, the forest fire burned part of their house. It was ruined.

5. Jeff was sleeping when _____, he heard a loud noise.

Writing: A story about a personal experience

◯ PLAN
Plan your personal story for a website. Use the list in the Focus on Content box and make notes.

◯ WRITE
Write your story for the website. Use your notes and the blog to help you. Write about 120 words.

◯ CHECK
Can you say "yes" to these questions?

- Did you include the information from the Focus on Content box?
- Did you use adverbs like *suddenly* to make the writing more dramatic?

| Home | Stories | Music | Movies | Chat |

CHASING THE STORMS

Tornadoes bring heavy rain and terrible winds – the strongest tornadoes travel at 400 kilometers per hour and are 80 kilometers wide. They are very destructive. Storm chasers are people who follow the tornadoes and try to get as close as possible. Today's interview is with Todd Robson, a storm chaser in Tornado Alley.

What is Tornado Alley?
It's the large area in the middle of the United States. It goes from Iowa in the north to Louisiana in the south. Most of the world's tornadoes happen in Tornado Alley. Every year, there are 1,000 or more tornadoes here!

Why are there so many tornadoes in Tornado Alley?
The summers are really hot, and there are lots of thunderstorms. Those are favorable conditions for tornadoes. Most tornadoes in Tornado Alley happen between March and August, but they can happen at any time of the year.

What's it like living in Tornado Alley?
New buildings in Tornado Alley have to have strong roofs and good foundations. A lot of people have special shelters underground – storm cellars – that protect them from tornadoes. And most neighborhoods have loud tornado sirens that warn them that a tornado is nearby.

Why are you a storm chaser?
Well, it's really exciting, but it isn't just a hobby. It's my job, too. Scientists need to understand storms better so that we can predict when they're coming and warn people.

I've read about storm-chasing tours. Do they really exist?
Yes! People can pay to go on storm-chasing trips. It's scary, and it can be a bit dangerous, but it's fun. Most of our tours are from April to June, and we drive all over Tornado Alley looking for storms. It's incredible!

Culture: Tornado Alley

1. Look at the photo. What kind of extreme weather do you see? What do you think the people in the car are doing?

2. Read and listen to the interview. Check your answers in Exercise 1.

3. Read the interview again. Complete the summary.

   Todd Robson is a storm chaser in ^{1}_____. Tornadoes bring strong winds and ^{2}_____. They can travel at ^{3}_____. There are more than ^{4}_____ tornadoes in Tornado Alley each year, where the summers are ^{5}_____ and there are lots of thunderstorms. Many people have ^{6}_____ that protect them from tornadoes. Some people chase storms because it's exciting, but scientists want to understand them better to ^{7}_____ when they're coming. If you want to chase storms, the best time to do it is from ^{8}_____ to June.

4. **YOUR TURN** Work with a partner. Ask and answer the questions.

   1. Why do you think people want to watch storms?
   2. Do you know anyone who's afraid of storms?
   3. Would you like to go on a storm-chasing tour? Why? / Why not?

DID YOU KNOW...?
If you're near a tornado, the safest place is underground – in the basement of a house or in a special shelter.

BE CURIOUS Find out about some scientists who study tornadoes. What is an F5 tornado? (Workbook, p. 87)

Discovery EDUCATION

8.3 STORM CHASERS

UNIT 8 REVIEW

Vocabulary

1. **Match the words with the definitions.**

    1. ___ earthquake
    2. ___ avalanche
    3. ___ hurricane
    4. ___ eruption
    5. ___ flood

    a. powerful movements below the Earth's surface
    b. an explosion inside a volcano
    c. very strong winds that can cause a lot of damage
    d. a large quantity of water that suddenly covers land and houses
    e. a large quantity of ice or snow falling down a mountain

Grammar

2. **Complete the paragraph with the past perfect forms of the verbs.**

    | notice | read | see | ski | start | ✓ travel |

    Last year, I was skiing in Utah with my family. We ¹ _had traveled_ to Utah before, but this was our first visit to this ski resort. My sister and I ² _____ avalanche warning signs in other areas, but there were no signs where we were that day. We ³ _____ down the hill, and a minute later, I heard a loud sound. I ⁴ _____ in a book that avalanches were loud, but this sounded like a train. A loud train! Suddenly, I saw a huge wall of snow coming down the hill after us. I shouted at my sister to ski fast and to follow me. We ⁵ _____ most of the way down the hill, as fast as we could go, when the avalanche reached us. We were covered in snow and couldn't find a way to escape. Luckily, some people ⁶ _____ us, and they had called a rescue crew.

3. **Complete the sentences and questions with the past perfect or simple present forms of the verbs.**

    1. I _didn't see_ (not see) sharks until I _had left_ (leave) the ocean.
    2. After we _____ (be) hiking for three hours, it _____ (start) raining.
    3. The hikers _____ (not see) the landslide warning signs before they _____ (begin) walking down the hill.
    4. The emergency workers _____ (not stop) looking for survivors until they _____ (make) sure everyone was safe.
    5. She _____ (not drink) all the water in her bottle, so she _____ (share) some of it with her friend.
    6. We _____ (feel) terrible when we saw all the houses the hurricane _____ (destroy).

Useful language

4. **Complete the conversation.**

    | don't | Let me | Oh | ✓ What's the | what to do |

    Maria: Kate! Wake up! Look at that!
    Kate: What? ¹ _What's the_ matter?
    Maria: There's a spider in our tent. A big one. Look over there!
    Kate: ² _____, no! Now what?
    Maria: I don't know ³ _____! Do you?
    Kate: Well, first of all, ⁴ _____ panic.
    Maria: I'm trying not to. But look at it. It's huge!
    Kate: I know. OK. Hang on. ⁵ _____ think.
    Maria: Let's cover it with a towel and throw it outside.
    Kate: Good idea. Get your towel.
    Maria: My towel? Are you serious? Get your towel.
    Kate: Maria, any towel is OK. Let's get going!

PROGRESS CHECK: Now I can . . .

☐ discuss natural disasters.
☐ ask and answer questions about past experiences.
☐ discuss past events.
☐ ask about and discuss personal problems.
☐ write about a difficult past experience.
☐ discuss tornadoes and people who chase tornadoes.

9 He SAID, She SAID

Discovery EDUCATION

BE CURIOUS

- Social Networks
- What do you think about celebrity gossip?
- The Language of the Future?
- Pictures with Meaning

1. Describe what you see in this picture.

2. What kinds of things do you and your friends like to talk about?

3. When you're not together, how do you communicate with your friends?

UNIT CONTENTS

Vocabulary Reporting verbs; Communication methods
Grammar Quoted speech vs. reported speech; reported questions
Listening Short conversations

Vocabulary: Reporting verbs

1. Match the words with the definitions.

1. _e_ say
2. ___ explain
3. ___ remind
4. ___ whisper
5. ___ tell
6. ___ shout
7. ___ announce
8. ___ promise
9. ___ suggest
10. ___ complain

a. to speak very quietly (7 letters)
b. to express an idea for someone to consider (7 letters)
c. to say something very loudly (5 letters)
d. to make someone remember something (6 letters)
e. to tell someone about a fact, thought, or opinion (3 letters)
f. to say you're unhappy or don't like something (8 letters)
g. to say you will certainly do something (7 letters)
h. to make something easy to understand (7 letters)
i. to share news, stories, or information with someone (4 letters)
j. to say something officially (8 letters)

2. Listen, check, and repeat.

3. Complete the sentences with words from Exercise 1.

1. I usually forget to clean my room on Saturdays. My mother has to _remind_ me.
2. My brother's action figure was broken when he bought it. My father went to the store to _____, and he got his money back.
3. After my baby sister finally fell asleep, my mother asked us to _____ so we wouldn't wake her up.
4. I love it when my grandmother comes over. She likes to _____ me stories from when she was little.
5. Mr. Black is a great teacher. He can _____ really hard concepts so that we can understand them.
6. Jessica usually stays out too late, but this time she _____ her parents she would be home on time.

Speaking: Tell about a time when you . . .

4. YOUR TURN Work with a partner. Ask and answer the questions.

1. When was the last time you shouted? Where were you, and why did you shout?
2. Do you know someone who complains a lot? Who? Do you usually agree with this person?
3. When was the last time you promised to do something? Did you do it? Why? / Why not?

> Once, when I was younger, I promised to make dinner with my little sister. We made dinner, but it was terrible!

Say it RIGHT!

When a word ends in the final consonants *d*, *l*, *m*, and *n*, put your tongue in the position to say that letter, but don't say it. Native speakers put more emphasis on the vowel. Practice these sentences:
*I don't understan**d**. Can you please explai**n**?*
*There's nothing to te**ll**. He didn't come ho**m**e.*

▶ Workbook, p. 58

Reading Communication Changes; Are Cell Phones Good for Teenagers?; The World Speaks One Language
Conversation Comparing different accounts of a story
Writing An essay about social networking sites

The Reality of COMMUNICATION TODAY

COMMUNICATION CHANGES
by Amanda Mitchell

Teenagers love their cell phones and social networking sites, but there's conflict at home because of it. I talked to kids, parents, and experts to find out what's going on.

1. ___ "My cell phone is a great way for me to communicate with my friends," student Sarah Davis says. Sarah explained that she wanted to hang out with her friends after school – at the mall or in the park – but these days it wasn't easy. She said her mother, Becky, worried about her going out alone. "So, we go to social networking sites and hang out together that way." Becky isn't happy about it. "That's all she does," she complains.

2. ___ In the past 30 years, parents have become more concerned about security issues. Becky explained that kids in her generation hung out together every day. They rode their bikes to the mall, to each other's houses, or to the park. "But I just don't think that's safe anymore," she says.

3. ___ Psychologist Dr. Richard Turner said that conflict about cell phone use is becoming a common problem in families. "These kids grew up with cell phones. At the same time, parents are uncomfortable with the constant cell phone use. Obviously, families need to find a balance between safety concerns and a teenager's need to be with friends."

4. ___ Students are busier than they used to be. This is another reason why they spend time on social networking sites. "Universities like students who are active and engaged," student Mike Owens explains. That means that Mike does sports or other activities every day after school. "There's just no time to hang out with my friends. We use social networking sites instead," Mike laughs. He said that his parents sometimes get upset about this. "But what can I do? It's the reality!"

DID YOU KNOW...?
The first handheld cell phones were used as car phones. They cost $4,000 to $9,000 in today's money and were so big and heavy that people called them "The Brick."

Reading: A magazine article

1. Read the possible paragraph headings for an article. What do you think the article is about?

   a. Conflict in families
   b. Then and now
   c. No free time
   d. A great way to communicate

2. Read and listen to the article. Match the headings (a–d) in Exercise 1 with the paragraphs.

3. Read the possible paragraph headings for an article again. Answer the questions.

   1. Why isn't it easy for Sarah to hang out with her friends at the mall?
   2. Why does Becky complain about Sarah's cell phone use?
   3. Where did Becky and her friends hang out 30 years ago?
   4. What does Dr. Turner say is becoming a source of conflict in many families?
   5. What kind of students do universities look for?
   6. What does Mike do after school?

4. **YOUR TURN** Work with a partner. Ask and answer the questions.

   1. Where's your favorite place to hang out with your friends?
   2. What social networking sites do you use most? Why?
   3. What do you imagine social networking sites will be like in 10 years?

Grammar: Quoted speech vs. reported speech

5. Complete the chart with the words in the box.

can   Future with *will*   Present perfect   Simple past   ✓ Simple present

Use reported speech to tell others what another person said.

	Quoted speech	Reported speech
1. Simple present	"It **isn't** right," she said.	She said that it **wasn't** right.
2. _____	"We **spent** the whole day together," she told me.	She told me that they **had spent** the whole day together.
3. _____	"We**'ve had** a cell phone for 12 years," he said.	He said that they **had had** a cell phone for 12 years.
4. _____	"I**'ll text** you when I get to the party," he promised.	He promised that he **would text** me when he got to the party.
5. _____	"I **can send** you an email," she whispered to her friend.	She whispered that she **could send** her friend an email.

> Check your answers: Grammar reference, p. 114

6. Look at the chart in Exercise 5. What does the verb in quoted speech change to in reported speech? Complete the table.

	Quoted speech	Reported speech
1.	Simple present	Simple past
2.	can	_____
3.	Present perfect	_____
4.	Simple past	_____
5.	will	_____

NOTICE IT
In quoted speech, put the comma inside the quotation marks when the quote is first, and outside the quotation marks when the quote comes second.

"I'm using my computer right **now**," she said.
She **said,** "I'm using my computer right now."

7. Write these sentences in reported speech form.

1. "Social networking sites are a great way to talk to my friends," said Daniel.
   Daniel said that social networking sites were a great way to talk to his friends.

2. "I learned how to create video games," explained Sophie.
   _____

3. Mike announced, "Students can use their cell phones."
   _____

4. "I'll volunteer next Saturday," promised Sarah.
   _____

5. Travis said, "I've never been to Europe."
   _____

Speaking: Face-to-face

8. YOUR TURN Work with a partner. Ask and answer the questions. Make notes of the answers your partner gives.

How often do you see your friends? What do you do together? Will you hang out this weekend?

9. Use your notes from Exercise 8 to write your partner's answers to the questions in reported speech. Then tell another pair of students about your partner.

> Jack said that he saw his friends on weekends and that they usually went to the mall. He said that they would go to the movies this weekend.

BE CURIOUS Find out about social networks. What are the three social networking sites that the video talks about? (Workbook, p. 88)

Discovery EDUCATION

9.1 SOCIAL NETWORKS

Workbook, pp. 58–59

Stop chatting and pay ATTENTION!

Listening: Short conversations

1. **Work with a partner. Look at the four pictures. Ask and answer the questions.**
   1. Where are the people?
   2. What is the relationship between the people in each picture?
   3. What do you think they're talking about?

2. **Listen to four short conversations. Match the pictures in Exercise 1 to the conversations.**

   1. _____ 2. _____ 3. _____ 4. _____

3. **Listen again. Answer the questions.**
   1. Nicole doesn't want to study. What does she want to do? Why does her mother think it's important to study hard?
   2. What is Joe texting Steve about? What does Joe think about his soccer skills?
   3. Why did Rachel have to go home? What did Rachel tell Mr. Peterson about the rules?
   4. Where are Paul and Addison going? What did Greg say would happen if they got to the concert early?

Vocabulary: Communication methods

4. **Complete the sentences with the correct words. Then listen and check your answers.**

blog post	forum	social network post
chatting	✓microblog post	text message
email	phone call	video chat

   1. My brother doesn't like to express himself in really short sentences, so he won't write a *microblog post*. He writes a long _____ every week, though, about whatever he's interested in.
   2. I can hear you pretty well, but I'm having trouble seeing you. I don't think the _____ is working. Let me send you an _____ instead.
   3. There was an article about the dress code on the school's online _____ today. I was _____ with Lisa about it in class, and Mr. Brown asked us to be quiet.
   4. It's been so long since I made a _____. I don't like to talk that much. I'd rather send a _____ from my phone.
   5. I like to write a _____ a few times a day to say how I'm feeling or to share funny videos with my friends.

5. **YOUR TURN** Work with a partner. What forms of communication do you like best? Why?

Grammar: Reported questions

6. Complete the chart.

In reported questions, the verbs usually change tenses as in reported speech.
The word order in reported questions is the same as in an affirmative sentence.

Direct speech questions	Reported questions
"Why **do** you **have** makeup on?"	He asked her why she __had__ makeup on.
"Which blog post **did** you **read**?"	She asked me which blog post I _____.
"How **have** you **been**?"	He asked me how I _____.
"When **will** you **chat** with me?"	She asked me when I _____ with her.
"Who **can help** them send a text message?"	He asked who _____ them send a text message.
Use if in Yes/No reported questions.	
"Are you on your way?"	He asked **if** we were on our way.
"Did you see what happened?"	She asked _____ I had seen what happened.

> Check your answers: Grammar reference, p. 114

7. Circle the correct answer.

1. "Where is your cell phone?" She asked **if / where** my cell phone was.
2. "Will you write that blog post today?" My teacher asked **if / when** I would write that blog post today.
3. "Can you do a video chat with a cell phone?" My grandmother asked **can / if** I could do a video chat with a cell phone.
4. "What did you do last night during the game?" Leah asked **if / what** I had done last night during the game.

8. Write the sentences as reported questions.

1. Devon asked me, "How are you doing?"

   Devon asked me how I was doing.

2. Nicolas asked John, "Where have you been?"

   _____

3. My parents asked me, "Do you want to eat breakfast?"

   _____

4. I asked my friends, "When can we hang out?"

   _____

> **Get it RIGHT!**
> In reported questions, don't use the auxiliary verb *do*.
> He asked me how **I created** my website.
> NOT: ~~He asked me how **did I create** my website.~~

Speaking: How often do you turn off your cell phone?

9. Write five questions to ask your friends. Write about these things:

| text | turn off your cell phone | video chat | write blog posts | write microblog posts |

10. YOUR TURN Work with a partner. Ask and answer your questions from Exercise 9.

> Have you ever written a blog post?
>> Yes, I have.

11. Tell another pair of students about the questions your partner asked you.

> Marco asked me if I had ever written a blog post.

Workbook, pp. 60–61

REAL TALK 9.2 WHAT DO YOU THINK ABOUT CELEBRITY GOSSIP?

That's not what I HEARD!

Conversation: What do you think about celebrity gossip?

1. **REAL TALK** Watch or listen to the teenagers. Write the correct numbers.

   1. _____ of the teenagers said they didn't like celebrity gossip at all.

   2. _____ of the teenagers said that it depended on the situation or the topic.

2. **YOUR TURN** What do you think about celebrity gossip? Where do you hear the gossip you're interested in: social media, TV, online news, or another source?

3. Listen to Zoe and Cole talking about some celebrity news. Complete the conversation.

USEFUL LANGUAGE: Comparing different accounts of a story

- That's not what I heard!
- Well, Diana said that
- That's definitely not what happened.
- I asked Natalie what had happened, and she said that
- ✓ According to
- How did you come up with that idea?

Zoe: ¹ _According to_ Hollywood Tonight, the police arrested Ashley Hill last night.

Cole: I heard that, too.

Zoe: It says that Ashley cut Jonah Clark's hair off while he was asleep, and then stole his car.

Cole: ² _____

Zoe: What? How do you know?

Cole: ³ _____ Ashley had borrowed her boyfriend's car. She didn't steal it. The problem is, she doesn't have a driver's license.

Zoe: She was probably with Shawn Evans when it happened.

Cole: Shawn Evans? ⁴ _____ She doesn't even know Shawn Evans.

Zoe: Yes, she does. They've been friends since they were on that TV show.

Cole: Oh yeah, that's right. Why do you think she was with Shawn last night?

Zoe: ⁵ _____ Shawn and Ashley are more than friends. They started dating about two weeks ago.

Cole: Where did Diana hear that? ⁶ _____ Hollywood Tonight just said that her boyfriend was Jonah Clark!

Zoe: This is pretty confusing. Let's see if Ashley posted anything online about it.

Cole: She can't post anything. She's in jail. Remember?

4. Practice the conversation with a partner.

5. **YOUR TURN** Work with a partner. Take turns comparing different accounts of the story.

According to this site, Max Marker hit a photographer last night.

Student A	Student B
You read online that your favorite singer got angry and tried to hit a photographer.	You hear from a friend that the photographer got angry and tried to hit your favorite singer.

No way. That's definitely not what happened. I heard that . . .

ARE CELL PHONES GOOD FOR TEENAGERS?

by Avery Bradley

Twenty years ago, cell phones were mostly used by adults for work. Now, it's almost impossible to find a teenager without one. But are cell phones good for teenagers?

There are many good things about cell phones. First, they help teenagers communicate with friends and family anytime, anywhere. Sending text messages is quick and cheap. Cell phones also help organize your life – you have your calendar, photos, and social networking sites all in one place!

However, there are problems with cell phones, too. For one thing, if you forget to check your phone and miss text messages, your friends might think you're mad at them. In addition, you might not always get a signal, especially if you're not in a city. Finally, using your cell phone all the time can get really expensive.

Overall, I think cell phones are a great way for teenagers to communicate. We just need to be careful when we use them.

Reading to write: An essay about cell phones

6. Look at the title of the essay above. What do you think the essay is about? Read the essay to check.

> **Focus on CONTENT**
> When you write an essay, you can include this information:
> - An introduction
> - A paragraph with arguments in favor
> - A paragraph with arguments against
> - A conclusion, including your opinion

7. Read Avery's essay again. Answer the questions.
   1. How does the writer get the reader's attention in the introduction?
   2. How many arguments in favor of cell phones are there?
   3. How many arguments against cell phones are there?
   4. What is Avery's opinion about cell phones for teenagers?

> **Focus on LANGUAGE**
> **Introducing a series of arguments**
> *First, In addition, For one thing, also, Finally*

8. Find the phrases from the Focus on Language box in Avery's essay.

9. Complete the sentences with the correct words.

also	finally	First
✓ For one thing	In addition	

   1. I recommend this cell phone. ¹ _For one thing_, it's a smartphone. It's ² _____ on sale, and ³ _____, it's small and light.
   2. The new model has two improvements. ⁴ _____, it has a lot more memory. ⁵ _____, the battery will last longer.

Writing: An essay about social networking sites

PLAN
Plan an essay with the title "Are Social Networking Sites a Good Way for Teenagers to Communicate?" Use the list in the Focus on Content box and make notes.

WRITE
Write your essay. Use your answers to Exercises 7 and 8 to help you. Write about 150 words.

CHECK
Can you say "yes" to these questions?
- Have you included all the paragraphs mentioned in the Focus on Content box?
- Have you included words and phrases to introduce a series of arguments?

THE WORLD SPEAKS ONE LANGUAGE

Almost everywhere you go in the world, you see English. It's on signs, advertisements, and on T-shirts. It's everywhere! Online, you see even more English. Why? Because it's a world language: a language known and spoken in lots of countries.

How many people speak and understand English? Statistics show that there are 375 million native speakers of English in the world. In some places, like India, Hong Kong, and Kenya, people speak lots of different languages, and English is one of them. Finally, linguists have said that there are more than a billion people who speak English as a foreign language, and that figure is increasing. In many countries, such as Denmark, Singapore, and Israel, more than 80 percent of the people speak English.

Do you like to travel? International tourists can't speak the language of every country they dream of visiting. Most countries, however, write signs, menus, and tourist pamphlets in at least two languages: the native language of that country and English. Tourists may not speak Arabic, for example, but when they visit Egypt, they can still eat great food, take tours, and have a wonderful time if they speak English.

Online, English is important, too. In 2013, researchers said that 55 percent of the most popular websites used English as their main language. If you set up a blog, for example, more people will find out about you and read your posts if you write in English. Over 95 percent of all scientific articles, either online or published in science magazines, are in English. And that number is growing.

And what about the future? Will English always be the world's number one language? For the moment, yes. But if the Chinese economy continues to grow, will Mandarin turn into the next number one world language? We'll have to wait and see.

DID YOU KNOW...?
Soon there will be more people in China who speak English as a foreign language than there are native English speakers in the whole world.

Culture: The number one language

1. Look at the photo above. Where would you see this sign? Why do you think the sign is in English?

2. Read and listen to the article. Is English still the world's number one language?

3. Read the article again. Are the sentences true (*T*) or false (*F*)?

   1. English is everywhere because it's a world language. ___
   2. About 375 million people speak English as a foreign language. ___
   3. Most countries try to help tourists by creating material in English. ___
   4. Over half of the most popular websites use English as the main language. ___
   5. The author is sure that Mandarin will be the world's next number one language. ___

4. **YOUR TURN** Work with a partner. Ask and answer the questions.

   1. How much English do you see or hear where you live? Where do you see it?
   2. Do you ever use English on the computer or on your phone? What do you use it for?

BE CURIOUS Find out about the Mandarin language. How many written characters are there in Mandarin, and how many do most people use? (Workbook, p. 89)

Discovery EDUCATION

9.3 THE LANGUAGE OF THE FUTURE?

UNIT 9 REVIEW

Vocabulary

1. Complete the sentences with the correct words.

| announce | ✓ explain | shout |
| complain | remind | whisper |

1. I don't understand our homework. Can you ___explain___ it to me?
2. Ken and Emily often _____ about people who use cell phones all the time. They really don't like it.
3. The fans in the stadium usually _____ so loudly that the other team can't hear instructions from the coach.
4. Please don't talk loudly here! People are studying, and you need to _____.
5. When are the TV stations going to _____ the news about the election?
6. If I don't remember to call my mom, please _____ me.

Grammar

2. Rewrite the sentences below in reported speech.

1. "I'm blogging about the movie."
   She said she was blogging about the movie.
2. "I go online every day."
   He _____.
3. "I can video chat with you tonight."
   She _____.
4. "I have written 100 blog posts."
   He _____.
5. "I am thinking about Daniel."
   She _____.
6. "I will send Paul an email."
   He _____.

3. Rewrite the questions below as reported questions.

1. "Who are you talking to?"
   She _asked who I was talking to._
2. "What is Alicia thinking about?"
   He _____
3. "Do you have Will's phone number?"
   They _____
4. "When will he send them a text message?"
   She _____
5. "Have you posted the picture on your blog?"
   He _____
6. "Who can help her?"
   They _____

Useful language

4. Complete the conversation.

| According to | That's definitely |
| Steve said that | That's not |

Tyler: Hey, Rob. I just heard about Ryan.
Rob: What did you hear?
Tyler: ¹_____ Ryan had been cheating on a test with his cell phone, and Ms. Harris caught him.
Rob: ²_____ not what happened.
Tyler: What do you mean?
Rob: ³_____ Jared, Ryan saw someone else cheating, and he told Ms. Harris about it.
Tyler: Hmm. ⁴_____ what I heard.
Rob: Ryan never cheats. And, I don't think he even has a cell phone. He lost his last week.
Tyler: Well, where is Ryan now? Let's just ask him and find out the truth!

PROGRESS CHECK: Now I can . . .

☐ talk about different ways of speaking.
☐ discuss social networking.
☐ talk about different communication methods.
☐ compare stories.
☐ write an essay about cell phones.
☐ discuss language use throughout the world.

CLIL PROJECT
9.4 PICTURES WITH MEANING, p. 120

10 Don't Give Up!

Discovery EDUCATION
BE CURIOUS

- Lifeguard and Athlete
- Have you ever given a class presentation?
- Circus Star

1. Describe what you see in this picture.

2. What do you think this runner did to prepare for the race?

3. Have you ever worked very hard toward a specific goal? What did you do?

UNIT CONTENTS

Vocabulary Goals and achievements; emotions related to accomplishments
Grammar Reflexive pronouns; causative *have/get*
Listening Challenging situations

Vocabulary: Goals and achievements

1. **Write the words next to the definitions.**

achieve	commitment	face	performance	reward
challenge	✓ deal with	goal	progress	skill

   1. To take action to solve a problem: <u>D E A L   W I T H</u>
   2. Something you want to do successfully in the future: _ _ _ _
   3. How well someone does something: _ _ _ _ _ _ _ _ _ _ _
   4. To succeed in doing something good: _ _ _ _ _ _ _
   5. To give something in exchange for good behavior or good work: _ _ _ _ _ _
   6. To deal with a difficult situation: _ _ _ _
   7. An ability to do an activity well because you have practiced it: _ _ _ _ _
   8. Development and improvement of skills or knowledge: _ _ _ _ _ _ _ _
   9. Something that is difficult and tests your ability: _ _ _ _ _ _ _ _ _
   10. A willingness to give your time and energy: _ _ _ _ _ _ _ _ _ _

2. **Listen, check, and repeat.** 🔊 10.01

3. **Circle the correct answers.**

   1. You ran 5 kilometers last week and 10 kilometers this week. That's real **progress / goal**!
   2. My father **dealt with / achieved** something no one in his family had done before: He went to college and became a doctor.
   3. Your **commitment / performance** on this test was incredible. You got 100 percent right!
   4. This class isn't easy. It will **challenge / achieve** you to work harder than you've ever worked before.
   5. Bianca didn't study for her chemistry test, so she had to **reward / face** the consequences: a bad grade.
   6. My **goal / skill** in life isn't to be rich or famous. I just want to be good at what I do.

   > **Spell it RIGHT!**
   > Notice that *ie* and *ei* can both represent the sound /i:/.
   > ach*ie*ve, bel*ie*ve
   > c*ei*ling, rec*ei*ve

Speaking: Go for it!

4. **YOUR TURN** Work with a partner. Ask and answer the questions.
   1. What is one academic or personal goal that you have for the next 12 months?
   2. Do you have an unusual skill? What is it?
   3. Have you ever been challenged to do a difficult or incredible thing? What?

   > *One of my academic goals for the next 12 months is to get better grades in science.*

▶ Workbook, p. 64

Reading Make Your Dreams Come True; Achieving My Goal; Olympics for the Brain
Conversation Reassuring someone
Writing A personal action plan

Dream BIG!

Make Your DREAMS Come True

by Kyle Stewart, school counselor at West High School in Franklin, Pennsylvania

In my 22 years as a high school counselor, I've talked to thousands of teenagers. Many of them have goals, from traveling around the world to changing the world. While some teenagers achieve the goals they set for themselves, others don't. If you have a dream, here's how to make it happen:

First, decide on a clear goal. What exactly do you want to do? Make sure it's your dream and not someone else's. Your father wants you to be a doctor. Do you want to be a doctor, too? If you do, great. You will need your own commitment to do the hard work of reaching your long-term goals.

Then choose a date to reach your goal. For example, do you want to go to college a year early? Then you may want to take extra classes now. Set a deadline, and challenge yourself to meet that deadline.

I've found that most people benefit from writing about their goals. A written list reminds people to work on their goals and helps them see their progress! Start by writing down your goal, your deadline, and the steps you need to take to make your dream a reality.

Finally, put your plan into action. Start taking the steps you wrote on your list. You have to do this work yourself. No one can do it for you. Remember to review your written goals at least once a week. And then, dream your dreams and never give up!

Reading: An online article

1. **Look at the title of the article. Do you have a dream that you'd like to come true? What could you do about it?**

2. **Read and listen to the article. Number the steps below in the correct order (1–4).**

   a. ___ Set a date to accomplish your goal.
   b. ___ Make your plan happen.
   c. ___ Decide for yourself what your goal is.
   d. ___ Get a pen and paper and start writing.

3. **Read the article again. Are the sentences true (T) or false (F)?**

   1. Kyle Stewart is a teenager with a dream. ___
   2. All of the students that Kyle talks to achieve their dreams. ___
   3. It's important to make sure that your goal is something you want for yourself. ___
   4. Students should decide a date by which they want to achieve their goal. ___
   5. Writing down the goal is not an important step. ___
   6. Nobody else can put your plan into action. You have to do it. ___

4. **YOUR TURN** Choose one of the goals below or a goal of your own. How could you achieve this goal? Discuss your steps with a partner.

be a scientist	improve your grades	make new friends
get fit and healthy	learn a musical instrument	save the environment

   I want to make some new friends, and I want to do it by the end of this year.

   Maybe you could join a new club!

DID YOU KNOW...?

The first jobs of many famous people were very different from their dreams. Singer Mick Jagger worked in a mental hospital, actress Jennifer Aniston was a telephone salesperson, and actor Tom Hanks sold popcorn and peanuts.

Grammar: Reflexive pronouns

5. Complete the chart.

Use a reflexive pronoun when an object refers to the subject.

I like to challenge **myself** by measuring my progress every week.

You need to set a deadline for _____.

He wasn't pleased with **himself** when he heard criticism of his performance.

She taught _____ the skills she needed to write essays.

We decided to enjoy **ourselves** only after we had studied for the test.

Teenagers can help _____ to any of the career planning books we have.

Many people achieve the goals **they** set for **themselves**.

> Check your answers: Grammar reference, p. 115

6. Complete the sentences.

1. My sister rewarded *herself* with a long walk after she had studied for three hours.
2. We set _____ a deadline for finishing the big project.
3. I didn't do well on the test. I blame _____ for not studying harder.
4. To succeed in life, you need to believe in _____.
5. Those kids need to face challenges by _____. They can't always ask their parents to help them.
6. Edward scared _____ when he thought he had lost his homework.

7. Add a sentence with a reflexive pronoun and *by*.

1. Nobody in the group had time to work on the presentation except Adrian and Stephanie.
   They worked on it by themselves.
2. He didn't have help writing his essays for school.
   _____
3. Nobody helped Cristina do the project.
   _____
4. None of my friends wanted to study with me yesterday.
   _____
5. My sister and I didn't do our exchange programs together.
   _____
6. My best friend couldn't go shopping yesterday.
   _____

Reflexive pronouns with *by*

You can use reflexive pronouns with by *to say you did something "without help" or "alone."*

I don't cook much, but I made this dinner **by myself**. Do you like it?

Mike painted his house **by himself**. He didn't hire a professional painter.

Speaking: Achieve it!

8. YOUR TURN Work with a partner. Choose one of the goals below. Decide on five steps a person needs to take to achieve it.

a. Win a gold medal in the Olympic Games
b. Discover a cure for cancer
c. Win an Oscar for best actor in a movie

> To win a gold medal, you have to challenge yourself.

> Right, but you can't do it all by yourself. You need a coach!

Say it RIGHT! (10.03)

A consonant cluster is a group of consonants with no vowels. Pay attention to the pronunciation of consonant clusters with /l/. Listen and repeat the words.
myse**lf**, himse**lf**, themse**lv**es
ski**lls**, she**lls**, te**lls**

BE CURIOUS Find out about a lifeguard in Australia. What does Candice do to train for the life saving competition? (Workbook, p. 90)

Discovery EDUCATION
10.1 LIFEGUARD AND ATHLETE

Are you up to the CHALLENGE?

Listening: Challenging situations

1. Look at the topics below. How could they be "challenging situations"?

a. A homemade birthday cake
b. A video competition
c. An important test
d. A soccer championship

2. Listen to four short conversations. Match the topics in Exercise 1 with the conversations.

1. _____   2. _____   3. _____   4. _____

3. Listen again. Answer the questions.

1. What did Lauren and her team win? Why isn't Lauren jumping up and down?
2. What was the name of the competition that David entered? What bad thing happened while David was making the video?
3. Who is Jennifer making the birthday cake for? What kind of cake is Jennifer's friend going to have made?
4. Why had Logan missed a lot of school? Where is Logan's dad going to take him?

Vocabulary: Emotions related to accomplishments

4. Complete the sentences with the correct words.

| calm | ✓ disappointed | miserable | prepared | satisfied |
| confident | excited | nervous | proud | thrilled |

1. I'm _disappointed_ that I can't be in the play. I really wanted to do it.
2. After training every day for seven weeks, I know I'm _____ for the race.
3. I was _____ of my son for doing his homework every day this week.
4. Sabrina studied really hard for the test, so she was _____ that she would do well.
5. My sister got an amazing scholarship to a school in Australia. She's _____!
6. Don't worry so much about your presentation. Just stay _____.
7. I could get a new bike, but I'm pretty _____ with my old one.
8. I was so _____ about my new school that I couldn't sleep the night before the first day of classes.
9. Vince can't go to summer camp this year, and he feels _____ about it.
10. When I'm _____ about something, I wake up really early and have lots of energy.

5. **YOUR TURN** Choose five words from Exercise 4. For each word, tell a partner about a time you felt that emotion.

Grammar: Causative *have/get*

5. Complete the chart.

> *Use causative* have/get *in situations where someone else does something for you. You don't do it. You can use* get *or* have. *They have similar meanings.*
>
> Lauren is **getting** her knee **examined** now. (She isn't examining her own knee. A doctor is.)
>
> Jennifer **had** a cake _____ for her friend. (She didn't make it. A professional did.)
>
> David needs to **get** his camera _____. (He can't fix it. A professional can.)
>
> Logan will **have** his eyes _____. (He won't check them. A professional will.)
>
> *The past participle of* get *is gotten.*
>
> Has Sophia **gotten** Jason's cake made yet? No, she hasn't.

> Check your answers: Grammar reference, p. 115

6. Complete the sentences with causative *have/get* and the words in parentheses.

1. Derek gets bad headaches every night when he does his homework. He needs to ___get his eyes checked___ (check his eyes).
2. Veronica needed a photo of herself for her passport. She went to a photographer to _____ (take her photo).
3. To look good for the school dance, I'm going to _____ (cut my hair) this afternoon.
4. I'm going to _____ (paint my bedroom) bright pink so that I feel more motivated to study.
5. Your sister is really smart! Has she _____ (test) to see if she has an extra-high IQ?
6. Jim wasn't confident about the game because his shoulder hurt a lot. He should have _____ (examine his shoulder) before the game.

7. Read the situations and write sentences with causative *have/get*.

1. Mitch's only dress shirt is dirty. A dry cleaning company washed it.
   He got his shirt cleaned.
2. My computer is broken, and I really need it. A repair person is going to fix it tomorrow.
   _____
3. The cheerleader hurt her knee. A doctor bandaged it.
   _____
4. The students stayed up late getting their English project ready. A pizza place delivered a pizza to them.
   _____

Speaking: Let's have a party!

8. YOUR TURN Work with a partner. Choose one of the events below. Decide on six steps to make the event happen. You must do three by yourselves, and get other people to do three.

a. You're going to have a birthday party, and you will invite 200 people.
b. You're going to organize a concert where a local band will play for your community.
c. You're in charge of a school trip. Three classes are going together to visit an important monument or nature site outside your city.

> *For this birthday party, we need to get 200 invitations printed.*

> **Get it RIGHT!**
> When you get/have something done, you don't do it yourself.
> *I'm going to cut my hair.* = I'm going to cut my own hair.
> *I'm going to get/have my hair cut.* = Another person is going to cut my hair.

REAL TALK 10.2 HAVE YOU EVER GIVEN A CLASS PRESENTATION?

You'll do GREAT!

Conversation: Have you ever given a class presentation?

1. **REAL TALK** Watch or listen to the teenagers. Write the numbers 1–6 in the order that you hear about these things.

   a. ___ I'm worried about doing one.
   b. ___ We talked about summer camp.
   c. _1_ I talked about Indonesia last week.
   d. ___ We do one every Friday.
   e. ___ I don't know how to surf.
   f. ___ I talked about my family and friends.

2. **YOUR TURN** Have you ever given a class presentation? What was the best part? What was the worst?

3. Listen to Julia talking to her sister Ella about a presentation. Complete the conversation.

> **USEFUL LANGUAGE: Reassuring someone**
> I think I can help you.
> ✓ You've faced bigger challenges than this!
> Try not to worry about it.
> I'm sure you'll do fine.

Julia: What's the matter, Ella? You look miserable.
Ella: I'm not miserable, just nervous. I have to give a presentation in English class next week, and I'm scared.
Julia: Come on. A presentation?
¹ _You've faced bigger challenges than this!_
Ella: Yeah, but not in English. And never in front of people!
Julia: ² _____ Your English is good.
Ella: Yes, but I'm really shy. And some people in my class speak really great English. I'm worried they'll laugh at me.
Julia: You'll do great.
Ella: No, I won't! When I speak in class, I mix up the words and talk too fast.
Julia: Listen, ³ _____ Have you written the presentation yet?
Ella: Well, most of it. It's almost done.
Julia: Great, then. You can practice it on me and my friends. The more you practice, the better you'll do.
Ella: OK! That sounds like a good idea. I'll feel more confident then.
Julia: Exactly. ⁴ _____ You'll be fine.

4. Practice the conversation with a partner.

5. **YOUR TURN** Work with a partner. Take turns explaining one of the problems and reassuring your partner.
   - You have to sing a song in a talent show.
   - You're playing in the final of a tennis tournament.

Achieving MY GOAL
Posted by Jacob, October 15

In two years, when I'm 17, I am determined to be an exchange student in a Spanish-speaking country. In order to achieve this, I will begin taking Spanish classes next semester at school. I don't speak any Spanish, so I'll have to study hard every day. In addition, I'll do research on different study abroad programs. When I find the best one, and learn about the price and the way it works, I'll talk to my parents. I'll need help from them, and I hope they agree to help! I'll ask them if they can pay for part of the program. I also plan to get a job in the summer – this summer and the next. I'll work as much as I can and keep studying Spanish. Then I'll apply for the exchange program, filling out all the forms and getting all the documents needed. When I'm accepted, I'll apply for my passport, and a visa if necessary. Finally, the program will tell me what country I'm going to – Spain, Mexico, Argentina, or Peru. I'll study about the history and culture of that country. That way, I'll be really prepared.

Reading to write: Jacob's blog post

6. Look at the picture. What do you think Jacob's goal is? Read his action plan and check.

> ● *Focus on* **CONTENT**
> When you write about a goal, begin by describing your goal clearly. Then describe each step you need to take to achieve your goal. For some of the steps, you may need help from other people. Tell your readers who those people are and how they'll help you.

7. Read Jacob's blog post again. Number the steps (1–7) in the order he will take them.

a. ___ talk to his parents

b. ___ get a job

c. ___ start Spanish classes

d. ___ learn about the country

e. ___ apply for the program

f. ___ research programs

g. ___ apply for a passport and visa

> ● *Focus on* **LANGUAGE**
> When you write about a personal action plan, you can include some of these phrases:
> *I am determined to . . .*
> *In order to achieve this, I will . . .*
> *In addition, I will . . .*
> *I will need help from . . .*

8. Find the phrases in the Focus on Language box in Jacob's blog post and underline the entire sentence.

Writing: A personal action plan

▢ **PLAN**
Choose a goal you'd like to achieve. Write what the goal is and at least five steps toward achieving the goal.

▢ **WRITE**
Write your personal action plan. Use your notes from above to help you. You can also use Jason's blog post as a model.

▢ **CHECK**
Check your writing. Can you say "yes" to these questions?
- Is your goal described clearly?
- Did you write at least five steps toward your goal?

Olympics for the Brain

Do you want to win medals and earn scholarships? These things are not just for great athletes, but for hard-working students, too. How? Form a team and join Academic Decathlon®!

What is Academic Decathlon®?
It's an academic competition for students from all over the United States, and sometimes all over the world. Every year, teams of students study one topic – past themes have included Russia, the Great Depression, and energy alternatives. Then they compete in local, state, and national championships.

Who is on each team?
Teams include nine students, and each team must have three different types of students on it. Three members must be excellent students. Three members must be students who do well, but who aren't the school's top students. And three team members must be students who don't get great grades.

What happens in the competition?
Competitions aren't about being good at one subject area only. Every team member needs to be prepared to do five things. First, they need to deliver a speech related to the topic, and then answer questions. Then students need to answer questions about themselves in an interview. After that, they need to write an essay about the topic. They also need to take seven different tests in subject areas related to the topic. And finally, teams participate in a Super Quiz. Teams listen to questions and have seven seconds to answer them. It's the only part of the competition open to the public, and it's noisy, fun, and exciting.

Why do students love Academic Decathlon®?
Lots of reasons! Like athletes, these students enjoy working as a team. If you join a team, you'll meet other students from all over the country, and work very hard to get there. Most of all, you'll have fun!

Culture: United States Academic Decathlon®

1. **Answer the questions.**
   1. Have you ever won a medal? What was it for?
   2. Would you be interested in participating in an academic competition?

2. **Read and listen to the article. What kinds of students can participate in Academic Decathlon®?**

3. **Read the article again. Answer the questions.**
   1. Where do the students who compete come from?
   2. How many people are on a team?
   3. Do team members need to learn about one subject area or all subject areas?
   4. What do students have to answer questions about in the interview?
   5. Which part of the competition can the public watch?

4. **YOUR TURN** Work with a partner. Ask and answer the questions.
   1. What kind of academic competitions can you compete in where you live?
   2. Would you enjoy participating in Academic Decathlon®? What part of it sounds most interesting to you?

DID YOU KNOW...?
In 2013, Granada Hills Charter School in California became only the second public school ever to win the national US Academic Decathlon® title three years in a row.

BE CURIOUS Find out about a young girl who accomplished a difficult goal. What kind of diploma did she receive? (Workbook, p. 91)

Discovery EDUCATION

10.3 CIRCUS STAR

UNIT 10 REVIEW

Vocabulary

1. Complete the sentences.

| challenge | goal | rewarded |
| face | progress | ✓ skills |

1. Academic Decathlon® helps students develop their public speaking ____skills____.

2. When you want to accomplish an important _____, it's a good idea to write it down and look at it often.

3. Caleb doesn't like to do only easy things. He likes to _____ himself.

4. After several students in my class won an academic competition, the school _____ the whole class with a party.

5. You won't achieve your goal right away, but you can make a little _____ toward it every day.

6. Instead of ignoring or running away from your problems, it's always better to _____ them directly.

Grammar

2. Complete the sentences with reflexive pronouns.

1. After doing homework for seven hours on Saturday, Greta rewarded ____herself____ by going to a movie with her best friend.

2. What happened to his finger? Did he cut _____?

3. Even though I had a bad headache, I forced _____ to study hard.

4. Sarah and Olivia love math, and they challenge _____ to always learn more.

5. When we were little, my brother and I used to pretend we were astronauts. We called _____ "The Moon Boys."

3. Circle the correct answers.

1. When I decided to start exercising before school each morning, the first thing I did was ____.
   a. get fixed my alarm clock
   b. (have my alarm clock fixed)

2. Charles won a silver medal in the Olympics. When he came home, he ____.
   a. got it framed
   b. have framed it

3. Jada accidentally stepped on her cell phone and needed to ____.
   a. repair
   b. get it repaired

4. When are you going to ____? You need to do it soon, I think.
   a. take your passport picture
   b. get your passport picture taken

5. When my sister graduated from high school, my parents had a big party for her. They ____.
   a. had a big chocolate cake made
   b. make a big chocolate cake

Useful language

4. Complete the conversation.

| I'm sure | I think I can | worry about it | you've faced |

Matt: Dad, I'm really nervous. I want to try out for the basketball team tomorrow, but I've never played basketball except out in the driveway with you!

Dad: ¹_____ you'll do fine. Science nerds can play sports too, you know.

Matt: I don't know. I'm tall, but I'm not as tall as some of those guys. And they're all really good.

Dad: Basketball isn't all about height. Try not to ²_____ and just do your best.

Matt: Don't worry? That's all I do. I don't think I can do this.

Dad: Listen, ³_____ bigger challenges than this. Remember last year's science fair? That was harder than basketball tryouts.

Matt: No, I don't think so. I'm good at science.

Dad: ⁴_____ help you. Let's go outside and practice together.

Matt: OK. Thanks!

PROGRESS CHECK: Now I can . . .

- ☐ talk about goals and accomplishments.
- ☐ discuss emotions related to accomplishments.
- ☐ discuss steps toward achieving goals.
- ☐ reassure someone.
- ☐ write a personal action plan.
- ☐ discuss an academic competition.

Uncover Your Knowledge

UNITS 6–10 Review Game

TEAM 1
START

- Imagine you have a chance to meet a celebrity, living or dead. Use the second conditional to tell your teammate who you would meet and what you would do.
- Name five things that can happen in school.
- Think of two imaginary situations and ask your teammate what they would do in those situations.
- Say eight different materials that things can be made from.
- Identify four items in your classroom. Say what two of them are made of and what the other two are used for.
- Imagine that you saw a classmate cheating on a test. Explain the situation to your teammate and ask for advice on what to do about it.
- Tell your teammate how you would design and build an eco-friendly building. What would it be? How it would save energy?
- Ask your teammate two questions in the simple past passive. Use Where, When, How, or Who. Your teammate answers with a simple past passive statement.
- In 30 seconds, say two phrases that use the verb *do* and two phrases that use the verb *make*.
- What had you known about extreme weather disasters before this unit? Tell your teammate two things you had known, and two things you hadn't known.
- Tell a teammate that he or she has done something that upset you. Your teammate apologizes.

INSTRUCTIONS:

■ Make teams and choose game pieces.

■ Put your game pieces on your team's START.

■ Flip a coin to see who goes first.

■ Read the first challenge. Can you do it correctly?

   Yes → Continue to the next challenge.

   No → Lose your turn.

The first team to do all of the challenges wins!

TEAM 2
START

- **GRAMMAR**
- **VOCABULARY**
- **USEFUL LANGUAGE**

1. Tell a teammate two things you did, one before the other. Use the past perfect and simple past.

2. Role-play a conversation with your teammate. Tell them about a personal problem, and have them try to help you.

3. What three items would you want to have if you were lost in the woods? Explain why.

4. Report to your teammate three different things you heard people say yesterday.

5. How do you feel when you are getting ready for a big test? How do you feel when the test is over and you did well? Use at least four emotion words.

6. In 30 seconds, say three sentences that use reflexive pronouns.

7. Name at least one natural disaster that can occur in each area: forests, mountains, tropical islands, and flat areas.

8. Say three phrases you can use to reassure someone.

9. Have your teammate ask you a question. Then tell another teammate what your first teammate asked you.

10. Give six examples of verbs you can use to report speech in 30 seconds.

11. Role-play a conversation with your teammate. Say that something happened to a celebrity last night. Your teammate heard a different version of the story. Compare your stories.

12. Describe a goal you have achieved. Tell your teammate what your goal was, what challenges you faced, and how you dealt with them.

13. Use causative *have/get* to tell your teammate three things that other people do for you.

14. List all the different ways you communicated with people this week.

Units 6–10 Review | 105

Simple present and present continuous review, page 5

Use the simple present to describe what normally happens. This includes routines and facts.

It **sticks** to your face.	He/She/It **doesn't** live here.
I/You/We/They **like** cold weather.	I/You/We/They **don't like** hot weather.
I/You/We/They **get** home late.	I/You/We/They **don't go out** a lot.

Use the present continuous to describe something happening right now or these days.

I'**m wearing** a hat.	I'**m not wearing** boots.
He/She **is working** right now.	He/She **isn't studying** right now.
You/We/They **are eating** hot food these days.	You/We/They **aren't drinking** coffee.

1. **Write sentences in the simple present or the present continuous.**

   1. it / always / rain / in April _____
   2. Tonya / write / a paper right now _____
   3. they / not walk / to work these days _____
   4. I / eat / dinner at 6:00 p.m. every night _____
   5. Jack / not like / subzero weather _____
   6. we / play / soccer outside right now _____

Simple past and past continuous review, page 7

Use the simple past to describe actions and events in the past.

I/You/He/She/We/They **took** a plane over part of Panama.
I/You/He/She/We/They **didn't have** to stop for food.
I/You/He/She/We/They **started** the trip in Alaska.
I/You/He/She/We/They **didn't start** the trip in California.
We **made** our own food.
He **didn't break** his arm, but it hurt a lot.
What **did** you **miss** the most?

Use the past continuous to describe actions and events in progress in the past.

I **was spending** the night in Quito when I <u>heard</u> that the road was closed.
He **wasn't wearing** a helmet when he <u>fell</u>.
We **were riding** through Colorado when Robert <u>hurt</u> his arm.
They **were eating** their lunch by the road when the storm <u>started</u>.
You **weren't talking** to me when I <u>dropped</u> my phone.
What **were** you **doing** last night when the electricity <u>went</u> out?

2. **Complete the sentences with the simple past or past continuous.**

   1. Jackie _____ (ride) her bike when she _____ (fall).
   2. We _____ (give) a lot of money to an education program last year.
   3. Paul and Oliver _____ (watch) TV when it _____ (start) to hail.
   4. I _____ (not study) when you _____ (call) me.
   5. My sisters _____ (not do) their homework when I _____ (get) home.
   6. She _____ (hear) about the blizzard at 10:00 a.m.

have to/don't have to, page 15

> Use have/has to to say that it is necessary to do something.
> Use don't/doesn't have to to say that it is not necessary to do something, but you can do it if you want to.

Affirmative	Negative
I/You/We/They **have to get** more sleep.	I/You/We/They **don't have to get up** early on Saturdays.
He/She **has to get up** early on Saturdays.	He/She **doesn't have to help** with the housework.

1. **Write sentences with the correct form of** *have to*. ✔ = yes, ✗ = no.

   1. I / have / more time for myself / ✔ _____
   2. Ben / help / around the house / ✔ _____
   3. Carol / shop / for clothes this weekend / ✗ _____
   4. They / get up / early tomorrow / ✔ _____
   5. You / work / late tonight / ✗ _____
   6. She / wash / the dishes / ✗ _____

Modals of obligation – *should, ought to, had better*, page 17

> Should, ought to, and had better have similar meanings. Use them to say what is a good or right thing to do.
>
> Use should and shouldn't for a personal opinion.
>
> I/You/He/She/We/They **should try** to work out more.
>
> I/You/He/She/We/They **shouldn't get** so stressed out.
>
> Use ought to and ought not to when you're talking about duty or the law.
>
> I/You/He/She/We/They **ought to call** the police about the car accident.
>
> I/You/He/She/We/They **ought not to enter** that part of the airport.
>
> Use had better and had better not to give very strong advice.
>
> I/You/He/She/We/They **had better start** studying now.
>
> I/You/He/She/We/They **had better not be** late for the test tomorrow.

2. **Complete the sentences with the affirmative or negative of the word or phrase in parentheses.**

   1. Kyle _____ relax. He's too stressed out about school. (should)
   2. You _____ apologize to Jenny. You made her feel terrible. (had better)
   3. Vic and Mary _____ go camping. They have a lot of homework this weekend. (should)
   4. We _____ tell your parents about what happened. They need to know. (ought to)
   5. They _____ take their cameras to the museum. You can't take photos there. (ought to)
   6. Jen _____ call Frank right now. He's at a job interview. (had better)

Verb + -ing form (gerund) review, page 25

We can use the -ing form of a verb after some verbs to talk about things we like or don't like.

Common verbs followed by -ing forms:
like, love, hate, enjoy, (not) mind

		-ing form	
I/You/We/They	love	drawing	pictures in my free time.
	don't like	going	to museums.
He/She	enjoys	looking	at sculptures.
	hates	helping	around the house.
	doesn't mind	doing	housework.

1. Complete the conversations with the correct form of the verbs in the box.

   don't like / go   enjoy / meet   hate / do   love / work   not mind / look

   1. **A:** Does your brother like art?
      B: Not really, but he _____ at murals.
   2. **A:** Who washes the dishes at your house?
      B: I do. And I _____ it!
   3. **A:** How is your brother's new job?
      B: Great. He _____ at the pizza place.
   4. **A:** Did you see the new sculpture at the museum?
      B: No, I didn't. I _____ to museums.
   5. **A:** Isn't your mother an artist? Could you introduce me to her?
      B: Sure. She _____ new people.

-ing forms (gerunds) as subjects, page 27

You can use the -ing form as the subject of a sentence. The verb is singular.

Playing several instruments at once <u>takes</u> a lot of energy.
Singing at the same time I play instruments <u>is</u> hard.
Being here at the festival <u>is</u> really special to me.

For the negative, use not *before the -ing form.*

Not enjoying some kinds of music <u>is</u> normal.
Not playing music <u>makes</u> me sad.

2. Put the words in the correct order to make sentences.

   1. is / the trumpet / playing / difficult
      _____
   2. me into trouble / practicing / the piano / gets / not
      _____
   3. easy / finding / isn't / a good keyboard player
      _____
   4. before a concert / it hard to play the flute / makes / eating
      _____
   5. getting / ruins / a good night's sleep / not / my day
      _____

Present perfect with *already*, *yet*, and *just*, page 35

We can use already *in affirmative sentences in the present perfect.*

I/You/We/They **have already been** at sea for four days.

He/She **has already cooked** three meals for the others on the ship.

The ship/It **has already left** the port.

We can use yet *in negative sentences in the present perfect.*

I/You/We/They **haven't found** turtles **yet**.

He/She **hasn't visited** the ship **yet**.

It **hasn't rained yet**.

Use just *with the present perfect to say that something happened very recently.*

I/You/We/They **have just seen** dolphins.

He/She **has just boarded** the ship.

It **has just gotten** dark.

1. Circle the correct words to complete the sentences.

1. Donna has **just** / **yet** bought a mountain bike.
2. I've **already** / **yet** gone sailing twice this summer.
3. Carlos and Doug haven't left for summer camp **just** / **yet**.
4. She hasn't gone on a safari **already** / **yet**.
5. We've **already** / **just** packed our suitcases for the cruise. We packed them a week ago!
6. It has **just** / **yet** started raining, so we can't go ballooning now.

Present perfect with *for* and *since*, page 37

Use the present perfect with for *or* since *for past actions and events continuing into the present.*

Use for *with a period of time such as* a week, two months, *or* five years.

I/You/We/They **have been** here **for** three days.

I/You/We/They **haven't seen** Tom **for** three days.

He/She **has worked** at the rafting company **for** a month.

He/She **hasn't gone** on a trip **for** two years.

Use since *with a specific date or time.*

I/You/We/They **have been** here **since** last Wednesday.

I/You/We/They **haven't taken** a vacation **since** last June.

He/She **has lived** in Colorado **since** 2010.

He/She **hasn't called** me **since** last Monday.

2. Complete the sentences with the present perfect of the verbs in parentheses and *for* or *since*.

1. Mario _____ (known) Josh _____ two years.
2. Ken and Lisa _____ (not eat) _____ 8:00 a.m.
3. We _____ (wait) for Cindy _____ an hour.
4. I _____ (live) in Mexico _____ 2008.
5. You _____ (not see) me _____ three weeks.

Future review – *will, be going to,* present continuous, page 45

Use will, be going to, *and the present continuous to talk about the future.*
Use will *for actions and events that we decide to do in the moment of speaking.*

Are you going running now? I **will go** with you.
I/You/He/She/We/They **will go** to the park.
I/You/He/She/We/They **won't go** to the store.

Use going to *for planned actions and events. They may be in the near future or in a more distant future time.*

I'm **(not) going to share** a room with other students.
He/She **is (not) going to fly** to Las Vegas next month.
You/We/They **are (not) going to be** in different schools next year.

Use the present continuous for planned actions and events, usually in the very near future.

I **am (not) traveling** to New York soon.
He/She **is (not) having** dinner with her mother tonight.
You/We/They **are (not) going** to the wedding tomorrow.

Be going to is used much more than will in conversation.

1. Complete the sentences with the given form of the verbs in parentheses.

   1. Kendra _____ a test tomorrow. (take – *present continuous*)
   2. Wait for me! I _____ ready in five minutes. (be – *will*)
   3. Sally and Mark _____ a movie tonight. (not see – *going to*)
   4. He _____ to Rio de Janeiro tonight. (not fly – *present continuous*)
   5. My cousins _____ me at the circus on Friday. (meet – *going to*)

Modals of probability – *must, can't, may, might, could,* page 47

Use must *for something you're almost certain of.*
Use can't *for something you believe is impossible.*
Use might, may, *and* could *for something that you believe is possible.*

I/You/He/She/It/We/They	**must be** really terrifying.
	must be terrified.
	must not be relaxed.
	can't be from France.
	may/might/could be upstairs.
	may/might not go to the barbecue.
	may/might/could be sick.

2. Circle the correct answer. Sometimes more than one answer is possible.

   1. I ____ be in class tomorrow. I don't feel well.
      a. could   b. might not   c. must   d. may not

   2. You ____ be exhausted. You only slept an hour last night.
      a. can't   b. must not   c. must   d. might not

   3. Eva ____ be confused about our homework. She just explained it to me.
      a. can't   b. could   c. may   d. might not

   4. We ____ go on the roller coaster. I don't think we're tall enough.
      a. must   b. might not   c. may not   d. could

   5. They ____ be surprised. They knew we were planning a party.
      a. could   b. may   c. can't   d. might

Second conditional, page 57

Use the second conditional to describe imaginary situations and possible consequences.

Imaginary situation	Possible consequences
if + simple past	*would (not)* + base form of the verb
If I **changed** the school rules,	students **wouldn't wear** uniforms.
If you **missed** class,	you **would be** assigned to detention.
If she **didn't** like the class,	she **wouldn't go**.

Many American English speakers use *were* rather than *was* after I, he, she, and it, especially in a more formal style.

Formal style	Informal style
If I **were** rude to my teacher, my parents would be very mad at me.	If I **was** always punctual, I wouldn't be assigned to detention so much.

The *if* clause can come at the beginning or end of the sentence. If it's at the beginning, it's followed by a comma.

If you missed class, she would be assigned to detention.
You would be assigned to detention **if** you missed class.

1. **Write second conditional sentences.**

    1. If / you / break / the rules / you / be sent / to the principal's office
       _____

    2. If / Sara / not wear / her uniform / she / be assigned / to detention
       _____

    3. Carl / not get / extra credit / if / he / cheat / on the assignment
       _____

    4. We / be / in trouble / if / we / bully / students
       _____

Second conditional *Wh-* questions, page 59

Use *Wh-* questions in the second conditional to ask about imaginary situations and possible consequences.

What	would your teacher do	if	one of your classmates **cheated** on a test?
Who	would you talk to	if	you **had** a serious problem with a friend?
When	would you go to school	if	you **chose** the days you went?
If	you wanted to do something fun this weekend,	where	would you **go**?
If	you got a new pet,	why	would you **choose** one kind of pet over another?

2. **Complete the second conditional questions with *what*, *who*, *when*, or *where* and the words in parentheses. Use each question word once.**

    1. _____ (you / do) if _____ (you / have) a difficult test to study for?

    2. If _____ (Sheri / go) to New York, _____ (she / go)? In the summer?

    3. If _____ (you / have) a party, _____ (it / be)? At a restaurant or at your house?

    4. _____ (you / ask) for help if _____ (you / not understand) your homework? Your teacher or your friend?

Simple present passive, page 67

Use the passive when it is not important who does the action, or when you don't know who does it.

To form the simple present passive, use is/are + past participle.

Active	Passive
Affirmative	
They **make** this wall of bottles.	This wall **is made** of bottles.
People **use** car tires to build strong walls.	Car tires **are used** to build strong walls.
Negative	
They **don't make** that bottle of plastic.	That bottle **isn't made** of plastic.
People **don't build** the houses with bricks.	The houses **aren't built** with bricks.

1. Complete the sentences in the simple present passive with the verbs from the box.

| call | make | not build | not grow | recycle |

1. The blocks _____ of cement.
2. This cotton _____ in cold places.
3. Those plastic bottles _____ to make furniture.
4. These houses _____ quickly. It takes a long time.
5. The new exhibit at the museum _____ "Reused Art."

Simple past passive, page 69

Use the passive when it is not important who did the action, or when you don't know who did it.

To form the simple past passive, use was/were + past participle.

Active	Passive
Affirmative	
We **built** the EcoHouse in 1985.	The EcoHouse **was built** in 1985.
We **updated** the appliances two months ago.	The appliances **were updated** two months ago.
Negative	
We **didn't install** a recycling bin until last year.	A recycling bin **wasn't installed** until last year.
They **didn't install** solar panels 60 years ago.	Solar panels **weren't installed** 60 years ago.
Use by with the passive to show who did the action.	
The EcoHouse **was designed by** the museum.	
The most energy **was consumed by** the heater.	
Questions and answers with the passive	
When **was** the EcoHouse **built**?	It **was built** in 1985.
Was the EcoHouse **built** in 1985?	Yes, it **was**.
Were the old apartments **destroyed** this year?	No, they **weren't**.

2. Complete the conversations with the simple past passive.

1. **A:** _____ the program _____ (install) on your computer?
   B: Yes, it _____. It _____ (do) yesterday by the computer tech.
2. **A:** Where _____ the pottery _____ (discover)?
   B: It _____ (find) in a pyramid. Then it _____ (take) to a lab by an archeologist. It _____ (not put) in a museum.
3. **A:** _____ the houses _____ (build) in the 1990s?
   B: No, they _____. They _____ (made) in the 1980s.

Past perfect, page 77

> Use the past perfect to refer to something that happened before a specific time in the past. To form the past perfect, use **had** + past participle.

Affirmative	Negative
I/You/He/She/We/They **had read** a book about it.	I/You/He/She/We/They **hadn't heard** about it before then.
I/You/He/She/It/We/They **had been** fairly quiet for several years.	I/You/He/She/It/We/They **hadn't been** there before.
What **had** I/you/he/she/we/they **heard** about volcanoes before?	
Why **hadn't** I/you/he/she/we/they **researched** anything about Indonesia before?	

Contractions had = 'd   had not = **hadn't**

1. Write sentences and questions in the past perfect.

1. Carolina / hear / about the tornado before her parents / .
   _____

2. what / you / learn / tsunamis before class / ?
   _____

3. Tyler / not read / about the forest fires before / .
   _____

4. they / flown / out of the city before the earthquake / .
   _____

5. why / you / not bring / your bike inside before the hurricane / ?
   _____

Past perfect and simple past, page 79

> The young man's parents **called** the police after he **had been** gone for three days.
> The boy **had drunk** the liquid from all the contact lens cases when they **found** him.
> The boy **didn't tell** his story until he **had drunk** a lot of water.
>
> 1. We **can** use the past perfect and the simple past in the same sentence.
> 2. We use the **past perfect** for the action that was completed first.

2. Write sentences with the information in the chart. Use the past perfect and the simple past and the words in parentheses.

First Activity	Second Activity
1. they put on sunscreen	they go to the beach
2. I not buy a sleeping bag	my friend ask me to go camping
3. she cut her arm	she find the first-aid kit
4. we get lost	we not look at the map
5. he not find his flashlight	the lights went out

1. (before) _____
2. (when) _____
3. (after) _____
4. (until) _____
5. (before) _____

Quoted speech vs. reported speech, page 87

Use reported speech to tell others what another person said.

	Quoted speech	Reported speech
Simple present	"It **isn't** right," she said.	She said that it **wasn't** right.
Simple past	"We **spent** the whole day together," she told me.	She told me that they **had spent** the whole day together.
Present perfect	"We**'ve had** a cell phone for 12 years," he said.	They said that they **had had** a cell phone for 12 years.
Future with *will*	"I**'ll text** you when I get to the party," he promised.	He promised that he **would text** me when he got to the party.
can	"I **can send** you an email," she whispered.	She whispered that she **could send** him an email.
Present continuous	"I**'m texting** my friends," he explained.	He explained that he **was texting** his friends.
Past continuous	"I **was checking** my email," she said.	She said that she **had been checking** her email.

1. Read the quoted speech. Then circle the correct answer in the reported speech.

1. "I'll clean my room tomorrow." Leo said that he **could clean** / **would clean** his room tomorrow.

2. "I didn't do my homework." Todd explained that he **hadn't done** / **wouldn't do** his homework.

3. "I'm terrified of earthquakes." Julie announced that she **was** / **will be** terrified of earthquakes.

4. "I can help you." My sister promised me that she **helped** / **could help** me.

Reported questions, page 89

In reported questions, the verbs usually change tenses as in reported speech. The word order in reported questions is the same as in an affirmative sentence.

Direct speech questions	Reported questions
"Why **do** you **have** makeup on?"	He asked her why she **had** makeup on.
"Which blog post **did** you **read**?"	She asked me which blog post I **had read**.
"How **have** you **been**?"	He asked me how I **had been**.
"When **will** you **chat** with me?"	She asked me when I **would chat** with her.
"Who **can help** them send a text message?"	He asked who **could help** them send a text message.
"What **are** you **doing**?"	He asked me what I **was doing**.
"Where **were** you **going**?"	She asked me where I **had been going**.
Use if *in Yes/No reported questions.*	
"Are you on your way?"	He asked **if** we were on our way.
"Did you see what happened?"	She asked **if** I had seen what happened.

2. Put the words in the correct order to make reported questions.

1. why / she sent her / Yolanda / so many text messages / asked Maria

   _____

2. asked / I / if / my friend / on my blog post / he would comment

   _____

3. forum / asked Sue / which / she had joined / Lorenzo

   _____

Reflexive pronouns, page 97

Use a reflexive pronoun when an object refers to the subject.

I like to challenge **myself** by measuring my progress every week.
You need to set a deadline for **yourself**.
All of **you** should challenge **yourselves** at this job.
He wasn't pleased with **himself** when he heard criticism of his performance.
She taught **herself** the skills she needed to write essays.
We decided to enjoy **ourselves** only after we had studied for the test.
Teenagers can help **themselves** to any of the career planning books we have.
Many people achieve the goals **they** set for **themselves**.
An education is important, and **it** can pay for **itself** if you get a good job.

1. **Circle the correct answers.**

   1. Maria taught **herself** / **myself** / **himself** to play the piano.
   2. You should reward **ourselves** / **yourself** / **myself** for your hard work.
   3. My parents usually deal with their problems **yourself** / **themselves** / **ourselves**.
   4. Please don't help me. I want to do it by **myself** / **herself** / **yourself**.
   5. Liz and I are very pleased with **herself** / **themselves** / **ourselves**.
   6. Will Eddie teach **myself** / **himself** / **yourself** the computer skills he needs?

Causative *have/get*, page 99

Use causative have/get *in situations where someone else does something for you. You don't do it.*
You can use get *or* have*. They have similar meanings.*

	have/get	object	past participle	
Lauren	is **getting**	her knee	**examined**	now.
Jennifer	**had**	a cake	**made**	for her friend.
David	needs to **get**	his camera	**fixed**.	
Logan	will **have**	his eyes	**checked**.	

2. **Write sentences about what Sandy did yesterday and what she will do tomorrow.**

Yesterday	Tomorrow
have / tablet / fix	have / hair / cut
get / clothes / clean	get / elbow / examine
get / homework / check	have / bike / repair

1. *Sandy* _____
2. *She* _____
3. _____
4. _____
5. _____
6. _____

CLIL PROJECT

The San PEOPLE

1. Label the pictures with the correct words.

Bushmen   hunt   Kalahari Desert   South Africa

a _____   b _____   c _____   d _____

1.4 LIFE IN THE DESERT

2. Watch the video. Complete the phrases with the correct adjectives.

animal   bright   difficult   high   young

1. _____ temperatures
2. a _____ place to live
3. a _____ future
4. _____ tracks
5. a _____ springbok

3. Match the phrases to make sentences.

1. The Kalahari Desert _____
2. The San people have lived _____
3. Recently the South African government _____
4. They get their food _____
5. From the footprints, _____

a. from plants and animals.
b. Isaac can tell the size of the animal.
c. in the Kalahari for thousands of years.
d. is a place of high temperatures and little rain.
e. gave a part of the Kalahari to the Khomani San.

PROJECT Learn about a group of people who live close to nature. Some choices are: the Inuit, the Saami, Australian Aborigines, or native South Americans in the Amazon rain forest. Find out more about them and answer the questions below. Present your information to the class.

- What is their name?
- Where do they live?
- What kinds of food are popular in the region?
- How do they get food?
- What kinds of animals live in the region?
- What are some difficulties of living in the region?
- What festivals or celebrations do they have?
- How is their life changing?

Renaissance GREATS

1. Label the pictures with the correct words.

| architecture | astronomy | the Medicis | perspective | three-dimensional |

a _____ b _____ c _____ d _____ e _____

2. Watch the video. Put the sentences 1–6 in the correct categories.

Medieval   Renaissance
_____   _____
_____   _____
_____   _____

1. Paintings didn't look realistic.
2. Rich families gave a lot of money to artists.
3. Paintings looked flat.
4. More important things were bigger in paintings.
5. Paintings were as realistic as possible.
6. Paintings looked three-dimensional.

Discovery EDUCATION
3.4 ART IN PERSPECTIVE

3. Complete the paragraph with the correct words.

| created | painters | painting | perspective | realistic |

Across Europe, ¹_____ began to use ²_____ in their work. Filippo Brunelleschi was the first Italian to do this. He ³_____ a ⁴_____ of this building that looked exactly like the real thing. This was the beginning of ⁵_____ art.

PROJECT

Leonardo da Vinci, Michelangelo, Filippo Brunelleschi – these are three great artists of the Renaissance. Choose one of them, or think of another, and make a poster. Include the following information on your poster, and then present to your class.

- A picture of your artist
- The years they lived
- Two interesting facts about their life
- A picture of a painting or a building they created
- Describe two things they painted, built, created, or discovered

Guided TOURS

1. Which sentences are true about living in the city? Which sentences are true about the country? Label the sentences *city* or *country*.

1. There are more things to do, during the day and at night. _____
2. You can enjoy the beauties of nature. _____
3. The streets can be crowded and noisy. _____
4. Sometimes people try to steal your money. _____
5. You know your neighbors and other people. _____
6. People are friendlier and say hello to you. _____
7. Places like schools and hospitals are closer to your home. _____

Discovery EDUCATION
5.4 CITY OR COUNTRY?

2. Watch the video. Complete the sentences with the correct words.

| big | cultural | fashionable | freezing | quiet | small | stylish |

1. In Russia, many people live in the countryside or in _____ towns.
2. But recently, more and more people are moving from the countryside to _____ cities.
3. There are _____ shops and _____ restaurants.
4. But there are some _____ places in cities.
5. In Moscow, people can relax by the river – even in the _____ months of winter.
6. _____ events bring people together.

PROJECT Write a guide to your city or town. Tell visitors what's different about your part of the world. Use the questions below.

Why go? Give three reasons.
_____

How do you get there? Describe the best routes by plane, train, bus, and car.
_____

What can you see? Name three things.
_____

What can you do? Describe two activities.
_____

Rethinking the CAR

1. Match the words with the correct definitions.

1. _____ fossil fuel
2. _____ carbon dioxide
3. _____ the environment
4. _____ battery
5. _____ renewable energy
6. _____ solar power

a. electricity that comes from the sun's heat
b. energy that comes from the sun, water, or wind
c. fuel from under the ground, like gas, coal, and oil
d. it gives energy to make radios, cars, and toys work
e. the air, water, or land where people, animals, and plants live
f. we produce this gas when we burn things or when we breathe out

2. Watch the video. Complete the sentences with the correct words.

| cell | efficient | factory | fossil | pollution | renewable |

1. Oil is a type of _____ fuel.
2. When you burn things, you get air _____.
3. New electric cars are more energy _____.
4. The batteries for the Coda car come from a _____ in China.
5. You can carry a _____ phone in your pocket.
6. Wind power is a type of _____ energy.

Discovery EDUCATION
7.4 DRIVING INTO THE FUTURE

3. Match the countries 1–4 with the car companies a–d.

1. _____ China
2. _____ Germany
3. _____ Japan
4. _____ USA

a. BMW
b. Chevy & Ford
c. BYD
d. Nissan

PROJECT

In groups, think of ways you and your classmates can help the environment. Here are some ideas:

- Recycle your old computers and cell phones
- Save energy in your home (turn off lights when you leave the room, take a two-minute shower, unplug appliances when you're not using them)
- Join an environmental group
- Take the bus, ride a bike, or walk to school

Make a presentation and show your ideas to the others in the class. Then ask the class to vote on the best ideas.

Ancient SYMBOLS

CLIL PROJECT

1. **Match the words with the correct definitions.**

   | archeologist | hieroglyphics | skeleton | strap | tomb |

   1. The bones of a human or animal body _____
   2. A person who studies very old places and things _____
   3. Egyptian writing from thousands of years ago _____
   4. A stone structure for a dead body of a person _____
   5. A narrow piece of leather or other strong material. You use it to connect something, like a sandal _____

   Discovery EDUCATION
   9.4 PICTURES WITH MEANING

2. **Watch the video. Number the sentences 1–5 in the order that you hear them.**

   a. Mansour Bourek is an archeologist. ____
   b. And here's a goose, a leaf, a mouth, and a strap from a sandal. ____
   c. His team of archeologists come to work inside the tomb. ____
   d. This skeleton has been here for over 2,000 years. ____
   e. Ahmed's family lives above one of the biggest tombs. ____

3. **Match the words with the correct hieroglyphics.**

   | goose | hill country | sun | to cry |

   1 _____   **2** _____   **3** _____   **4** _____

   PROJECT

   About 200 years ago, French soldiers discovered an ancient stone in Egypt with a story written on it. Scientists determined that the story was in three different languages: Greek, Demotic script (the common writing used in ancient Egyptian documents), and in hieroglyphics. The scientists knew how to read Greek, so they were able to understand the hieroglyphics! They named the stone the Rosetta Stone.

   Now create your own Rosetta Stone. Write a story about what you think life was like in ancient Egypt. Do research and see if you can translate your story into hieroglyphics.

Irregular verbs

Base Verb	Simple Past	Past Participle
babysit	babysat	babysat
be	was, were	been
become	became	become
begin	began	begun
bleed	bled	bled
blow	blew	blown
break	broke	broken
bring	brought	brought
build	built	built
burn	burned/burnt	burned/burnt
buy	bought	bought
catch	caught	caught
choose	chose	chosen
come	came	come
cost	cost	cost
cut	cut	cut
deal	dealt	dealt
dive	dived/dove	dived
do	did	done
draw	drew	drawn
dream	dreamed/dreamt	dreamed/dreamt
drink	drank	drunk
drive	drove	driven
eat	ate	eaten
fall	fell	fallen
feel	felt	felt
fight	fought	fought
find	found	found
fly	flew	flown
forget	forgot	forgotten
freeze	froze	frozen
get	got	gotten
give	gave	given
go	went	gone
grow	grew	grown
hang	hung	hung
have	had	had
hear	heard	heard
hide	hid	hidden
hit	hit	hit
hold	held	held
hurt	hurt	hurt
keep	kept	kept

Base Verb	Simple Past	Past Participle
know	knew	known
leave	left	left
let	let	let
lie	lay	lain
lose	lost	lost
make	made	made
mean	meant	meant
meet	met	met
pay	paid	paid
put	put	put
read	read	read
ride	rode	ridden
ring	rang	rung
rise	rose	risen
run	ran	run
say	said	said
see	saw	seen
sell	sold	sold
send	sent	sent
set	set	set
show	showed	shown
shut	shut	shut
sing	sang	sung
sit	sat	sat
sleep	slept	slept
speak	spoke	spoken
spend	spent	spent
spread	spread	spread
stand	stood	stood
steal	stole	stolen
stick	stuck	stuck
swim	swam	swum
take	took	taken
teach	taught	taught
tell	told	told
think	thought	thought
throw	threw	thrown
understand	understood	understood
wake	woke	woken
wear	wore	worn
win	won	won
write	wrote	written

Credits

The authors and publishers acknowledge the following sources of copyright material and are grateful for the permissions granted. While every effort has been made, it has not always been possible to identify the sources of all the material used, or to trace all copyright holders. If any omissions are brought to our notice, we will be happy to include the appropriate acknowledgements on reprinting.

p. 2-3 (B/G): Shutterstock Images/John McCormick; p. 3 (a): Alamy/©Piero Cruciatti; p. 3 (b): Shutterstock Images/egd; p. 3 (c): Shutterstock Images/James BO Insogna; p. 3 (d): Alamy/©Matthew Chattle; p. 3 (e): Alamy/©blickwinkel; p. 3 (f): Shutterstock Images/Igumnova Irina; p. 3 (g): Getty Images/Sam Yeh/AFP; p. 4 (B/G): Shutterstock Images/Kathriba; p. 4 (TL): Getty Images/National Geographic; p. 4 (TR): Alamy/©RIA Novosti; p. 5 (CL): Alamy/©Jeff Schultz/Alaska Stock; p. 6 (B/G): Shutterstock Images/Yulia Glam; p. 7 (CR): Shutterstock Images/Andrey_Popov; p. 8 (L): Alamy/©Roy Johnson; p. 9 (TR): Shutterstock Images/Raymona Pooler; p. 10 (TL): Alamy/©Chris Howarth/South Atlantic; p. 10 (B/G): Shutterstock Images/Freesoulproduction; p. 11 (1): Shutterstock Images/Ashraf Jandali; p.11 (2): Shutterstock Images/Rarach; p.11 (3): Alamy/©Barry Diomede; p. 11 (4): Shutterstock Images/OHishiapply; p. 11 (5): Alamy/©EB Images/Blend Images; p. 11 (6): Alamy/©Paul Maguire; p. 12-13 (B/G): Corbis/JGI/Jamie Grill; p. 13 (a): Shutterstock Images/Syda Productions, p. 13 (b): Alamy/©Tetra Images; p. 13 (c): Alamy/©Kuttig – People; p. 13 (e): Shutterstock Images/Pressmaster; p.13 (g): Alamy/©Juice Images; p. 13 (f): Shutterstock Images/Masson; p. 13 (g): Superstock/age footstock; p. 13 (h): Getty Images/Image Source; p. 13 (i): Shutterstock Images/kuznetcov_konstantin; p. 14 (TL): Shutterstock Images/Lasse Kristensen; p. 15 (TR): Alamy/©PCN Photography; p. 16 (TR): Shutterstock Images/Lucky Business; p. 16 (a): Shutterstock Images/Ruslan Guzov; p. 16 (b): Shutterstock Images/Dragon Images;p. 16 (c): Shutterstock Images/Pressmaster; p. 16 (d): Shutterstock Images/Creatista; p. 16 (e): Shutterstock Images/Photographee.eu;p. 16 (f): Getty Images/Nick Dolding; p. 16 (g): Alamy/©Bjorn Andren/Robert Matton AB; p. 17 (TR): Shutterstock Images/Alexander Raths; p. 18 (TL): Alamy/©Kumar Sriskandan; p. 18 (BL): Corbis/Hill Street Studios/Blend Images; p. 19 (TR): Alamy/©Sverre Haugland; p. 20 (B/G): Shutterstock Images/William Perugini; p. 20 (T): Alamy/©AJSH Photograph; p. 21 (BR): Shutterstock Images/Andreasnikolas; p. 22-23 (B/G): Alamy/©JL Images; p. 23 (a): Alamy/©Jeff Gilbert; p. 23 (b): Alamy/©Michele and Tom Grimm;p. 23 (c):Alamy/©Arco Images GmbH; p. 23 (d): Alamy/©Paul Lovichi Photography; p. 23 (e): Alamy/©eddie linssen; p. 23 (f): Alamy/©Nagelestock.com; p. 23 (g): Alamy/©Tony French; p. 23 (h): Alamy/©Andrew Aitchison; p. 23 (i): Shutterestock/Grynold; p. 23 (j): Alamy/©Christina K; p. 24 (TL): Shutterstock Images/Jag_cz; p. 24 (T): Alamy/©Kevin Britland; p. 25 (BL): Alamy/©LWA/Dann Tardif/Blend Images; p. 26 (TL): Alamy/©i stage; p. 26 (a): Alamy/©Aki; p. 26 (b): Shutterstock Images/Furtseff; p. 26 (c): Shutterstock Images/Vereshchagin Dmitry; p. 26 (d): Shutterestock/Christian Bertrand; p. 26 (e): Shutterstock Images/mphot; p. 26 (f): Shutterstock Images/Dario Sabljak; p. 26 (g): Shutterstock Images/Chromakey; p. 26 (h): Alamy/©lem; p. 26 (i):Shutterstock Images/vvoe; p. 26 (j): Shutterstock Images/ Visun Khankasem; p. 27 (CR): Alamy/©Graham Salter/Lebrecht Music & Arts; p. 28 (L): Shutterstock Images/Warren Goldswain; p. 29 (TL): Alamy/©david pearson; p. 30 (TR): Alamy/©ZUMA Press, Inc.; p. 30 (B/G): Shutterstock Images/Fluke samed; p. 32-33 (B/G): Getty Images/Vetta/Scott Hailstone; p. 33 (a): Alamy/©J.R.Bale; p. 33 (b): Superstock/age footstock; p. 33 (c): Getty Images/Ken Chernus/Taxi; p. 33 (d): Shutterstock Images/Greg Epperson; p. 33 (e): Alamy/©PHOTOEDIT; p. 33 (f): Alamy/©Age Fotostock Spain S.L.; p. 33 (g): Alamy/©Dmitry Burlakov; p. 33 (h): Shutterstock Images/PhotoSky; p. 33 (i): Alamy/©ZUMA Press, Inc.; p. 34 (TL): Alamy/©Gaspar Avila; p. 34 (BL): Alamy/©ZUMA Press, Inc.; p. 35 (CR): Getty Images/Tetra Images; p. 36 (TL): Getty Images/Philip and Karen Smith; p. 36 (BL): Alamy/©Westend61 GmbH; p. 37 (TR): Alamy/©Cultura; p. 38 (TL): Alamy/©Hemis; p. 38 (CL): Shutterstock Images/Strahil Dimitrov; p. 38 (BL): Shutterstock Images/Graphichead; p. 39 (TR): Corbis/Radius Images; p. 40 (T): Shutterstock Images/Pichugin Dmitry; p. 40 (a): Shutterstock Images/Bildagentur Zoonar GmbH; p. 40 (b): Alamy/©Howard Davies; p. 40 (c): Robert Harding Picture Library/Stuart Black/AgeFotostock; p. 40 (d): Alamy/©John Elk III; p. 40 (e): Shutterstock Images/Konrad Mostert; p. 40 (B/G): Shutterstock Images/Sasapee; p. 42-43 (B/G): Corbis/2/Andrew Bret Wallis/Ocean; p. 43 (a): Shutterstock Images/Dmitrijs Bindemanis; p. 43 (b): Shutterstock Images/Matteo photos; p. 43 (c): Alamy/©Robin Beckham/BEEPstock; p. 43 (d): Shutterstock Images/Jayakumar; p. 43 (e): Shutterstock Images/Jag_cz; p. 43 (f): Shutterstock Images/Lisa F. Young; p. 43 (g): Alamy/©Phil Degginger; p. 43 (h): Shutterstock Images/Blend Images; p. 43 (TR): Shutterstock Images/Andresr; p. 44 (1): UNIVERSAL/THE KOBAL COLLECTION/BOLAND, JASIN; p. 44 (2): UNIVERSAL/THE KOBAL COLLECTION/MOSELEY, MELISSA; p. 44 (3): HAMMER FILM PRODUCTIONS/THE KOBAL COLLECTION; p. 44 (4): MIRAMAX/THE KOBAL COLLECTION; p. 44 (5): 20TH CENTURY FOX/THE KOBAL COLLECTION/FOREMAN, RICHARD; p. 44 (6): CODE RED PRODUCTIONS/THE KOBAL COLLECTION; p. 44 (7): NEW REGENCY PICTURES/THE KOBAL COLLECTION; p. 46 (TL): Alamy/©Gunter Marx; p. 46 (BL): Alamy/©Ruby; p. 46 (BL): Alamy/©GeoStills; p. 47 (TR): Alamy/©Gunter Marx; p. 48 (B/G): Shutterstock Images/Kamira; p. 49 (TR): Shutterstock Images/Pincasso; p. 50 (TR): Alamy/©Adrian Turner; p. 50 (B/G): Shutterstock Images/Shchipkova Elena; p. 51 (TR): Shutterstock Images/Jacek Chabraszewski; p. 52-53 (B/G): Corbis/Herbert Meyrl/Westend61; p. 54-55 (B/G): Getty Images/Kevin Spreekmeester; p. 56 (TC): Shutterstock Images/Feng Yu; p. 57 (B): Alamy/©Agencja Fotograficzna Caro; p. 58 (CL): Alamy/©Denise Hager Catchlight Visual Services; p. 58 (TL): Shutterstock Images/Sean Locke Photography; p. 59 (CR): Alamy/©Richard G. Bingham II; p. 60 (TL): Shutterstock Images/IPranoffee; p. 60 (BL): Getty Images/Chris Schmidt; p. 60 (BC): Alamy/©Tony Cordoza; p. 60 (BR): Alamy/©Marjorie Kamys Cotera/Bob Daemmrich Photography; p. 61 (TL): Shutterstock Images/Ermolaev Alexander; p. 62 (B/G): Shutterstock Images/Albund; p. 62 (TL): Alamy/©Picture Partners; p. 62 (BL): Alamy/©Denise Hager Catchlight Visual Services; p. 63 (TR): Shutterstock Images/Dmitry Kalinovsky; p. 64-65 (B/G): Shutterstock Images/Albachiaraa; p. 65 (a): Shutterstock Images/Lanych; p. 65 (b): Shutterstock Images/Luchi_a; p. 65 (c): Shutterstock Images/K.Miri Photography; p. 65 (d): Shutterstock Images/Coprid; p. 65 (e): Shutterstock Images/Stockphoto Graf; p. 65 (f): Shutterstock Images/FreeBirdPhotos; p. 65 (g): Shutterstock Images/DigitalMagus; p. 65 (h): Shutterstock Images/Praisaeng; p. 65 (i): Shutterstock Images/Vadim Ratnikov; p. 65 (j): Shutterstock Images/Coprid; p. 65 (k): Shutterstock Images/John Kasawa; p. 66 (TL): Alamy/©jay goebel; p. 67 (CR): Alamy/©eye35.pix; p. 68 (TL): Alamy/©Bubbles Photolibrary; p. 69 (CR): Shutterstock Images/Minerva Studio; p. 70 (BC): Shutterstock Images/Pressmaster; p.70 (BR): Alamy/©PhotoAlto sas; p. 70 (TL): Alamy/©Jim West; p. 71 (TL): Alamy/©Purestock; p. 72 (TR): Alamy/©Justin Hannaford; p. 72 (CR): Alamy/©Chris Cooper-Smith; p. 72 (T): Shutterstock Images/CoolR; p. 72 (B): Shutterstock Images/Imagevixen; p. 73 (1): Alamy/©Cristina Fumi Photography; p. 73 (2): Shutterstock Images/Felix Rohan; p. 73 (3): Shutterstock Images/Alex Staroseltsev; p. 73 (4): Shutterstock Images/MNI; p. 73 (5): Shutterstock Images/Elena Blokhina; p. 73 (6): Shutterstock Images/Mama_mia; p. 74-75 (B/G): Corbis/Wave; p. 75 (a):Shutterstock Images/Lafoto; p. 75 (b): Shutterstock Images/st.djura; p. 75 (c): Shutterstock Images/Morten Normann Almeland; p. 75 (d): Shutterstock Images/Vaju Ariel; p. 75 (e): Shutterstock Images/Gts; p. 75 (f): Alamy/©Zacarias Pereira Da Mata; p. 75 (g): Shutterstock Images/chaoss; p. 75 (h): Shutterstock Images/jo Crebbin; p. 75 (i): Alamy/©Avico Ltd; p. 76 (T): Alamy/©Keith J Smith; p. 77 (TR): Shutterstock Images/Sekar B; p. 78 (TL): Alamy/©Paul Mayall Australia; p. 78 (a): Shutterstock Images/Gresei; p. 78 (b): Shutterstock Images/Brian A Jackson; p. 78 (c): Shutterstock Images/Nikitabuida; p. 78 (d): Alamy/©BSIP SA; p. 78 (e): Shutterstock Images/Tony740607; p. 78 (f): Shutterstock Images/Grynold; p. 78 (g): Shutterstock Images/Tatiana Popova; p. 78 (h): Shutterstock Images/Ti Santi; p. 78 (i): Alamy/©D.Hurst; p. 79 (TR): Getty Images/Nacivet; p. 80 (TL): Shutterstock Images/Lamreal-kobzeva; p. 80 (CL): Shutterstock Images/scyther5; p. 80 (BL): Shutterstock Images/Ervin Monn; p. 81 (TL): Alamy/©Blend Images; p. 82 (TR): Corbis/Jim Reed/Jim Reed Photography - Severe &; p. 82 (T): Shutterstock Images/Minerva Studio; p. 82 (B/G): Shutterstock Images/Minerva Studio; p. 83 (BL): Shutterstock Images/Gorillaimages; p. 84-85 (B/G): Alamy/©Science Photo Library; p. 85 (CR): Alamy/©JGI/Jamie Grill/Blend Images; p. 86 (T): Shutterstock Images/Littleny; p. 87 (BR): Getty Images/Mark Bowden; p. 88 (a): Shutterstock Images/Syda Productions; p. 88 (b): Alamy/©Blend Images; p. 88 (c): Getty Images/Yellow Dog Productions; p. 88 (d): Getty Images/iStockphoto; p. 89 (CR): Getty Images/Debra Roets/Le Club Symphonie; p. 90 (TL): Shutterstock Images/Goodluz; p. 91 (TR): Shutterstock Images/Stephen Coburn; p. 92 (TL): Alamy/©Liquid Light; p. 92 (ML): Alamy/©Kathy deWitt; p. 92 (BL): Alamy/©Tim Graham; p. 92 (B/G): Shutterstock Images/FrameAngel; p. 94-95 (B/G): Corbis/Pete Saloutos/Image Source; p. 96 (TL): Shutterstock Images/Arieliona; p. 97 (TR): Alamy/©Redsnapper; p. 98 (TR): Alamy/©Steve Lindridge; p. 99 (CR): Alamy/©Paul/F1online Digitale Bildagentur GmbH; p. 100 (TL): Alamy/©Robert Harding World Imagery; p. 100 (BL): Alamy/©Bob Daemmrich; p. 101 (TL): Alamy/©Steve Skjold; p. 102 (T, B/G): Alamy/©Zuma Press; p. 104-105 (B/G): Corbis/Marc Dozier; p. 120 (BR): Alamy/©The Print Collector; Back cover: Shutterstock Images/fluke samed.

Front cover photography by Alamy/©Martin Strmiska.

The publishers are grateful to the following illustrators:

Q2A Media Services, Inc. p. 6, 116, 120; Martin Sanders p. 28.

All video stills by kind permission of:

Discovery Communications, LLC 2015: p. 2 (1, 3, 4), 5, 10, 11, 12 (1, 3), 15, 20, 22 (1, 3, 4), 25, 30, 31, 32 (1, 3), 35, 40, 42 (1, 3, 4), 45, 50, 51, 54 (1, 3), 57, 62, 64 (1, 3, 4), 67, 72, 73, 74 (1, 3), 77, 82, 84 (1, 3, 4), 87, 92, 93, 94 (1, 3), 97, 102, 116, 117, 118, 119, 120; Cambridge University Press: p. 2 (2), 8, 12 (2), 18, 22 (2), 28, 32 (2), 38, 42 (2), 48, 54 (2), 60, 64 (2), 70, 74 (2), 80, 84 (2), 90, 94 (2), 100.

Uncover 3 Combo
Kathryn O'Dell

Workbook

CAMBRIDGE UNIVERSITY PRESS

Discovery EDUCATION

Table of Contents

1	Life on the Edge	2
2	First Things First!	8
	Review: Units 1 and 2	14
3	Art All Around Us	16
4	Sign Me Up!	22
	Review: Units 3 and 4	28
5	Yikes!	30
6	Difficult Decisions	36
	Review: Units 5 and 6	42
7	Smart Planet	44
8	Run for Cover!	50
	Review: Units 7 and 8	56
9	He Said, She Said	58
10	Don't Give Up!	64
	Review: Units 9 and 10	70
	Video worksheets	72

1 Life on the Edge

VOCABULARY Extreme weather

1 Complete the sentences and the crossword.

ACROSS

2. We didn't go for a boat ride because of high ___winds___.

4. There was a lot of _____ and lightning during the storm.

6. We couldn't see the road very well because of the _____. It was very thick.

7. It started to _____ during the storm. We were afraid the windows might break from the ice.

DOWN

1. I didn't have school today because of the _____.

3. It was over 35°C during the _____ wave.

5. The game was canceled because of _____ rain.

2 Complete the weather report with words and phrases from Exercise 1.

Worldwide Weather

There is a ¹___blizzard___ in Anchorage, Alaska, today. Expect 25 to 50 centimeters of snow by the end of the day. ²_____ of 80 kilometers per hour are blowing the snow around.

³_____ is coming down quickly in several cities in southern Germany. Falling ice can damage cars and hurt people.

Today in Mexico City there is ⁴_____ falling at about 3 centimeters per hour. Right now, it's quiet, but expect ⁵_____ at night.

The Golden Gate Bridge is closed in San Francisco because of ⁶_____. Drivers can't see very far in front of them. Be careful on the roads.

There is a ⁷_____ in Dubai with temperatures over 40°C.

3 What kinds of extreme weather do you think can happen in these places?

1. ___high winds,___ _____

2. _____

3. _____

GRAMMAR Present tense review – simple present and present continuous

1 **Look at Eva's weekend schedule. Complete the sentences about her routine with the simple present forms of the verbs.**

Friday	Saturday	Sunday
go to class	work at food court	visit grandparents
study with Kyle at library	hang out with friends	make lunch with grandma

1. Eva _____*goes*_____ to class on Fridays. She ____*doesn't go*____ to class on Saturdays and Sundays.
2. Eva and Kyle _____ at Eva's house. They _____ at the library.
3. Eva _____ at the food court on Saturdays. She _____ at the bike shop.
4. Eva and her friends _____ after work.
5. Eva _____ her grandparents on Sundays.
6. Eva and her grandma _____ lunch. Her grandpa _____ lunch.

2 **Put the words in the correct order to make sentences. Change the verbs to the present continuous.**

1. right / the snow / now / melt
   The snow is melting right now.
2. fly / Jake / to Alaska
   _____
3. in the park / play / they / basketball
   _____
4. my / I / skateboard / not ride
   _____
5. vacation / plan / a / we
   _____
6. and Tara / coats / not wear / Ed
   _____

3 **Check (✓) if the activities are routines or happening right now.**

	Routine	Right now
1. I'm driving in a blizzard.		✓
2. Dennis goes to the beach with his friends.		
3. Sarah drives to class.		
4. You aren't visiting your cousins.		
5. We are going to the beach with our friends.		
6. Mark and Penny visit their grandparents.		

4 **Complete the conversation with the simple present or present continuous forms of the verbs.**

Tina: Hi, Leo. What are you doing these days?

Leo: I ¹___*am taking*___ (take) a class at the community center, and I ²_____ (play) on a new soccer team. I ³_____ (be) really busy.

Tina: What class?

Leo: It ⁴_____ (be) a meteorology class. You know, a class about weather.

Tina: I see. What are you studying?

Leo: Well, right now, we ⁵_____ (learn) about weather changes around the world.

Tina: That sounds interesting.

Leo: Yeah. The weather ⁶_____ (change) a lot these days. I ⁷_____ (read) a chapter about extreme weather right now.

Tina: Speaking of weather, I have to go! It ⁸_____ (start) to rain.

Leo: Oh, no. I guess I ⁹_____ (not go) to my soccer game now. We ¹⁰_____ (play) at the park every Tuesday, but we ¹¹_____ (not go) when it rains!

VOCABULARY Basic needs

1 Label the pictures with the correct words.

> clothes
> communication
> education
> entertainment
> ✓ food and drink
> health care
> a home
> money
> transportation

1. _food and drink_
2. _____
3. _____
4. _____
5. _____
6. _____
7. _____
8. _____
9. _____

2 Complete the sentence with the words and phrases from Exercise 1.

1. My cousin wants to buy ___*a home*___ in our neighborhood, but he doesn't have enough _____ yet.
2. There are many _____ options in this city – buses, trains, and subways.
3. I'm getting a good _____ at Clinton High School.
4. I need to buy some new _____ for school.
5. Texting is a more popular form of _____ than talking on the phone for teens.
6. Do you go to the movies for _____?
7. You can get _____ at the food court in the mall.
8. My parents have good _____. Their doctor is excellent.

3 Answer the questions with your own information.

1. What do you usually do for entertainment?
   I usually watch movies on my computer.
   _____

2. How much money do you spend every week?
   _____
   _____

3. What form of transportation do you use to get to school?
   _____
   _____

4. What is the main form of communication you use with your friends?
   _____
   _____

5. What kind of clothes do you like to wear?
   _____
   _____

GRAMMAR Past tense review – simple past and past continuous

1 Write sentences with the simple past.

1. Larry / get / home late last night
   Larry got home late last night.

2. We / not go / to the concert
   _____

3. I / send / Jen three text messages
   _____

4. They / ride / their skateboards to school
   _____

5. You / not call / last night
   _____

6. Sandra / wear / jeans to school
   _____

7. I / not be / at school yesterday
   _____

8. My cousin / arrive / from Argentina last night
   _____

2 Complete the sentences with the past continuous forms of the verbs.

1. Laura *was studying* (study) during the blizzard.
2. Vic and Dan _____ (ride) the bus together.
3. We _____ (not walk) outside when it started to hail.
4. I _____ (not wear) a coat when it got cold.
5. You _____ (shop) when I called you.
6. Frank _____ (wear) a helmet when he fell off his bike.

3 Complete the sentences with the simple past or past continuous forms of the verbs.

1. I *didn't watch* (not watch) the news last night. I was too busy!
2. Torrey _____ (see) the tornado before it hit the town.
3. I put on a hat, but the wind _____ (blow) it off my head.
4. Jess _____ (not wear) a raincoat when the rain came, so she got really wet.
5. Sam _____ (listen) to the radio when he heard the weather report.
6. Reggie _____ (not be) afraid of storms until he experienced high winds.

4 Correct the sentences and questions.

1. Marcos ~~use~~ *used* to play in the snow.
2. We use drive to California every summer.
3. Rita not used to take the bus to school.
4. Did you used to camp in the mountains?
5. I used to bought new clothes at the mall.
6. Jack and Paul use to watch TV on Saturday mornings.

5 Complete the text with the simple past, past continuous, or *used to*.

On the Edge

Tonya Harris lives on the edge – on the edge of a mountain! One time, she and her younger brother ¹ *were playing* (play) soccer outside when her brother ² _____ (kick) the ball off the mountain. He ³ _____ (chase) the ball when Tonya ⁴ _____ (scream). She ⁵ _____ (stop) him from going over the edge of the mountain. Now that her brother is older, she doesn't worry about him, but she ⁶ _____ (worry) about him all the time!

Tonya's school is at the bottom of the mountain. When she was young, she ⁷ _____ (take) the bus to school, but now she rides her bike. Yesterday, she ⁸ _____ (ride) her bike when she ⁹ _____ (fall). She ¹⁰ _____ (break) her arm. Her parents ¹¹ _____ (drive) to work when they ¹² _____ (see) her. They ¹³ _____ (take) her to the doctor right away. Tonya ¹⁴ _____ (not go) to school yesterday. This morning, Tonya ¹⁵ _____ (go) back to school. While her friends ¹⁶ _____ (wait) for class to start, they ¹⁷ _____ (write) their names on her cast. Tonya likes her life on the edge of the mountain, but she's going to be more careful!

CONVERSATION — Agreeing and disagreeing

1. Circle the correct answers.

1. **A:** This weather is crazy, ____?
   B: Yeah. It's an incredible blizzard.
   a. don't you think   b. I disagree

2. **A:** Do you think it's going to snow more?
   B: ____. I think the blizzard is over.
   a. I disagree   b. I don't think so

3. **A:** I hate winter weather.
   B: ____. I love the snow!
   a. See what I mean   b. I disagree

4. **A:** The snow is so high!
   B: ____? I told you it was 30 centimeters!
   a. See what I mean   b. I don't think so

5. **A:** I can't wait for spring. ____?
   B: Actually, I like the winter.
   a. Don't you agree   b. See what I mean

2 Circle the correct phrases.

Tim: Can you believe this blizzard? It's the biggest one so far this year, ¹**I don't think so / don't you think**?

Donna: Yes, I think you're right. There's at least 30 centimeters of snow on the ground! It'd be better to live somewhere warm. ²**Don't you agree / I disagree**?

Tim: ³**See what I mean / I don't think so**. I really like the cold weather.

Donna: Really? I prefer a warmer place. There's so much more to do in warm weather!

Tim: ⁴**I disagree / Don't you agree**! I do a lot in the winter. There are so many winter activities here – like snowboarding and skiing.

Donna: We did have fun on the ski trip last weekend.

Tim: ⁵**I don't think so / See what I mean**? Winter is great.

Donna: Yeah, I guess so. But this blizzard is terrible! It's too cold to ski or snowboard.

Tim: That's true.

READING TO WRITE

1 Number the parts of a persuasive email in order from 1–3.

____ Explain why you think your readers should do what you're suggesting.

____ State your position again in a different way.

____ State your position on a topic.

2 Circle the correct words.

To: martin@net.cup.org
From: lydia@net.cup.org
Subject: Cuernavaca is the best!

Hi Martin,
I'm living in Cuernavaca in Mexico now. I love it. I think it's the best city in Mexico!
¹**First of all** / Second, it's like spring all year. ²**The best part** / **For example**, there are a lot of flowers and plants everywhere – all year long.
³**For example** / **Second**, there's a lot to do and see in Cuernavaca. ⁴**For instance** / **First of all**, there are historic buildings, carnivals, and a lot of markets.
⁵**The best part** / **For example** is the people. There are many places to meet friends. I met two new friends at the skate park yesterday!
Cuernavaca really is a great place to live. I hope you can visit me this year.
Your cousin,
Lydia

3 Match the sentences. Then write them in the correct places in the email.

1. The best part is all of the places to eat. ____
2. First of all, there are many things to do outside. ____
3. Second, there are many things to do inside. ____

a. For example, you can go to sports events and parks.
b. For instance, there are many museums in Chicago.
c. Chicago has food from all over the world!

To: evelyn@net.cup.org
From: talia@net.cup.org
Subject: Come to Chicago!

Hi Evelyn,
I want you to come visit me in Chicago on your school break! Chicago is one of the best cities to visit.
_____
_____
_____
_____
_____

So please come visit me. We'll have lots of fun!
Your friend,
Talia

Unit 1 | 7

2 First Things First!

VOCABULARY Priorities

1 Put the words in the correct order to make phrases about priorities.

1. out / working

   working out

2. out / weekend / on / staying / the / late

   _____

3. with / hanging / friends / out

   _____

4. clothes / for / shopping

   _____

5. the / helping / house / around

   _____

6. something / doing / creative

   _____

7. for / time / having / yourself

   _____

8. friends / online / chatting / with

   _____

9. enough / sleep / getting

   _____

2 What are the people doing? Write sentences using eight of the phrases from Exercise 1.

1. Carol is communicating with Jim and Vicky on her computer.

   She's chatting with friends online.

2. Brad went to bed at 9:00 p.m. last night. It's 8:00 a.m., and he's still in bed.

   _____

3. Jenny and Mark are exercising at the gym.

   _____

4. Mandy is looking at T-shirts and jeans.

   _____

5. Trent and Sue are cleaning the kitchen and washing clothes.

   _____

6. It's Saturday at 11:00 p.m. Wendy is at a concert.

   _____

7. Carlos is talking at a café with Luke, Dana, and Cindy.

   _____

8. Luisa is painting a picture.

   _____

3 Answer the questions with your own information.

1. What do you do when you have time for yourself?

   When I have time for myself, I read in the park.

   _____

2. How late do you stay out on the weekends?

   _____

   _____

3. Where do you hang out with friends? What do you do?

   _____

   _____

4. Do you help around the house? What do you do?

   _____

   _____

5. Do you like shopping for clothes? Where do you go?

   _____

   _____

GRAMMAR have to/don't have to; must

1 Look at Matt and Carrie's To Do list and write sentences about their chores. ✓ = have to, ✗ = not have to.

To Do Weekend chores and activities		
Matt	Carrie	Both
shop for clothes ✓	work out ✗	help around the house ✓
fix the computer ✓	practice the piano ✓	work in the yard ✗
go to soccer practice ✗	take the dog for a walk ✓	do homework ✓

1. _Matt has to shop for clothes._
2. _____
3. _____
4. _____
5. _____
6. _____
7. _____
8. _____
9. _____

2 Write sentences about the skate park rules with *must* and *must not*.

Do . . .	Don't . . .
• wear a helmet • take turns on the ramps • throw away trash	• bring food or drink into the skate area • use the park after 9:00 p.m. • ride bikes on the ramps

1. _You must wear a helmet._
2. _____
3. _____
4. _____
5. _____
6. _____

3 Write two sentences for each picture with the words from the box and the correct form of (*not*) *have to* or *must* (*not*).

you / turn off / your phone
she / call / her mother now
you / use / your phone
she / call / her mother later

1. _____
2. _____

3. _____
4. _____

4 Write sentences about your chores with (*not*) *have to*.

Have to
1. _I have to wash the dishes._
2. _____
3. _____
Don't have to
4. _____
5. _____
6. _____

5 Write sentences about rules for a library with *must* (*not*).

Dos
1. _____
2. _____
Don'ts
3. _You must not run in the library._
4. _____

Unit 2 | 9

VOCABULARY Emotions

1 Find six more words for emotions.

S	H	I	O	P	R	O	F	G	W	U	M	K	P
T	B	S	P	Z	J	X	G	V	R	Q	I	A	Q	N
R	R	L	R	N	B	A	A	W	F	U	L	W	C	Z
E	M	I	O	M	D	D	Y	B	N	A	T	O	E	F
S	L	U	U	I	G	Z	K	P	D	Y	N	N	X	V
S	Z	U	D	U	N	A	W	E	P	G	E	D	H	L
E	M	B	A	R	R	A	S	S	E	D	R	E	A	B
D	I	S	U	R	H	I	Q	U	R	B	A	R	U	D
O	F	Z	S	C	K	R	J	G	E	F	P	F	S	P
U	E	T	E	R	R	I	F	I	E	D	K	U	T	M
T	H	W	N	N	X	H	T	S	T	M	H	L	E	O
G	V	K	A	S	L	S	T	P	R	H	X	E	D	T

2 Complete the sentences with the correct words.

awful
embarrassed
exhausted
proud
✓ stressed out
terrified
wonderful

I have so much to do this week. I'm really
¹ _stressed out_ ! First of all, I have to
give a speech in my class on Friday. I'm
² _____ because I really don't
like speaking in front of people. I worked on
the speech for hours last night, and today I'm
³ _____ . Last time I gave a
speech, I was so ⁴ _____
because I forgot what to say. It was
⁵ _____ ! But I'm going to
practice a lot this time. I hope it's going to be
⁶ _____ . I want to make my
parents ⁷ _____ .

3 How do you think the people feel in these situations? Use some of the words from Exercise 2. Sometimes more than one answer is possible.

1. John forgot his teacher's name. _embarrassed_
2. Linda is scared of spiders, and there is a huge one under her bed. _____
3. Abby has three tests tomorrow, and she has to take care of her younger brothers tonight. _____
4. Oliver's sister scored three goals in a soccer game. _____
5. Danny didn't get enough sleep last night. _____

4 How do you feel in these situations? Use words from Exercise 2.

1. You did well on a test. _____
2. You're riding a roller coaster. _____
3. You have to give a speech. _____
4. Your friend won an award. _____

GRAMMAR Modals of obligation – *should, ought to, had better*

1 Complete the advice with *should* (*not*) and the verbs.

Mike G My friends are going sky diving tomorrow, but I don't want to go. I'm terrified! What should I do?

Sara Li You ¹_____ (be) embarrassed. It's OK if you don't want to go.

Dave I agree. You ²_____ (tell) your friends you don't want to go.

Paula S I disagree. You ³_____ (try) it. It might be really fun!

Steven You ⁴_____ (go) with them on the plane. It will be fun. But, if you get scared, you ⁵_____ (jump). You ⁶_____ (do) anything that you don't want to do. You can decide when you get there.

10 | Unit 2

2 Look at the pictures and complete the sentences with *ought (not) to* and the correct verbs.

No Parking

1. We ___ought not to park___ here.

Turn your cell phones off

2. You _____ your cell phone off.

You can't take big bags on the plane

3. I _____ this bag on the plane. I'll have to check it.

Please be quiet

4. You _____ quiet in the library.

Don't sit on the grass

5. They _____ on the grass in the park.

3 Write sentences with *had better (not)*. ✓ = yes, ✗ = no.

1. Terry / hang out / with his friends tonight / ✗

   ___Terry had better not hang out with his___
   ___friends tonight.___

2. Josh and Mia / shop / for clothes before school starts / ✓

   _____

3. We / get / home on time / ✓

   _____

4. You / chat / online very long / ✗

   _____

5. Serena / help / around the house / ✓

   _____

6. I / get / too stressed out / ✗

   _____

It's + adjective + infinitive

4 Correct the sentences.

1. ~~It~~ *It's* easy to be proud of your friends.
2. It's no difficult to ride a bike.
3. You shouldn't to stay out late.
4. It's important have time for yourself.
5. It fun not to shop for clothes.
6. You ought call the police about the robbery.
7. It's important is quiet in the library.
8. You had better to get enough sleep.

5 Read the sentences. Then write sentences with similar meanings with the modals.

1. It's a good idea for John to work out. (should)

   ___John should work out.___

2. My cousin needs to call me. (had better)

   _____

3. You can't drive on that side of the road. (ought not to)

   _____

4. We can't stay out too late. (had better not)

   _____

5. It's required that I buy a ticket before I get on the bus. (ought to)

   _____

6. It's a bad idea for Lori to chat online with her friends for hours. (shouldn't)

   _____

CONVERSATION — Helping someone to do something

1 Put the words in order to make sentences.

1. show / let / you / me
   Let me show you.

2. at / very / that / I'm / like / not / good / things
   _____

3. if / you / like / I'll / give / a hand / you
   _____

4. really / simple / it's / pretty
   _____

5. not / how / it / I'm / sure / to do
   _____

2 Complete the conversation with the sentences from Exercise 1.

Sam: Hey, Dee.

Dee: Hi, Sam. It looks like you're having problems with your phone.
¹ *I'll give you a hand if you like.*

Sam: That'd be great. I need to get my email on my phone, but
² _____
Do you know how?

Dee: Yeah, I do. I just did it with my new phone last week.
³ _____

Sam: Well, you might think it's easy, but
⁴ _____
I'm really terrible with technology.

Dee: It's really not difficult to do.
⁵ _____
You'll see.

Sam: OK. Thanks.

Dee: So, first, go to "Settings" and click on "Email." Then click on "Add account" and enter your email address.

Sam: Wow. That *was* easy. Thanks.

READING TO WRITE

1 Complete Lucas's blog post with *a few*, *a little*, *too many*, or *too much*.

Last month, I was really stressed out. I was involved in ¹ _too many_ activities. I was taking three classes, working part-time at the mall, working out at the gym, and playing on a soccer team. I was doing ² _____! I only had ³ _____ time to hang out with my friends. At the end of the week, I was exhausted, and I really missed my friends.

I made some changes in my lifestyle. I made sure that I had ⁴ _____ minutes for myself each day. Every morning, I read before breakfast, and at night, I took ⁵ _____ time to play video games. I also made sure I was getting enough sleep. Then I started doing some of my needed activities with friends. I started working out with ⁶ _____ friends and studying for my classes with my best friend. I still have ⁷ _____ to do, but at least I'm seeing my friends more!

---

2 Read Lucas's blog post again. Answer the questions.

1. What was Lucas's problem?

   _____

2. What four things caused his problem?

   _____
   _____
   _____
   _____

3. What three steps did Lucas take to solve his problem?

   _____
   _____
   _____

3 Read Lucas's blog post again. Check (✓) the advice he would give other people.

If you are involved in too many activities, . . .

☑ you have to have time for yourself.
❑ you shouldn't work out.
❑ you should try to do some of your activities with other people.
❑ you can study with friends.
❑ you shouldn't study so much.
❑ you had better quit your job.
❑ you should sleep less to make time to get all of your work done.
❑ you ought to get enough sleep.

4 Complete the end of Lucas's blog post with the phrases you checked in Exercise 3.

If you're like me and are involved in too many activities, I have some advice for you. ¹ _You have to have time for yourself._ For example, read a book, ride your bike, or play video games for a few minutes.

² _____
_____

For instance, you can work out with people in your family, or
³ _____
_____

⁴ _____
_____
_____ In fact, most teens need eight to 10 hours of sleep.

REVIEW UNITS 1–2

1 Write two correct sentences for each picture.

> I hate storms with heavy rain.
> I hope this heat wave ends soon.
> ✓ I love blizzards.
> I'm exhausted from working in the hot weather.
> I'm stressed out from driving in bad weather.
> I'm terrified of thunder and lightning.
> It's wonderful to see all of the snow.
> The hail is awful.

1. *I love blizzards.*
   _____

2. _____
   _____

3. _____
   _____

4. _____
   _____

2 Complete the sentences with the simple present or simple past forms of the phrases.

> do something creative
> ✓ not get enough sleep
> not help around the house
> shop for clothes
> stay out late on the weekend
> work out

1. I usually *don't get enough sleep* during the week. I go to bed late and get up early.

2. I often _____. I hang out with friends Friday and Saturday nights.

3. Last week, my sister and I _____ at the mall. I spent $100.

4. Dan _____ at the gym for two hours yesterday.

5. They usually _____ when they're stressed out, like take photos.

6. Kelly _____ last weekend because she wasn't home.

3 Complete the sentences with the present continuous forms of the verbs. Then label each situation with the correct category.

> Clothes and money
> Education
> Entertainment
> Food and drink
> ✓ Health care
> Transportation

1. The doctors *are helping* (help) sick people in another country right now. *Health care*

2. Felipe _____ (study) law these days. _____

3. Shelly _____ (take) the bus right now because the train _____ (not run). _____

4. We _____ (have) sushi and tea in a Japanese restaurant right now. _____

5. Adam and Elsa _____ (watch) a comedy at the movie theater. _____

6. I _____ (not pay) for jeans and these T-shirts with cash. I _____ (use) my credit card. _____

4 Complete the paragraph with the simple past or past continuous forms of the verbs.

Last night, I ¹ _was sleeping_ (sleep) when it ² _____ (start) to rain. I ³ _____ (walk) to the window when I ⁴ _____ (hear) thunder. My parents ⁵ _____ (watch) a movie on TV when I ⁶ _____ (scream). They ⁷ _____ (run) to my room. They ⁸ _____ (wonder) what happened when they ⁹ _____ (see) that I was terrified of the thunder! After that, we ¹⁰ _____ (watch) the movie together, and then I ¹¹ _____ (go) to bed. I ¹² _____ (fall) asleep when my cat ¹³ _____ (jump) on my bed. I definitely ¹⁴ _____ (not get) enough sleep last night!

5 Circle the correct answers.

1. Julie is sick. She **had better** / had better not see a doctor.
2. We **must** / **must not** pay with a credit card. This restaurant only takes cash.
3. You **have to** / **don't have to** help around the house today. It's a mess!
4. Nelson and Ben **should** / **shouldn't** stay out so late. They're always exhausted in the morning.
5. We **ought to** / **ought not to** wear helmets when we ride our bikes on that road. It's dangerous.
6. You **must** / **must not** do your homework before you can hang out with friends.
7. Wendy **has to** / **doesn't have to** walk to school. She takes the bus.
8. You **had better** / **had better not** be late to class. The teacher is strict about being on time.
9. We **should** / **shouldn't** buy Tim a gift. It's his birthday tomorrow.
10. Ray **ought to** / **ought not to** drive without a license.

6 Write sentences with your own opinions. Use *it's (not)* + adjective + infinitive.

1. easy / ride / a bike
   It's easy to ride a bike. OR
   It's not easy to ride a bike.

2. fun / go / to amusement parks
   _____

3. smart / spend / money on an education
   _____

4. difficult / learn / English
   _____

5. important / have / time for yourself
   _____

6. hard / get / enough sleep
   _____

7. boring / watch TV / every weekend
   _____

7 Circle the correct answers.

1. **A:** Do you know how to fix a computer?
   B: No. _____
   a. I'm not very good at things like that.
   b. It's really pretty simple.

2. **A:** It's difficult to lift this heavy box.
   B: Wait. _____
   a. Let me show you.
   b. I'll give you a hand if you like.

3. **A:** It's hot in here. _____
   B: Yeah, but I like hot weather.
   a. I don't think so.
   b. Don't you think?

4. **A:** Our homework is confusing.
   B: I know. _____
   a. I'm not sure how to do it.
   b. I disagree.

5. **A:** I really want to beat this video game! Can you help me?
   B: Sure. _____
   a. I'm not very good at things like that.
   b. I'll give you a hand if you like.

6. **A:** Well, I'm glad we left at 6:00 like you wanted. These are great seats!
   B: _____ It's always good to go early.
   a. Don't you think?
   b. See what I mean?

3 Art All Around Us

VOCABULARY Visual arts

1 **Match the clues on the left with the things and people on the right. Some items have more than one answer.**

1. a person __e__, ____
2. done on a wall ____, ____
3. done with a pencil ____
4. always done on a computer ____
5. a lot of art in one place ____
6. art made with the hands that isn't flat ____, ____
7. usually in a book ____

a. digital art
b. pottery
c. exhibition
d. comics
e. living statue
f. mural
g. sculpture
h. drawing
i. portrait painter
j. graffiti

2 **What kind of art are the materials below used for? Label the pictures with some of the words from Exercise 1.**

1. __pottery__
2. _____
3. _____
4. _____
5. _____
6. _____

3 **Complete the sentences with some of the words from Exercise 1.**

1. A famous Diego Rivera _____ is at the Detroit Institute of Arts. It's a painting of factory workers painted on a wall in the museum.
2. My grandmother is a _____. She paints pictures of famous people.
3. I am a _____ in New York City. I dress up as the Statue of Liberty.
4. There's a great _____ of modern art at the museum.

4 **Answer the questions with your own information.**

1. What kind of art do you like to see at exhibitions?
   I like to see Renaissance art at exhibitions.
2. What kind of art do you have in your home or room?
   _____
3. Do you have an art class or did you take an art class in the past? What kind of art do/did you make?
   _____
4. Do you like comics? Why? / Why not?
   _____

GRAMMAR Verb + -ing form (gerund) review

1 **Correct the sentences. Use the simple present and the -ing form of a verb (gerund).**

1. John loves ~~go~~ *going* to museums.
2. Isabel enjoying taking art classes.
3. We not like watching living statues. It's boring.
4. I don't mind to help my dad when he paints.
5. Cal and Vera hate draw pictures.
6. Marcia loves read comics. She reads them all the time.

16 | Unit 3

2 Complete the two sentences about each picture with the correct verbs. Use the simple present and the *-ing* form of a verb.

| ✓ like | look | ✓ make | not enjoy |

1. Kate ___likes making___ pottery.
   She _____ at sculptures.

| hate | love | play | ride |

2. Joe _____ his skateboard.
   He _____ soccer.

| run | enjoy | not like | get |

3. Sparky _____ in the park.
   She _____ a bath.

| love | not mind | play | walk |

4. Dina and Ki _____ soccer in the park. They _____ to school.

3 Put the words in order to make sentences. Change the correct verbs to the *-ing* form.

1. enjoy / on the weekends / Stacey / shop / for clothes
   Stacey enjoys shopping for clothes
   on the weekends.

2. camp / and Dan / in the mountains / Tyler / love
   _____
   _____

3. to / go / I / art exhibitions / don't enjoy
   _____
   _____

4. around / don't mind / the house / we / help
   _____
   _____

5. of her cat / Donna / paint / loves / portraits
   _____
   _____

6. watch / hate / horror movies / you
   _____
   _____

4 Write sentences that are true for you with the simple present and the *-ing* form of a verb. Use the phrases *(not) like, (not) love, hate, (not) enjoy,* or *not mind*.

1. ride a bike
   I love riding a bike.

2. go to museums
   _____

3. watch living statues
   _____

4. draw pictures
   _____

5. take photos
   _____

6. help around the house
   _____

VOCABULARY Musical instruments

1 Look at the pictures and complete the crossword.

2. c	e	l	l	o

ACROSS

2.
5.
6.
7.
8.
9.
10.

DOWN

1.
3.
4.

2 Check (✓) the items that are true for each instrument. Sometimes more than one answer is possible.

	You use your mouth to play this.	You use your hands to play this.	It has strings.
1. a trumpet	✓	✓	
2. drums			
3. a guitar			
4. a keyboard			
5. a cello			
6. a piano			
7. a flute			
8. a harmonica			
9. a violin			
10. a saxophone			

3 Look at the pictures in Exercise 1 again. Write sentences about the instruments the people are playing. Use the present continuous.

1. *Tia is playing a guitar.*
2. _____
3. _____
4. _____
5. _____
6. _____

18 | Unit 3

GRAMMAR -ing forms (gerunds) as subjects

1 Write the *-ing* forms of the verbs.

1. draw _drawing_
2. take _____
3. run _____
4. make _____
5. feel _____
6. shop _____
7. care _____
8. play _____

2 Complete the sentences with the *-ing* forms of the verbs from Exercise 1.

1. _Drawing_ outside is very relaxing.
2. _____ the drums loudly is fun.
3. _____ for animals is a big responsibility.
4. _____ is really good exercise.
5. _____ for clothes can take a lot of time.
6. _____ pottery is harder than it looks.
7. _____ photos is Sonya's favorite thing to do.
8. _____ exhausted is not good for you.

3 Write the activities in the order you like doing them. Use the *-ing* forms of the verbs. 1 = the activity you like the best.

> chat with friends
> do something creative
> play a musical instrument
> ride on a roller coaster
> visit a museum

1. _____
2. _____
3. _____
4. _____
5. _____

Verbs + prepositions + *-ing* forms (gerunds)

4 Write sentences. Use verbs + prepositions + *-ing* forms.

1. not apologize / for / make / mistakes isn't a good idea

   Not apologizing for making mistakes isn't a good idea.

2. you need to / concentrate / on / study

   _____

3. our lessons / consist / of / make / pottery and jewelry

   _____

4. Janice / feel / like / play / her guitar right now

   _____

5. not believe / in / have / time for yourself can have negative results

   _____

6. I / decide / against / go / to the concert

   _____

5 Answer the questions with your own ideas. Use *-ing* forms as subjects or use a verb + a preposition + the *-ing* form of a verb.

1. What do you think about painting?

   Painting is hard, but some people are good at it.

2. When do you concentrate on studying?

   _____

3. What's your opinion about exercising?

   _____

4. What do you worry about?

   _____

5. What have you apologized for doing?

   _____

6. What do you think about learning to play an instrument?

   _____

CONVERSATION — Inviting a friend and arranging to meet

1 Circle the correct words.

1. **How** / Should about going to the Museum of Modern Art tomorrow?
2. **How / What** time should we meet?
3. **Should / Sounds** good.
4. **What / Should** I ask my brother to take us?
5. **That's / Sounding** a good idea.

2 Complete the conversation with the phrases from Exercise 1.

Mateo: Hi, Sara. ¹ *How about going to the Museum of Modern Art tomorrow?*

Sara: Really? I thought you hated going to museums.

Mateo: Well, I usually do, but there's a really cool digital art exhibition. They have pictures of skateboarders that an artist created on a computer.

Sara: Cool! I'd like seeing that.

Mateo: OK. The museum is kind of far, but we can ride our bikes.

Sara: ² _____ He won't mind driving.

Mateo: ³ _____ I can come to your house then. ⁴ _____

Sara: Well, he doesn't like getting up early. How about 11:00 a.m.?

Mateo: ⁵ _____

READING TO WRITE

1 Answer the questions with information from the poster.

ROCK WITH US!
DOKK is playing this Friday!
Come and hear our new songs on Friday, April 10, at 9:00 p.m. at Newtown Park.

1. What's the name of the band?
   _____
2. What kind of music do they play?
   _____
3. When are they playing?
   _____
4. Where are they playing?
   _____

2 Circle the correct words.

Gina: How ¹(was) / were the concert last night?

Barry: It ²was / were great! I love listening to live music.

Gina: Who played?

Barry: DOKK. The band's name ³is / are from the first letters of the members' names – Donna, Olivia, Kevin, and Kim.

Gina: Cool. Where ⁴is / are the band from?

Barry: They ⁵is / are from Austin, Texas. They write their own music. Donna ⁶is / are an amazing drummer, Kevin and Kim play the guitar, and Olivia sings. Last night, they ⁷was / were amazing! I liked the concert because they played my favorite songs, and they played their new songs, too.

Gina: ⁸Is / Are it your favorite band?

Barry: Well, no. My favorite band ⁹is / are The Three Joshes, but I like DOKK a lot. They ¹⁰is / are really popular. There ¹¹was / were a big crowd last night. I think there ¹²was / were over 500 people at the concert.

Gina: Wow! Next time they play, let me know, and I'll go with you.

3 Complete Barry's blog post about the concert. Use the information in the poster from Exercise 1 and the conversation from Exercise 2.

LAST WEEKEND'S CONCERT
Posted on April 8

I went to a great concert last weekend at ¹ _Newtown Park_ . There were ² _____ people at the concert. Most of them were teenagers. A band named ³ _____ played. They are a ⁴ _____ band from Austin, ⁵ _____ . There are ⁶ _____ people in the band. Their band name is from ⁷ _____ of their names. The concert was ⁸ _____ ! I liked it because they played my ⁹ _____ . Their ¹⁰ _____ were also really good. If they play in your city, you have to go see this band!

4 Sign Me Up!

VOCABULARY Adventure travel

1 Find eight more words associated with travel activities.

N	H	I	M	H	K	C	C	A	M	W	U	M	K	M
B	B	S	O	Z	J	R	A	F	T	I	N	G	Q	N
T	B	L	U	N	B	U	I	C	R	U	I	S	E	Z
O	A	I	N	M	D	I	Y	B	N	A	B	N	L	R
S	C	U	T	I	G	Z	I	N	G	Y	A	T	A	O
H	K	S	A	I	L	I	N	G	P	G	L	E	S	C
M	P	F	I	Y	C	B	Q	X	A	G	L	R	L	K
R	A	S	N	R	H	I	Q	U	R	B	O	M	M	C
G	C	Z	B	C	K	M	O	U	N	F	O	Y	O	L
T	K	Y	I	X	D	E	P	C	N	E	N	A	T	I
D	I	W	K	N	X	S	A	F	A	R	I	F	P	M
G	N	K	I	S	I	S	L	E	R	P	N	E	S	B
I	G	X	N	T	S	A	F	A	N	A	G	S	U	I
Y	P	Y	G	B	Q	F	N	H	B	O	G	P	F	N
T	S	U	M	M	E	R	C	A	M	P	D	I	A	G

2 Check (✓) the activities that involve water.

1. ❏ go backpacking
2. ❏ go on a cruise
3. ❏ go ballooning
4. ❏ go mountain biking
5. ❏ go on a safari
6. ❏ go rafting
7. ❏ go rock climbing
8. ❏ go sailing
9. ❏ go to summer camp

3 Complete Javier's email with some of the expressions from Exercise 2. Use the simple past.

To: Tim
From: Javier
Subject: My summer at camp

Hey Tim,

I'm so glad that I ¹ _went to summer camp_. At first, I didn't want to be away from home this summer, but I'm having a great time. There are a lot of cool activities here. Last week, we ² _____ on the lake. We took two boats so that everyone at camp could go. We also ³ _____ on the Red River. It was very fast! I ⁴ _____, too. I had to wear a helmet and use ropes to get to the top of the mountain! On Saturday, we ⁵ _____. My bag was really heavy because I brought a lot of water and food for the hike. On Sunday, we ⁶ _____ on some trails. I was glad that I brought my bike to camp, so I didn't have to rent one.

Yesterday was the best! We ⁷ _____. It was amazing! We were so high up in the sky.

I can't believe that you ⁸ _____. Did you see any elephants, lions, or giraffes? Write soon and tell me all about your trip.

Your friend,
Javier

4 Answer the questions with your own information.

1. Which activities from Exercise 2 have you done?

   I have gone rafting, and I have gone on a cruise.

   _____

2. Which activities would you like to do?

   _____

3. Which activities wouldn't you want to try?

   _____

GRAMMAR Present perfect with *already*, *yet*, and *just*; present perfect questions

1 Read the sentences. Circle the answer that correctly explains each situation.

1. The boat hasn't left yet.
   a. The boat left.   (b. The boat didn't leave.)
2. They've already left for summer camp.
   a. They are at home.   b. They aren't at home.
3. We have just seen lions on a safari.
   a. We saw lions a few minutes ago.   b. We saw lions a week ago.
4. They haven't cleaned the boat yet.
   a. They won't clean the boat.   b. They will probably clean the boat later.
5. Calvin has just told me about his trip.
   a. Calvin told me about his trip recently.   b. Calvin told me about his trip a while ago.

2 Rewrite the sentences and questions with the words in parentheses.

1. Have you left the house? (yet)
   Have you left the house yet?
2. I have told Todd our travel plans. (already)
   _____
3. Jenna has taken a picture of a monkey. (just)
   _____
4. They haven't gone rafting. (yet)
   _____
5. Has Sheila called you? (yet)
   _____

3 Put the words in order to make sentences.

1. decided / rafting / just / to go / we / have
   We have just decided to go rafting.
2. about / already / sailing / seen / that documentary / I / have
   _____
   _____
3. his / Peng / packed / yet / hasn't / bags /
   _____
   _____
4. have / already / the cruise / for / my parents / left
   _____
   _____
5. summer camp / has / from / Carolina / gotten back / just
   _____
   _____
6. about / you / your / yet / told me / trip / haven't
   _____
   _____

4 Look at the picture. Write sentences about Emma's activities. Use *already* and *yet*.

To Do
buy sunglasses
call my grandma ✓

1. pack her suitcase
   Emma has packed her suitcase already.
2. pack her tablet
   She _____
3. shut down her tablet
   _____
4. clean her room
   _____
5. buy sunglasses
   _____
6. call her grandma
   _____

VOCABULARY Phrasal verbs related to travel

1. Complete the sentences with a word or phrase from each box.

come	✓look	around	✓out
find	look	back	out
give	make	forward to	sure
look	take	off	up

1. _Look out_! That rock is going to fall.
2. We're closed. Please _____ tomorrow.
3. I want to _____ more about rock climbing in this area.
4. Don't _____. With a little practice, you'll be great at mountain biking.
5. Our plane will _____ in about an hour.
6. Please _____ you wear a helmet when you're biking.
7. Many people _____ summer vacation.
8. Let's _____ the nature center after we hike.

2 Correct the sentences.

1. I'm not looking forward ~~of~~ _to_ going home.
2. Sharon has already found in about the rock climbing class.
3. You need to take sure you wear hiking boots on the trails.
4. I don't want to give out, but this is really hard.
5. Did your plane take up on time?
6. David hasn't looked back from Ecuador yet.
7. I want to go to the market and find around a little.

3 Complete the quiz questions with some of the phrasal verbs from Exercise 1. Then circle the answers that are true for you.

1. Who _makes sure_ you get up on time?
   a. I do.
   b. My parents.
   c. My brother or sister.

2. What do you _____ the most?
   a. Vacation.
   b. Weekends.
   c. Concerts.

3. When do you _____ on something?
   a. Never!
   b. When it is too hard.
   c. When it takes too much time.

4. Which of these things would you most like to _____ about?
   a. Nature trails in my area.
   b. Rock climbing adventures.
   c. Sailing classes.

5. When do you like to _____ in a store the most?
   a. When I'm buying something for myself.
   b. When I'm buying something for my family.
   c. When I'm buying something for a friend.

GRAMMAR Present perfect with *for* and *since*

1 Write the expressions in the correct places in the chart. Add *for* or *since*.

✓a week	last Tuesday	2013	a month
two days	5:00 p.m.	six hours	April

for	since
for a week	

2 Circle the correct words.

1. Lia has been a rock climbing instructor **for / (since)** 2010.
2. Jordan's been in Jamaica **for / since** two weeks.
3. You haven't called me **for / since** three days.
4. Britt hasn't been rafting **for / since** July.
5. I haven't seen Marcos **for / since** 3:00.
6. Have you been studying **for / since** an hour?

3 Complete the paragraph with the present perfect forms of the verbs and *for* or *since*.

River Valley Summer Camp

Join us this summer at our wonderful camp. River Valley Summer Camp ¹ _has been open_ (be open) _since_ 2001. Hundreds of teens ² _____ (enjoy) our camp _____ over 10 years.

Meet Martin: He ³ _____ (be) a camp leader _____ 2012. He ⁴ _____ (teach) rafting classes _____ five years. This year, he will lead our new river rafting adventures.

Meet Aya: She ⁵ _____ (cook) delicious meals for our camp _____ last June. You'll love the food at River Valley.

Meet Max and Judy: They ⁶ _____ (know) each other _____ eight years. They met at River Valley eight years ago, and they got married last year. Now they run the sailing classes together.

⁷ _____ you _____ (want) to come to a summer camp _____ a long time? Sign up for River Valley today!

How long . . . ? and the present perfect

4 Look at Eric's activities. Write questions with *How long* and the present perfect. Then answer the questions.

live in Kenya	2009
work at a nature center	two years
be a safari guide	a month
teach nature classes	July
have his website about safaris	2012

1. *How long has Eric lived in Kenya?*
   He's lived in Kenya since 2009.
2. _____
3. _____
4. _____
5. _____

5 Answer the questions with your own information.

1. How long have you lived in your city?
   I've lived in my city since I was five years old.
2. How long has your family lived in your house?
   _____
3. How long have you been a student?
   _____
4. How long have you studied English?
   _____
5. How long have you and your best friend known each other?
   _____
6. How long have you owned a computer?
   _____

CONVERSATION Signing up for an adventure activity

1 Circle the correct phrases.

Emily: Hello. ¹**Does the price include / Can I ask you a few things about** the ballooning trip?

Guide: Sure. What would you like to know?

Emily: ²**How long is / Where can I sign up** the trip?

Guide: It's from 2:00 to 6:00, but you're only in the air for about two hours. First, we give you safety information about ballooning.

Emily: OK. ³**What about / Is it only for** adults?

Guide: No. But if you're under 18, an adult must be with you.

Emily: I see. ⁴**What do I need to bring / Where can I sign up?**

Guide: Not much. But you should wear a jacket. It can be cold up in the air. It's an amazing experience.

Emily: ⁵**How long is / What about** cameras? Can I bring mine?

Guide: Of course. You just have to be really careful with it. You don't want it to fall out of the balloon!

2 Complete the conversation with the correct phrases.

> ✓ Can I ask you a few things about
> Does the price include
> How long is
> Is it only for
> Where can I sign up

Noah: ¹ *Can I ask you a few things about* the rock climbing trip?

Guide: Of course.

Noah: ² _____ experienced climbers?

Guide: No, not at all. It's for beginners, too.

Noah: Great. ³ _____ equipment?

Guide: Yes, it does. We provide helmets, knee pads, and everything else you need.

Noah: OK. ⁴ _____ it?

Guide: You can choose a two-hour or four-hour adventure. It's a lot of fun, and our guides will help you with everything.

Noah: Sounds great. ⁵ _____ ?

Guide: Right here!

READING TO WRITE

1 Read the sentences that compare house parties in Ecuador and the United States. Match the sentences that are about the same topics.

Ecuador	The United States
1. People wait for the host to serve them food. _d_	a. Guests sometimes bring food to the party.
2. People usually play music and dance. ___	b. Parties can be big or small.
3. The host usually makes all of the food. ___	c. Most people dress casually.
4. Younger people often wear informal clothing, but older people often dress up. ___	d. The host often puts food on a table, and guests help themselves.
5. Parties are various sizes – from a few people to many friends. ___	e. People often listen to music while they talk.

2 Complete the sentences with the correct words.

also	either . . . or
although	however
✓ both . . . and	not only . . . but also . . .

¹ _Both_ people from South America _and_ Asia often shake hands when they greet people from the United States or Canada.

When people in Asia meet for the first time, they often give each other business cards. ² _____ people in South America don't always give each other business cards, they may exchange phone numbers and emails.

In South America, people ³ _____ kiss each other on the cheek _____ hug each other. In Asia, ⁴ _____, people do not touch each other when they say hello. They bow. ⁵ _____ do they bow when they say hello, _____ they _____ bow when they say goodbye.

3 Write the pieces of the article from Exercise 2 under the correct headings.

GREETINGS IN SOUTH AMERICA AND ASIA

Typical greetings

In South America, people _____

Greeting people from other countries

Exchanging information

Unit 4 | 27

REVIEW UNITS 3–4

1 Look at the pictures and complete the puzzle. Find out what John did on vacation by filling in the gray boxes.

John went _____ on vacation.

```
      1
      c  r  u  i  s  e
   2
         3
         4
   5
   6
         7
```

1.
2.
3.
4.
5.
6.
7.

2 Write the words in the correct places in the chart.

backpacking	graffiti	a safari
ballooning	a harmonica	sailing
a cello	✓ a mural	a saxophone
drums	pottery	a sculpture

Art	Music	Travel
a mural		

3 Complete the sentences with the simple present forms of the phrases. Use a verb + -ing form (gerund).

hate / come back
✓ love / find out
not enjoy / make sure
not like / give up
not mind / look around

1. Lauren ____*loves finding out*____ about new places.
2. Terrance _____ home after vacation.
3. I _____ when I try something new.
4. My brother _____ when I go shopping.
5. My mother _____ I've done my chores.

4 Complete the sentences with the -ing forms of the verbs. Add a preposition when necessary.

¹ ____*Being*____ (be) a portrait painter is an amazing job. I love it, and I think ² ____*about drawing*____ (draw) all the time! I studied digital art in high school, but in college, I concentrated ³ _____ (learn) to draw. ⁴ _____ (not follow) my dream would have been a mistake. Now my work consists ⁵ _____ (paint) portraits of interesting people. ⁶ _____ (work) with new people can be difficult. They have to sit for hours, and ⁷ _____ (sit) still is difficult, especially for children. My clients may get tired, but I don't worry ⁸ _____ (be) bored. I love my job, and I always will!

5 Look at Alexis's To Do list. Then complete sentences about her activities. Use the present perfect with *already* and *yet*. ✓ = She's done it.

TO DO:
✓ go to the photo exhibition with Anna
practice the violin
pack clothes for summer camp
✓ buy my dad's birthday present
help around the house with Josh
✓ do my homework

1. Alexis and Anna *have already gone to the photo exhibition.*
2. Alexis _____
3. She _____
4. She _____
5. Alexis and Josh _____
   _____
6. Alexis _____

6 Complete the conversation with the present perfect forms of the verbs and *already*, *yet*, or *just*.

Rick: Hey, Carla. ¹___*Have*___ you ___*had*___ dinner ___*yet*___? (have / yet)

Carla: No, I ²_____. But I ³_____ _____ lunch. (finish / just)

Rick: Oh, OK. Well, do you want to go out for dinner in a few hours?

Carla: Sounds good. ⁴_____ you _____ at that new Mexican restaurant _____? (eat / yet)

Rick: Yes, I ⁵_____. I ⁶_____ _____ there three times. (be / already)

Carla: But ⁷_____ you _____ the chicken tostadas _____? (try / yet)

Rick: No, I ⁸_____. Let's go and I'll try them!

7 Write questions for the answers. Then complete the answers with *for* or *since*.

1. *How long has she been on a safari?*
   She's been on a safari *for* ten days.
2. _____
   They've lived in Chicago _____ 2006.
3. _____
   I've played the saxophone _____ six months.
4. _____
   We've known Raul _____ three years.
5. _____
   He's worked at the summer camp _____ June.

8 Complete the conversations with the correct phrases.

Does the price include
✓ How about going
How long is
Is it only for
What do I need to bring
What time should we meet

1. **A:** What do you want to do today?
   B: ___*How about going*___ to the digital art exhibition at the museum?
2. **A:** _____ the backpacking trip?
   B: Five days.
3. **A:** _____?
   B: A warm jacket and hiking boots.
4. **A:** _____ transportation?
   B: Yes, it does. We take you to the river on a bus.
5. **A:** _____ beginners?
   B: No, it isn't. We have classes for advanced climbers.
6. **A:** _____?
   B: How about 6:00 p.m.?

5 Yikes!

VOCABULARY Fears

1 Circle seven more words about fears.

clthedarksnaelevatorstsngpqflyingbirectclownsvathoptdsnakesingheiinsectstgifpsmnheightsabtwlfqpbirdsflatnf

2 Look at the pictures. Complete the sentences with the correct fears from Exercise 1.

1. Tao and Sherry are afraid of ____heights____, and they're afraid of _____.

2. Vic is afraid of _____ and _____.

3. Alicia is afraid of _____ and _____.

4. Ed is afraid of _____ and _____.

3 Circle the correct words in the quiz. Then check (✓) the answers that are true for you. Add your points.

How fearful are you?

		Always true 3 points	Sometimes true 2 points	Never true 1 point
1	I take the stairs because I hate riding in (elevators) / the dark.			
2	I don't like hiking because **snakes / flying** scare me.			
3	I don't go to the circus because I'm afraid of **insects / clowns**.			
4	I can't walk on high bridges because I'm afraid of **heights / clowns**.			
5	I sleep with a nightlight because I'm afraid of **heights / the dark**.			
6	**Snakes / Birds** scare me when they fly over my head.			
7	I'm afraid of **elevators / flying**. I hate planes!			
8	I don't like to sit on the ground because I'm afraid of **insects / birds**.			

My points: _____

17–24 points: You're afraid of a lot of things. It can stop you from doing things.

9–16 points: You have some fears, but you can probably overcome them.

8 points: You aren't afraid of anything!

30 | Unit 5

GRAMMAR Future review – *will, be going to*, present continuous

1 Read the sentences and check (✓) the correct columns.

	Planned event	Decided at the moment of speaking
1. Hey, I think I'll go to the store with you.		✓
2. Paul is going to study in Mexico next year.		
3. I'm not working on Saturday.		
4. I don't know the answer. Janice will tell you.		
5. Sean is taking a test in an hour.		
6. I'm not going to go on the camping trip because I'm afraid of insects.		
7. No, I won't hike to the top of the mountain. I'm afraid of heights.		
8. Sakura is going to take a class about facing fears.		

2 Rewrite the sentences. Change the present continuous to *be going to* and use the words in parentheses.

1. Sandra is shopping with Rachel tomorrow. (next week)

   Sandra is going to shop with Rachel
   next week.

2. My brother is getting married in two days. (next year)

   _____

3. We are going to Rio de Janeiro next week. (in April)

   _____

4. I'm talking to the teacher in a few minutes. (after class)

   _____

5. Pam is going on a safari on Monday. (next month)

   _____

6. They're watching a movie tonight. (on Saturday)

   _____

3 Complete the conversations with the correct forms of *will* and the words in parentheses.

1. **A:** What are you going to do tomorrow?
   B: I don't know. Maybe ____*I'll go*____ (I / go) to the mall.

2. **A:** Do you and Don want to go to dinner with me after class?
   B: Sure. _____ (we / eat) with you.

3. **A:** Can I borrow your tablet?
   B: Sorry, I need it. But _____ (I / give) it to you when I'm done.

4. **A:** Where are you going on vacation?
   B: I'm not sure, but _____ (we / not choose) somewhere cold.

5. **A:** Do you want to take the elevator?
   B: No! I hate elevators. _____ (I / take) the stairs.

First conditional

4 Complete the paragraph with the first conditional.

Rita is afraid of snakes. If she
¹____*sees*____ (see) a snake, she
²_____ (not move).
If the snake ³_____ (move), she
⁴_____ (scream). If she
⁵_____ (scream), her brother
⁶_____ (hear) her. If Rita's
brother ⁷_____ (see) her with
the snake, he ⁸_____ (not help).
If he ⁹_____ (laugh), Rita
¹⁰_____ (cry). I hope Rita
doesn't see a snake!

VOCABULARY -ed and -ing adjective endings

1 Complete the chart.

	-ed	-ing
1.	embarrassed	embarrassing
2.		confusing
3.	interested	
4.		surprising
5.	exhausted	
6.		terrifying
7.	disgusted	
8.		relaxing

2 Complete the sentences with some of the words from Exercise 1. Then check (✓) if the sentences are true for you.

	Yes	No
1. I think space is _interesting_. There's always something new to learn about.		
2. I always feel _____ at the beach. The sound of the ocean makes me feel calm.		
3. Exercising is _____. I'm always tired after I work out.		
4. Yuck! I think snakes are _____.		
5. I was _____ on my last birthday! My parents had a party for me and invited all of my friends.		
6. I was _____ about my last test scores. I didn't do very well.		
7. I think clowns are _____. They really scare me.		
8. I'm never _____ in class. I always understand everything!		

3 Complete the sentences with the -ed or -ing adjective of the words in parentheses.

1. Martina is _disgusted_ (disgust) by insects.
2. Henry was _____ (exhaust) after he walked up eight flights of stairs.
3. Lori thinks her parents are _____ (embarrass) when they yell at her soccer games.
4. My little sister is _____ (terrify) of sleeping in the dark.
5. It was _____ (surprise) to find out Tara moved to Los Angeles.
6. Our homework assignment was _____ (confuse). No one understood the directions.
7. I'm not very _____ (interest) in science, but I love math.
8. Some people are afraid of flying, but I think it's _____ (relax).

GRAMMAR Modals of probability: must, can't, may, might, could

1 Read the sentences and check (✓) the correct columns.

	Almost certain	Impossible	Possible
1. Ramon must be from Mexico.	✓		
2. I might not have homework this weekend.			
3. We may not work tomorrow.			
4. Hillary can't be 16.			
5. My cousin could be at the mall.			
6. You must be exhausted.			

2 Match the sentences.

1. Laura wasn't in class today. _c_	a. She may not be hungry.
2. Kelly won't ride on roller coasters. ___	b. She could be busy.
3. Laila doesn't speak Japanese. ___	c. She might be sick.
4. Beth didn't order anything to eat. ___	d. She must be terrified of heights.
5. Nancy just ran 5 kilometers. ___	e. She can't be from Japan.
6. Mari didn't answer her phone. ___	f. She must be exhausted.

32 | Unit 5

3 Complete the conversation with *must*, *can't*, or *might*.

Julia: Do you know where Kayla is?

Mike: No, I don't. She __might__ be sick.

Julia: No, she ²_____ be sick. I talked to her this morning. She said she was coming to the party.

Mike: Hmm. How is she getting here?

Julia: She's taking the bus and then walking.

Mike: The bus ³_____ be late. It's usually on time, but you never know!

Julia: That ⁴_____ be true. She was already on the bus when I talked to her.

Mike: I see. Well, she ⁵_____ have to stop at the store on her way.

Julia: Oh, yeah! That ⁶_____ be it! She said she hadn't gotten a birthday card for Jacob yet.

Mike: Ah. Hey, do you think Jacob will be surprised?

Julia: I'm not sure. He ⁷_____ know about the party.

Mike: Really?

Julia: Yeah. His brother ⁸_____ keep a secret!

4 Write sentences with *must*, *can't*, or *may*.

1. Jenna / be / cold

   Jenna must be cold.

2. Isaac / go / rafting / or / go / ballooning

   _____

3. Jin-hee / be / finished with her book

   _____

4. You / be / exhausted

   _____

5. Nicole / fall off / her bike

   _____

5 Rewrite the sentences. Add the words in parentheses.

1. Paul is surprised. (might)

   Paul might be surprised.

2. It's 3:00. (must)

   _____

3. Cindy knows Julia. (could)

   _____

4. That roller coaster is terrifying. (must)

   _____

5. We expect to win the race. (can't)

   _____

6. You have the flu. (could)

   _____

CONVERSATION Expressing disbelief

1 Complete the phrases in the conversation.

Raul: Hi, Sofia. My friends and I are hiking up Cotopaxi this weekend.

Sofia: ¹N_o_ w_a_ _y_! That's cool.

Raul: Do you want to come?

Sofia: Sure. I'd love to! Can I invite Carolina?

Raul: Well, I don't know if she'd want to come. Cotopaxi is snowy once you get up high.

Sofia: So?

Raul: Well, Carolina is afraid of snow.

Sofia: ²T_ _ _'s im_ _ _ _ _ _ _ _! No one is afraid of snow.

Raul: It's true. There's even a name for it – chinophobia.

Sofia: Chinophobia? ³A_ _ y_ _ s _ _ _ _ _ _?

Raul: Yes, I am. It's a real thing, and Carolina has it.

Sofia: ⁴I d_ _'t b_ _ _ _ _ _ i_!

Raul: It's true. We were looking at this picture of snow one time, and she got really nervous.

Sofia: ⁵C_ _ _ o_! She got nervous just looking at snow?

Raul: Yes, she did!

Sofia: I'm going to call and ask her about it!

2 Circle the correct answers.

1. **A:** I climbed Cotopaxi in an hour.
   B: No **possible** / **(way)**! It takes expert climbers several hours.

2. **A:** Marcia is living in Quito for a year.
   B: Are you **serious** / **believing**? That's great.

3. **A:** Jorge took 10 bottles of water on the hike.
   B: **Believe** / **Come** on. His bag would have been too heavy.

4. **A:** Yolanda moved from the mountains to downtown Quito.
   B: I don't **impossible** / **believe** you. She hates busy cities.

5. **A:** There wasn't any snow on the top of Cotopaxi when we climbed it.
   B: That's **possible** / **impossible**. There's always snow on Cotopaxi.

READING TO WRITE

1 Circle the correct expressions.

To: sheri@net.cup.org
From: lisa@net.cup.org
Subject: What should I do?

Hello Sheri,

Thanks for writing. Your summer plans sound fun. ¹**Check this out / The fact**: I'm going to go to summer camp this year. It's in the mountains, and it's going to be really fun. The ²**problem / idea** is that we live for a month without any modern technology – no cell phones, no tablets, no lights! Cool, right? ³**The problem is that / Listen to** I promised to text my little sister every day. I haven't told her that I can't yet. I'm a little nervous to tell her because I know she's going to be upset. The ⁴**idea / truth** is that I'm looking forward to not using my phone, but I just don't know what to say to my sister. What do you think I should do?

Your friend,

Lisa

2 Match the categories with the sentences from Lisa's email.

1. _d_ Greeting		a. I haven't told her that I can't yet.
2. _____ Personal news		b. What do you think I should do?
3. _____ The problem		c. I promised to text my little sister every day.
4. _____ How you feel about the problem and why		d. Hello Sheri,
5. _____ What you have/ haven't done about the problem		e. I'm going to summer camp.
6. _____ A question to ask what your friend thinks		f. I'm a little nervous to tell her because I know she's going to be upset.

3 Write the email in the correct order.

Because of this, I don't think I can go to the festival.

Kevin

I'm really embarrassed, and I haven't told him yet.

Your friend,

The problem is that I have acousticophobia – I'm afraid of loud noises.

What do you think I should say to him?

✓ Hi Victor,

Check this out: My cousin's band is going to play in a music festival next month.

To: victor@net.cup.org
From: kevin@net.cup.org
Subject: A problem

Hi Victor,

_____
_____
_____
_____
_____
_____
_____
_____
_____
_____
_____
_____

6 Difficult Decisions

VOCABULARY School life

1 Complete the sentences and the crossword.

ACROSS

4. I don't mind wearing a ___uniform___ to school.
7. Many students aren't following the dress _____.
8. We're trying to win a _____ for "best project."
10. Sara was assigned to _____ for being late.

DOWN

1. Jack got sent to the principal's _____ for talking in class.
2. _____ is not allowed at our school. We must be kind to each other.
3. Tim was caught _____ on a test.
5. I'm getting extra _____ in my English class.
6. I'm always _____. I'm never late for class.
9. Our teacher talked to us about not being _____. She said we have to be more polite.

2 Complete the paragraph with the correct words or phrases.

be assigned	cheating
be punctual	follow
✓ be rude	get sent
bullying	wear

Hampton High School RULES

Do not [1] ___be rude___ to teachers or other students. [2] _____ is not allowed. Students must treat each other kindly. Students who are disrespectful will [3] _____ to the principal's office.

You must [4] _____. If you are late more than three times in one month, you'll [5] _____ to detention.

There is absolutely no [6] _____. Students must do their own work.

All students must [7] _____ the dress code.

You have to [8] _____ school uniforms.

3 Answer the questions with your own information.

1. Does your school have a dress code? Do you have to wear school uniforms?

   Our school has a dress code. Everyone has
   to wear a white shirt and black pants.

2. Why do students at your school get sent to the principal's office? Why are they assigned to detention?

   _____
   _____

3. Do you ever get extra credit in your classes? Which classes?

   _____
   _____

GRAMMAR Second conditional

1 Correct the second conditional sentences.

1. If I ~~would change~~ *changed* our school's dress code, I'd let students wear jeans every day.

2. If you bullied a student, you be assigned to detention.

3. If Sara does the best in the contest, she'd win the prize.

4. If we wasn't punctual, our teacher would be upset.

5. My teacher sends me to the principal's office if I broke the school rules.

6. Luke wouldn't pass the test if he not study.

7. Debbie would tell the teacher if she would see someone cheating.

8. I'd go to the soccer game I didn't have to study.

2 Complete the paragraph with the second conditional.

If Tim ¹ _____bullied_____ (bully) students,
he ² _____ (be) assigned to detention.
If he ³ _____ (be) assigned to detention,
his parents ⁴ _____ (be) angry. If his
parents ⁵ _____ (be) angry, they
⁶ _____ (make) him do chores. If Tim
⁷ _____ (have) to do chores, he
⁸ _____ (not be) happy. Tim had better not bully students!

3 Write second conditional sentences with the information in the chart.

	Imaginary situation	Possible consequence
1.	Leo / fail / his test	his parents / be / angry
2.	You / not call me	I / wonder / why
3.	Carla / win / the prize	she / be / happy
4.	Mark and Doug / not have / class	they / go / to the concert
5.	Jenny / go / on vacation	she / miss / her classes
6.	I / be rude / to my classmates	I / get sent / to the principal's office

1. *If Leo failed his test, his parents would be angry.*
2. _____
3. _____
4. _____
5. _____
6. _____

Second conditional yes/no questions

4 Write second conditional questions. Then answer the questions with your own information.

1. if / your friends / go / to a concert / your parents / let / you go with them

   Q: *If your friends went to a concert, would your parents let you go with them?*

   A: *Yes, they would.*   OR *No, they wouldn't.*

2. if / your friend / bully / another student / you / tell / the principal

   Q: _____
   A: _____

3. you / apologize / if / you / be / rude to a classmate

   Q: _____
   A: _____

4. your parents / be / angry / if / you / cheat / on a test

   Q: _____
   A: _____

VOCABULARY Expressions with *make* and *do*

1 Write the expressions in the correct places in the chart. Add *make* or *do*.

a difference	research
friends	something fun
✓ homework	the right thing
me a favor	you mad

do	make
do homework	

2 Complete the sentences with the correct expressions from Exercise 1.

1. Jacob likes to __do the right thing__ at school. He always follows the rules.
2. Charlotte is very friendly, and it's easy for her to _____.
3. Kyle really wants to _____ at his school. He started a "stop bullying" group.
4. I want to _____ this weekend. Let's go sailing!
5. Can you _____? I need help with my homework.
6. I never want to _____. I don't like it when you're angry.
7. My sister likes to _____ for school projects. She loves learning new things.
8. I can't go to the park. I have to _____.

3 Circle the correct words. Then write answers with your own information.

1. How often do you **do** / **make** homework? Where do you **do** / **make** it?
   I do homework every night. I do it at my desk.

2. Have you ever **done** / **made** a favor for someone? What did you **do** / **make**?
   _____
   _____
   _____

3. Do you **do** / **make** research online? When?
   _____
   _____
   _____

4. When do you **do** / **make** something fun? What do you **do** / **make**?
   _____
   _____
   _____

5. Do you **do** / **make** friends easily? How do you **do** / **make** new friends?
   _____
   _____
   _____

6. When your friends break the rules, do you **do** / **make** the right thing? What do you **do** / **make**?
   _____
   _____
   _____

7. Who **does** / **makes** you mad? Why?
   _____
   _____
   _____

8. Have you ever **done** / **made** a difference at your school? What was it?
   _____
   _____
   _____

GRAMMAR Second conditional Wh- questions

1 Match the questions with the answers.

1. What would you do if you didn't finish your homework? _d_	a. I'd go in August.
2. Who would you tell if someone bullied you at school? ___	b. I'd make new friends.
3. How would you do research if you had to write a paper? ___	c. I'd find information online.
4. If you went on vacation, when would you go? ___	d. I'd ask my teacher for more time.
5. If your friend was rude to you, what would you say? ___	e. I'd tell the principal.
6. What would you do if your family moved to a new city? ___	f. I'd tell her I was upset.

2 Circle the correct words.

Anna: Hey, David. What ¹**did / would** you do if your friend ²**asked / would ask** you to cheat on a test?

David: I'd say no! I'd never do that.

Anna: So, if your friend ³**cheated / would cheat**, who ⁴**did / would** you tell?

David: Hmm. I probably wouldn't tell anyone.

Anna: Really? Why ⁵**wouldn't / didn't** you tell anyone if your friend ⁶**did / would do** something wrong?

David: Well, I'd try to get my friend to do the right thing and tell someone.

Anna: That's a good idea.

3 Write the questions another way. Then answer the questions with your own information.

1. Where would you study if you had a test tomorrow?

    Q: _If you had a test tomorrow, where would you study?_

    A: _I'd study at the café._

2. If you broke your friend's computer, what would you do?

    Q: _____

    A: _____

3. If you did someone a favor, who would you help?

    Q: _____

    A: _____

4. Where would you celebrate if you had a party for your birthday?

    Q: _____

    A: _____

5. What would you do if you didn't have homework tonight?

    Q: _____

    A: _____

4 Complete the questions. Use the pictures and answers to help you.

1. Q: What _would Tony do if it rained_?

    A: He'd take an umbrella.

2. Q: Where _____?

    A: They'd go rafting in Costa Rica.

3. Q: _____

    A: She'd apologize to the teacher.

CONVERSATION Asking for and giving advice

1 Put the words in the correct order.

1. on / what's / going / ?
   What's going on?

2. advice / need / some / I / .
   _____

3. up / what's / sure / . / ?
   _____

4. do / what / I / should / ?
   _____

5. ask him / I / in person / you, / I'd / if / were / .
   _____

6. for it / you / asking him / have / tried / ?
   _____

2 Complete the conversation with the phrases from Exercise 1.

Haley: Hi, Brian. You look upset.
¹ *What's going on?*

Brian: Well, I'm really mad at Peter. I don't know what to do.
² _____

Haley: ³ _____

Brian: Well, Peter borrowed my tablet last week, and he hasn't given it back.
⁴ _____

Haley: ⁵ _____

Brian: Yes, I have. I sent him three text messages about it.

Haley: You know, maybe he didn't read the texts.
⁶ _____

Brian: Well, I guess that's a good idea.

Haley: Yeah. You might be getting mad for no good reason!

Brian: You're probably right. I'll go talk to him!

READING TO WRITE

1 Complete the article with the imperative form of the verbs.

be	invite	not wait
✓ follow	join	remember
go	not be	

HOW TO MAKE FRIENDS

It can be difficult to make friends, especially if you move to a new city. So, how can you make friends easily?

1 *Follow* this advice.

2 _____ places where there are a lot of teens. For example, go to a café or the library.

3 _____ a club. Do you like chess, sports, or photography? Find a club with your interests.

Find friends online with similar interests. But 4 _____ careful when you make friends online. Some people can be bullies online.

5 _____ to be friendly and smile when you meet new people. 6 _____ afraid to say hello and ask questions. 7 _____ for others to talk to you. You can be the one to start a conversation!

Stay in touch with new friends. Call, text, or email them. 8 _____ new friends to do things.

2 Read the article in Exercise 1 again. Circle the correct answers.

1. What's the title?
   a. Moving to a New City
   b. How to Make Friends
   c. Follow This Advice

2. What's the problem?
   a. Some people can be bullies online.
   b. It's hard to stay in touch with friends.
   c. It's sometimes hard to make friends.

3. Who does this problem affect?
   a. People who have moved to a new city.
   b. Teenagers who don't have any friends.
   c. People who want to make friends online.

4. What question does the article want to answer?
   a. Do you like making friends?
   b. How can you make friends easily?
   c. Why is it difficult to make friends?

3 Complete the article with the correct sentences.

Choose your friends carefully.
Don't be afraid to tell your friends they are wrong.
Get away from the situation.
✓ How can you avoid peer pressure?
Say "no" and mean it.

How to Avoid PEER PRESSURE

Peer pressure is when your friends try to make you do things that they are doing. Sometimes, they might not be doing the right thing.

1 *How can you avoid peer pressure?*
Follow this advice.

2 _____
_____

It's important to be strong if you don't want to do something. You might have to say "no" more than once.

3 _____
_____

If you walk away from something you don't want to do, your friends can't make you do it.

4 _____
_____

Hang out with friends that make good decisions.

5 _____
_____

They may listen to you and decide to do the right thing.

REVIEW UNITS 5–6

1 Complete each sentence with a word or phrase from each box.

confused	bullying
embarrassing	clowns
interesting	✓ did me a favor
✓ surprised	do research
terrified	snakes
terrifying	wear a school uniform

1. I was ___*surprised*___ when Rick ___*did me a favor*___. He never wants to help me.
2. I was _____ when the girls at school started _____ me. They were saying very mean things, and I was scared.
3. I think _____ are _____. I always scream when I see one outside in my yard.
4. I have to _____. I have to keep it on for my piano lesson because I don't have time to change. It's so _____!
5. I think it's _____ to _____. I love finding out about new things.
6. I'm _____. Sarah said she was afraid of _____, but she's posting pictures of them at the circus. It looks like she's having a good time.

2 Write the words in the correct places in the chart.

✓ elevators	relaxed
exhausted	the dark
getting extra credit	winning an award

Fears	*elevators*	
Feelings		
Rewards		

3 Complete the expressions with *do* or *make*.

1. ___*do*___ something fun
2. _____ me mad
3. _____ homework
4. _____ a difference
5. _____ friends

4 Look at the pictures. Complete the sentences with *be going to* and an expression from Exercise 3.

1. Isabel *is going to do something fun* this weekend.
2. Amy and Dan _____ at their new school.
3. You _____ if you don't clean your room.
4. Jeremy _____ after school.
5. I _____ in my community by helping others.

5 Circle the correct words.

1. Oh, no, you forgot to do your homework. You **can't** / (**must**) be really (**embarrassed**) / **embarrassing**.
2. This math problem is very **confused** / **confusing**. I think I **might** / **can't** have the wrong answer.
3. Ginger's vacation is **relaxed** / **relaxing**. She **may** / **might not** want to stay a few more days.
4. I'm **interested** / **interesting** in being a police officer, but it **must** / **must not** be very difficult.
5. Jen told me **surprised** / **surprising** news. She won an award. She **can't** / **might** be sad about that!
6. The race is going to be **exhausted** / **exhausting**. It **can't** / **could** take me an hour or more to finish.

6 Complete the conversations. Use *will* for decisions at the moment of speaking. Use the present continuous for planned events.

1. **A:** Do you want to go to a theme park this weekend?
   B: Sure. I ___'ll go___ (go) with you.
2. **A:** What are you going to do tomorrow?
   B: I _____ (shop) with my sister.
3. **A:** When are you going to Lima?
   B: We _____ (fly) there tomorrow.
4. **A:** Do you have homework tonight?
   B: I _____ (not know) until after my next class.
5. **A:** How are you getting home?
   B: I'm not sure. I think I _____ (walk).
6. **A:** Where is your brother staying tonight?
   B: He _____ (sleep) at my grandparents' house.

7 Complete the sentences with the correct forms of the verbs.

1. If Jim didn't stay up so late, he ___wouldn't feel___ (not feel) exhausted in the morning.
2. If Sara misses class again, she _____ (be) assigned detention.
3. If you _____ (not follow) the dress code, you'll be sent home.
4. If your best friend cheated on a test, what _____ you _____ (do)?
5. If Noah _____ (not be) rude, he wouldn't have to apologize.
6. If your classmates saw someone being bullied, _____ they _____ (tell) the teacher?
7. If you cheat on the test, you _____ (get) sent to the principal's office.
8. If you _____ (win) a prize, how would you feel?
9. If you are punctual, you _____ (not make) Mr. Gomez mad.
10. If you _____ (be) late to class, would you be embarrassed?

8 Complete the conversation.

Have you tried talking to him?	Come on!
Are you serious?	✓ I need some advice.
Sure. What's up?	What should I do?

Julia: Hey, Ryan.
¹ *I need some advice.*

Ryan: ² _____

Julia: Well, did you hear about Aaron? He was assigned to detention.

Ryan: ³ _____

Julia: Yes, I am. And he's not going to tell our parents.

Ryan: ⁴ _____
That doesn't sound like your brother.

Julia: I know.
⁵ _____

Ryan: ⁶ _____
You could tell him this: If he tells your parents before the principal does, it probably won't make them as mad.

Julia: That's a good idea.

7 Smart Planet

VOCABULARY Materials

1 Find 10 more words for materials.

M	H	I	T	H	K	W	O	A	M	W	U	B	B	M
B	A	N	O	Z	O	J	T	L	E	N	N	G	R	P
R	U	B	B	E	R	U	I	C	T	U	I	S	P	Z
O	A	I	N	V	B	I	Y	B	A	A	Q	N	L	R
T	C	C	O	T	T	O	N	N	L	Y	A	T	A	T
O	K	E	A	I	L	I	P	L	A	N	T	S	S	I
E	P	M	I	Y	C	B	A	S	T	I	D	A	T	K
R	B	E	N	R	W	O	O	D	R	B	R	I	I	C
A	R	N	B	O	A	M	O	U	N	F	O	M	C	I
N	I	T	I	O	T	E	P	L	A	E	N	A	H	R
T	C	C	K	N	E	S	A	G	L	A	S	S	E	M
G	K	K	I	S	R	S	L	S	I	T	T	O	G	J
I	S	D	N	U	S	A	P	A	P	E	R	U	F	L

2 Cross out the word that doesn't belong to each category.

1. **Water:** ocean   lake   ~~mountain~~   river
2. **Wood:** house   tablet   guitar   table
3. **Cement:** floor   house   road   car
4. **Plants:** waterfall   jungle   rain forest   farm
5. **Rubber:** tire   T-shirt   bath toy   balloon
6. **Metal:** fork   jewelry   book   chair
7. **Plastic:** magazine   bottle   keyboard   cup
8. **Glass:** window   mirror   pottery   light bulb

3 Complete the sentences with some of the materials from Exercise 1.

1. It's a ___cotton___ sweater.
2. I live in a _____ house.
3. It's a _____ jar.
4. I made a _____ airplane.
5. Do you like my new _____ boots?
6. Put those things in the _____ recycling bin.
7. _____ flows out of the fountain.
8. Use some _____ to start the fire.

4 Answer the questions with your own information.

1. What material is in the floors of your home?
   The floors in my home are wood.
2. What kind of bottle or can do you usually buy soda or juice in?
   _____
3. What kinds of clothes do you wear that are cotton?
   _____
4. What materials can you recycle in your area?
   _____

44 | Unit 7

GRAMMAR Simple present passive; infinitives of purpose

1 Correct the sentences.

1. My favorite T-shirt ~~are~~ *is* made from cotton.
2. Those cars are built be less harmful to the environment.
3. The animals in the wildlife park isn't hunted.
4. The water on the river not frozen because it's not cold enough.
5. Rubber is used to made erasers.
6. Plastic bottles aren't recycle at our recycling center.
7. These plants grown in a greenhouse.
8. Water isn't sell in plastic bottles at that store.

2 Write sentences with the simple present passive.

1. the buildings / design / in California
   The buildings are designed in California.
2. the fruit / grow / in Mexico
   _____
3. the cabinets / not make / of wood
   _____
4. the wall / not paint / green
   _____
5. the park / clean / every weekend
   _____
6. the glass bottles / not reused / at the market
   _____

3 Look at the pictures and answer the questions.

1. Where is the house built?
   It's built in a forest.
2. What is the house made of?
   _____
3. What is recycled at the recycling center?
   _____
4. What isn't recycled?
   _____
5. Where are the oranges grown?
   _____
6. Where is the tomato sauce made?
   _____

4 Write sentences with the information in the chart. Use the simple present passive and infinitives of purpose.

What?	Why?
those cotton T-shirts / make	keep / people cool
that house / design	save / energy
plastic bottles / recycle	make / furniture
bricks / use	build / houses
that wood / save	make / fires

1. *Those cotton T-shirts are made to keep people cool.*
2. _____
3. _____
4. _____
5. _____

VOCABULARY Eco-construction verbs

1 Circle seven more verbs.

abri(change)tapgladiscoverplasavebuimakbuildtsyinodestrreducelcdfkcotdesignrtobbssconsumeduceinstallrplasttowrci

2 Put the words in the correct categories. Some words can go in more than one category. Then add one more idea for each category.

- ✓ a house
- a new plant
- an air-conditioning unit
- clothes
- energy
- pollution
- the rain forest

Things you can . . .		Your ideas
1. build	a house	
2. change		
3. install		
4. reduce		
5. discover		
6. design	a house	
7. save		
8. consume		

3 Complete the sentences with the present continuous of the verbs from Exercise 1.

1. Mr. and Mrs. Henderson _are installing_ solar panels on their roof.

2. Jenny _____ money because she _____ her light bulbs to ones that don't use as much energy.

3. Tomás _____ a new way to recycle plastic.

4. Laura _____ a house for her parents.

5. They _____ a house in the city.

6. We _____ trash in our school by 50 percent.

46 | Unit 7

GRAMMAR Simple past passive

1 Check (✓) if the sentences are active or passive.

	Active	Passive
1. The houses were built in 2013.		✓
2. The company installed three recycling bins in the cafeteria.		
3. John's family doesn't grow corn on their farm.		
4. Our windows weren't replaced after the last storm.		
5. Large amounts of fuel were consumed by cars and trucks last year.		
6. Sara designed three new eco-friendly homes this year.		

2 Circle the correct words.

Make your home or business work for you, and let Eco-Friendly Now help you.

Last year, over 100 homes ¹**was made** / **were made** eco-friendly by our company.

Two-hundred and fifty solar panels ²**installed** / **were installed** in local businesses. The businesses ³**saved** / **were saved** thousands of dollars on their electric bills.

A new energy-saving technique ⁴**was developed** / **were developed** by our expert engineer. It ⁵**put** / **was put** in our first home last month.

We ⁶**changed** / **were changed** air conditioning systems in 25 homes, and bills ⁷**reduced** / **were reduced** by 40 percent.

Click here to read reviews that ⁸**was written** / **were written** by happy customers.

3 Complete the conversation with the simple past passive forms of the verbs.

Don: Hey, Kim. Are you going to join the School Improvement club?

Kim: What's that?

Don: Oh, it's a group at school that makes changes at our school. Last year, recycling bins ¹ _were put_ (put) in the cafeteria by the group.

Kim: That's cool. What other things ² _____ (do) by the group?

Don: Well, 100 trees ³ _____ (plant) around the school.

Eva: ⁴ _____ the garden _____ (create) by the group, too?

Don: Yes, it ⁵ _____. The garden ⁶ _____ (design) by one of the group members.

Eva: ⁷ _____ it _____ (design) by Julia Alvarez?

Don: No, it ⁸ _____. I think the plans ⁹ _____ (draw) by Mark Reynolds. Anyway, it's a great club.

Eva: How many people ¹⁰ _____ (involve) in the group last year?

Don: About 10. But we're trying to get at least 25 members this year.

Eva: OK. I'll join!

4 Write simple past passive sentences and questions. Add *by* when needed.

1. my dress / make / my grandmother / .
   My dress was made by my grandmother.

2. our house / not build / a famous architect / .
   _____

3. the company / start / a designer / ?
   _____

4. those potatoes / not grow / local farmers / .
   _____

5. when / solar panels / invent / ?
   _____

6. the plastic bottles / recycle / the students / .
   _____

7. where / the pottery / find / ?
   _____

8. lights / leave on / the children / ?
   _____

CONVERSATION Apologizing

1 Circle the correct words.

Ryan: This planting project was a great idea.

Carla: Yeah. The park is going to look so much better. Hey, Ryan, did you bring shovels for us?

Ryan: Oh, no. I forgot. I'm really ¹**sorry / fault**.

Carla: Ryan! How are we going to plant our trees? You said you'd bring them.

Ryan: I know. I didn't ²**forget / mean** to leave them at home.

Carla: Here comes Ms. Lee.

Ms. Lee: Hi, Carla and Ryan. What's going on? The other students have planted a lot of trees already.

Carla: My ³**sorry / apologies**. We forgot our shovels.

Ryan: It was my ⁴**fault / apologies**, Ms. Lee. I was supposed to bring the shovels, and I forgot.

Ms. Lee: Don't worry about it. You can borrow Javier's and Kayla's shovels. They're almost done.

2 Complete the conversation with the correct words.

| apologies | fault | mean | sorry |

Ana: Which flowers should we plant first?

Eric: Let's plant your flowers, Ana. Then we can plant Meg's. And finally mine. Meg, where are the flowers you brought?

Meg: Oh, I didn't bring any flowers. Was I supposed to?

Eric: We were all supposed to bring flowers.

Meg: Oh, I see. My ¹_____.

Eric: Now we don't have enough!

Meg: I didn't ²_____ to mess things up. I didn't know.

Eric: Well, the website about the planting project gave all of the information.

Ana: Eric, don't get mad at Meg. I invited her at the last minute. It was my ³_____. I forgot to tell her about the website, and I didn't tell her to bring flowers.

Eric: Oh, wow. I'm really ⁴_____, Meg.

Meg: That's OK. Hey, there's a garden center a few minutes away. I'll go buy some flowers now.

Eric: No! I'll go get them, Meg.

Ana: Hey, let's plant these flowers first, and then we'll all go!

48 | Unit 7

READING TO WRITE

1 Read the article. Then match the words to different words that refer to the same thing.

Riverdale Teens Have An Animal Adoption Day
by Jordan Pierce

Fifteen Riverdale High School students found homes for animals on Saturday, May 6. The teens worked with the Riverdale Animal Shelter to find homes for cats and dogs. They organized an Animal Adoption Day. They got 20 cats and dogs from the shelter and took them to Riverdale Park for the event. They set up a table there with signs and information about the animals.

All 20 animals were adopted by Riverdale families. The shelter was very happy with the results. It is going to continue working with the teenagers and have an Animal Adoption Day once a month.

1. Riverdale High School students __c__, _____, _____
2. animals _____, _____
3. the Riverdale Animal Shelter _____, _____
4. Animal Adoption Day _____
5. Riverdale Park _____

a. cats and dogs
b. the event
c. they
d. it
e. the teens
f. there
g. the teenagers
h. them
i. the shelter

2 Read the article in Exercise 1 again. Answer the questions.

1. What was the event?
   The event was an Animal Adoption Day.

2. When was it?
   _____

3. Where was it?
   _____

4. Who was involved?
   _____

5. What did they do?
   _____

6. What were the results?
   _____

7. What will happen next?
   _____

8 Run for Cover!

VOCABULARY Natural disasters

1 Put the letters in the correct order to make words.

1. O N T R O A D — _tornado_
2. D D L L I N A E S — _____
3. M S A T I N U — _____
4. R N H U I A C E R — _____
5. C N C O V L A I — _____
6. E T R F O S — _____
7. O L F O D — _____
8. U A T A E Q K E R H — _____
9. O R E P N U I T — _____
10. I F E R — _____
11. A A C E V A L N H — _____

2 Label the pictures with the correct words from Exercise 1.

1. _tornado_
2. _____
3. _____
4. _____
5. _____
6. _____
7. _____
8. _____
9. _____

3 Where do the natural disasters happen? Write the words in the correct places in the chart. Some words can go in more than one category.

✓ avalanche   forest fire   tornado
earthquake   hurricane   tsunami
flood   landslide   volcanic eruption

On land	In the air	In the ocean
avalanche		

4 When do the natural disasters happen? Check (✓) the answers that are true for your area. Then answer the questions.

	Often	Sometimes	Never
1. avalanches			
2. earthquakes			
3. floods			
4. forest fires			
5. hurricanes			
6. landslides			
7. tornadoes			
8. tsunamis			
9. volcanic eruptions			

1. Which natural disasters happen most often in your area?

   In my area, tornadoes happen most often.
   _____

2. Which natural disasters never happen in your area? Have you ever experienced them in other places?

   _____
   _____

50 | Unit 8

GRAMMAR Past perfect

1 Write the past perfect forms of the verbs.

1. plan _had planned_
2. be _____
3. not be _____
4. ski _____
5. not finish _____
6. not see _____
7. hear _____
8. feel _____

2 Complete the paragraph with verbs from Exercise 1.

Tell us your NATURAL DISASTER STORIES

Rachel Patterson:

My family ¹ _had planned_ a trip to Japan. Then we couldn't go because my father got sick. We finally went a year later. We ² _____ there for two days when an earthquake happened. I ³ _____ earthquakes in California before, but never one like this! We were at a restaurant, and I ⁴ _____ my lunch. It went flying across the room!

David Alba:

I ⁵ _____ snow before. But last week, I saw a lot of it! I went skiing in Denver, Colorado. I took ski lessons on the first day. My instructor ⁶ _____ all over the world, and she was a great teacher.

There ⁷ _____ an avalanche at the ski resort in over 10 years. However, on the second day, my instructor ⁸ _____ on TV that conditions were right for avalanches, so she cancelled our lessons. Later that day, no one was allowed to ski, and there was an avalanche! Luckily, I was safe!

3 Read the sentences. Then circle the answer that correctly explains each situation.

1. Elsa hadn't been to Costa Rica before her trip.
   a. She has been to Costa Rica more than once.
   b. She went to Costa Rica once.

2. The forest fire had started before breakfast.
   a. The forest fire started in the morning.
   b. The forest fire started in the afternoon.

3. Andrew had read an interesting article about tsunamis.
   a. Andrew read an article about tsunamis.
   b. Andrew didn't read an article about tsunamis.

4. Sun-hi hadn't told Paul about the hurricane.
   a. Paul knew about the hurricane.
   b. Paul didn't know about the hurricane.

5. June had finished the reading before school.
   a. June finished the reading.
   b. June didn't finish the reading.

6. The weather hadn't been good before the disaster.
   a. The disaster caused the weather to be bad.
   b. The disaster didn't cause the weather to be bad.

Past perfect *yes/no* questions

4 Write *yes/no* questions and answers in the past perfect. ✓ = yes, ✗ = no.

1. Dylan / hear / about the volcanic eruption / (✗)
   Q: _Had Dylan heard about the volcanic eruption?_
   A: _No, he hadn't._

2. you / be / to San Francisco before the earthquake / (✓)
   Q: _____
   A: _____

3. Sally / read / the article before class / (✗)
   Q: _____
   A: _____

4. your parents / tell / about the flood / (✗)
   Q: _____
   A: _____

5. the volcano / be / quiet for several months (✓)
   Q: _____
   A: _____

6. you and your brother / see / a tornado / before / (✓)
   Q: _____
   A: _____

VOCABULARY Survival essentials

1 Match the sentences to the pictures.

1. _g_
2. ___
3. ___
4. ___
5. ___
6. ___
7. ___
8. ___
9. ___

a. I always take a water bottle when I hike.
b. A penknife is useful on a camping trip.
c. You should wear sunglasses when it's sunny.
d. You should always wear sunscreen outside.
e. I cut my finger. I need a first-aid kit.
f. Your sleeping bag looks really warm.
g. Which way is north? Do you have a compass?
h. I need a flashlight. I'm afraid of the dark!
i. John had forgotten to bring a map on the hike.

2 Read the situations and circle the correct answers.

1. Gabriel is skiing in the mountains. It's really bright outside. What does he need?
   a. a compass   b. a first-aid kit   (c. sunscreen)

2. Carol is lost in a forest. She wants to find her way out before it's dark. What should she use?
   a. a penknife   b. a compass   c. a flashlight

3. Han is camping and sleeping in a tent. What does he need to stay warm?
   a. a flashlight   b. a sleeping bag   c. sunglasses

4. Mara fell and hurt her foot while snowboarding. What does she need?
   a. a water bottle   b. a penknife   c. a first-aid kit

5. Dan and Ethan need to cut a rope on their tent. What should they use?
   a. a penknife   b. sunscreen   c. a first-aid kit

6. Yae-won needs directions to the campgrounds. What should she use?
   a. a sleeping bag   b. a compass   c. a map

3 Answer the questions with words from Exercise 1.

1. Which two items protect you from the sun?
   _____
   _____

2. Which two items help you with directions?
   _____
   _____

3. Which two items would you most likely use at night?
   _____
   _____

4. Which two items would you most likely use for food or drink?
   _____
   _____

GRAMMAR Past perfect and simple past

1 Look at the timeline of Carl's trip. Complete the sentences with the past perfect or simple past. Use the past perfect for the event that happened first in each sentence.

9 a.m.
- pack his bags
- forget his sleeping bag
- leave for trip
- go fishing
- set up tent
- friends arrive
- start a fire
- cook the fish
- everyone eat
- go to bed

10 p.m.

1. Carl ___had packed___ had packed his bags a week before he ___left___ for his trip.
2. He _____ fishing before he _____ his tent.
3. He _____ his tent already when his friends _____ at the campsite.
4. A few minutes before Carl _____ the fish, he _____ a fire.
5. Everyone _____ a delicious fish dinner a few hours before they _____ to bed.
6. When Carl _____ to bed, he realized that he _____ his sleeping bag!

2 Circle the correct words. Use the past perfect for the event that happened first in each sentence.

1. On a long hike, John **dropped** / **(had dropped)** his compass 20 minutes before he **(realized)** / **had realized** it.
2. My sister **heard** / **had heard** about the hurricane before I **told** / **had told** her about it.
3. I **cut** / **had cut** my finger making dinner, and unfortunately, I **didn't buy** / **hadn't bought** a first-aid kit.
4. Sam and Jill were hungry on their hike because they **didn't pack** / **hadn't packed** any snacks before they **left** / **had left**.
5. When they **rescued** / **had rescued** the hikers, they **were** / **had been** lost for two days.
6. I was upset because after I **bought** / **had bought** my penknife, the store **had** / **had had** a big sale.

3 Write sentences with the simple past and past perfect. Use the past perfect for the event that happened first in each sentence.

1. Jessica / sign up / for a camping trip / after / her friend / tell her about it

   Jessica signed up for the camping trip
   after her friend had told her about it.

2. By the time / Raul / buy / his bike, / he / save / money for two months

   _____
   _____

3. I / not check / the weather report / before / I / go / hiking

   _____
   _____

4. We / pack / our suitcase / a week before / we / leave

   _____
   _____

5. Serena / not hear / about the tsunami / before / she / talk / to her brother

   _____
   _____

6. After / the news / be / on for an hour, / I / finally / hear / the weather report

   _____
   _____

CONVERSATION — Asking about and talking about personal problems

1 Circle the correct words.

1. Oh, **no** / know!
2. I don't **think** / **know** what to do!
3. Let me **think** / **panic**.
4. What's the **matter** / **wrong**?
5. **No** / **Don't** panic.

2 Complete the conversation with the expressions from Exercise 1.

Mae: Hey, Joe. What direction are we going in?

Joe: ¹ _Oh, no!_ I don't believe this!

Mae: ² _____

Joe: I can't find my compass! This is terrible!

Mae: ³ _____ Let's think about this calmly. When did you have it last?

Joe: ⁴ _____ Oh, I remember. I took it out of my bag at the beginning of the hike. I must have dropped it.

Mae: Well, it's no big deal. We can use the sun to see what direction we're going.

Joe: I know, but my grandfather had given me that compass before he moved to California. It's really special. ⁵ _____

Mae: Oh, now I see why you're so upset. Listen, we've only been hiking for 20 minutes. Let's go back and see if we can find it.

Joe: That'd be great. Thanks, Mae.

READING TO WRITE

1 Complete Kyle's story with the adverb form of the words in parentheses.

I'll never forget Friday, April 17. I was at my friend's house in the morning. We didn't have school that day because of high winds and heavy rain. I had heard on the news we might have a flood in our town, and ¹ _unfortunately_ (unfortunate), we did. The water was so high that our street was like a river. By noon, the rain had stopped, so my friend and I played in the street. ² _____ (natural), we thought it was fun. We didn't realize how bad things were. The water kept rising. ³ _____ (sudden), my parents showed up at my friend's house. They were really worried. They had left work early and said we had to go home ⁴ _____ (immediate). ⁵ _____ (fortunate), our house was OK, but many homes were destroyed. I felt terrible. On Saturday, I volunteered in my neighborhood to clean up the streets.

2 Read the article in Exercise 1 again. Circle the correct answers.

1. What happened?
   a. A hurricane destroyed many homes.
   b. There was a flood, but no homes were destroyed.
   c. (There was a flood, and homes were destroyed.)

2. When did it happen?
   a. On Friday, April 17
   b. On Saturday, April 17
   c. On Saturday, April 18

3. Where was Kyle when it happened?
   a. At home
   b. At a friend's house
   c. At school

4. How did Kyle feel about the flood?
   a. At first he thought it was fun, and then he felt bad.
   b. At first he felt bad, but then he thought it was fun.
   c. At first he felt terrible, and then he got really worried.

5. What happened at the end of the story?
   a. Kyle played in the water.
   b. Kyle helped clean up the streets.
   c. Kyle's parents took him home.

3 Complete Brianna's story with the correct sentences.

> Fortunately, there wasn't really an avalanche.
> I was really embarrassed.
> In the end, it turned out OK.
> ✓ Last Saturday was a terrible day.
> Suddenly, my sister shouted, "Avalanche!"
> Unfortunately, I broke Tara's snowboard.

₁ *Last Saturday was a terrible day.*

I went snowboarding on a mountain near my town.

My friend Tara let me borrow her snowboard.

² _____

I got really scared, and I ran into a tree.

³ _____

My sister was joking.

⁴ _____

The snowboard hit the tree when I ran into it, and it cracked. I called Tara that night to tell her.

⁵ _____

Snowboards are expensive, and I didn't have enough money to buy her a new one.

⁶ _____

My sister felt terrible about her joke, so she gave me money to buy Tara a new board!

Unit 8 | 55

REVIEW UNITS 7–8

1 Write the words in the correct places in the chart.

✓ cement, forest fire, plants, compass, hurricane, rubber, first aid kit, metal, tsunami, flashlight, penknife, volcanic eruption

Materials	Survival essentials	Natural disasters
cement	_____	_____
_____	_____	_____
_____	_____	_____
_____	_____	_____

2 Look at the pictures and complete the puzzle. Find out what the city did by filling in the gray boxes.

The city _____ their trash last year by 50 percent.

1. ¹t o r n a d o
2.
3.
4.
5.
6.
7.

1. 2. 3. 4. 5. 6. 7.

3 Complete each sentence with a word from each box. Use the simple present passive forms of the verbs.

build, design, make, recycle, turn, ✓ use

bricks, cotton, glass, paper, ✓ plastic, water

1. _Plastic is used_ to make this jewelry.

2. These shirts _____ of _____.

3. _____ bags _____ to help the environment.

4. This house _____ with _____.

5. The _____ lamps _____ by an artist.

6. The wheel _____ by _____.

56 | Review 4

4 Put the words in the correct order to make sentences. Change the verbs to the simple past passive.

1. by / the solar panels / install / an engineer / .
   The solar panels were installed by an engineer.

2. the flood / save / after / our dog / .
   _____

3. build / when / the house / ?
   _____

4. not discover / right away / the forest fire / .
   _____

5. little energy / the EcoHouse / by / consume / .
   _____

6. by / invent / an American / solar panels / ?
   _____

5 Correct the conversations. Use the past perfect.

1. **A:** Had you ~~hear~~ *heard* about the flood before the class?
   B: Yes, I ~~have~~ *had*.

2. **A:** What has you learned about Brazil before your trip?
   B: I had reading a lot about the food there.

3. **A:** Had Jake call you before he came over?
   B: No, he not.

4. **A:** Were Tom and Keiko been on a boat before their cruise?
   B: No, they haven't.

5. **A:** Where has you worked before you got this job?
   B: I had no worked anywhere. This is my first job.

6. **A:** Had you help on a volunteer project before?
   B: Yes, I hadn't.

7. **A:** What had happen before the flood?
   B: It has rained for several days.

8. **A:** Has you known about the tsunami before you went there?
   B: No, I not.

6 Complete the article with the simple past or past perfect forms of the verbs.

Samantha and her friend Lydia ¹____*went*____ (go) on a hike last Saturday. Samantha ²_____ (not be) in a forest before the trip, but Lydia ³_____ (go) many times. Lydia ⁴_____ (tell) Samantha about the forest before they ⁵_____ (get) there. Samantha ⁶_____ (not ask) Lydia what to bring before she ⁷_____ (pack) her bag for the trip. She ⁸_____ (take) a lot of water, some snacks, and her camera. On the hike, they ⁹_____ (walk) for about an hour when Samantha ¹⁰_____ (fall) and ¹¹_____ (cut) her knee. Unfortunately, Samantha ¹²_____ (not pack) a first-aid kit before they ¹³_____ (leave) for the hike, but, fortunately, Lydia had!

7 Complete the conversation.

Don't panic	I didn't mean to
I don't know what to do	I'm really sorry
Let me think	✓ What's the matter?

Rob: You look terrible. ¹____*What's the matter?*____

Ian: I'm really worried about the hurricane.

Rob: ²_____. The news said it probably won't be that bad.

Ian: No, I don't mean the hurricane here. I'm worried about the hurricane that hit Mexico. My grandparents live there.

Rob: Oh, ³_____ be rude. Now I see what you mean. ⁴_____.

Ian: That's OK. It's just that they aren't answering their phones, and ⁵_____.

Rob: Do you have the number for any of their neighbors?

Ian: Hmm . . . ⁶_____. Yes, my cousins live close by. I'll text them now. Thanks.

9 He Said, She Said

VOCABULARY Reporting verbs

1 Find nine more reporting verbs.

B	I	L	T	Z	J	O	G	V	A	Y	I	W
S	A	Y	P	N	B	P	R	O	M	N	S	H
O	N	I	S	U	G	G	E	S	T	A	T	I
G	N	U	W	I	S	Z	K	H	D	Y	N	S
G	O	U	P	U	S	T	L	O	P	G	E	P
E	U	F	R	Y	C	B	Q	U	A	G	M	E
R	N	S	O	R	H	I	L	T	R	B	A	R
G	C	O	M	P	L	A	I	N	E	F	N	M
P	E	Y	I	X	D	E	P	C	N	E	V	A
L	H	W	S	N	X	T	E	L	L	M	I	T
A	V	K	E	S	O	S	L	E	R	P	B	E
I	J	X	K	T	E	X	P	L	A	I	N	O
Y	R	E	M	I	N	D	L	A	N	G	P	

2 Circle the correct words.

1. Jennifer **said** / **reminded** she did well on her science test.
2. My dad **whispered** / **promised** me he'd drive us to the concert.
3. Who **suggested** / **announced** that we eat at this restaurant? It's great.
4. My brother always **explains** / **complains** about doing his chores.
5. Can you **promise** / **remind** me when our homework is due?
6. Diego **suggested** / **told** me about his vacation.
7. Please **whisper** / **shout** in the library. Talking loudly bothers people who are reading.
8. Lydia **told** / **explained** the computer program to us.
9. Tyrone **announced** / **said** his plans to get a summer job.
10. Maria was so surprised by a text message that she **shouted** / **told** in the middle of a store.

3 Complete the sentences with the simple past form of some of the verbs from Exercise 1.

1. During the game last week, the coach ___shouted___ loudly at the players, but they couldn't hear him.
2. I _____ my best friend that I would text her when I got home.
3. My brother _____ when it was his turn to take out the trash.
4. Yesterday Kai _____ to me that we should meet after class.
5. At the assembly, the principal _____ the winner of the class prize.
6. Mr. Sato _____ the assignment to us twice, because it was a little confusing.

4 Complete the sentences with your own information.

1. I usually whisper _when I'm talking in the library_.
2. I often have to explain things to _____.
3. When I complain, I usually complain about _____.
4. _____ sometimes has to remind me to _____.
5. People often shout when _____.
6. One time, _____ promised me _____.

GRAMMAR Quoted speech vs. reported speech

1 Add commas and quotation marks to the direct speech sentences in the correct places.

1. Veronica said, "I was really tired yesterday."
2. I've seen that movie John announced.
3. We'll come to your party they told us.
4. Mr. Valdez shouted You can't run in the hallway!
5. Sam whispered It's dark in here.

58 | Unit 9

2 Match the quoted speech sentences to the reported speech sentences. Use one reported speech sentence twice.

1. Maya said, "I won't call them." __d__	a. Maya said that she called them every day.
2. Maya said, "I'm calling them right now." ____	b. Maya said that she had called them.
3. Maya said, "I called them." ____	c. Maya said that she had been calling them.
4. Maya said, "I've called them." ____	d. Maya said that she wouldn't call them.
5. Maya said, "I call them every day." ____	e. Maya said that she was calling them right now.
6. Maya said, "I was calling them." ____	

3 Put the words in the correct order to make reported speech sentences.

1. was / explained / sick the day of the party / that she / Emily

   Emily explained that she was sick the day of the party.

2. could / me / chess / that he / Hiro / play / told

   _____

3. had / I / been / said / to Ecuador / I / that

   _____

4. was / Shelby / that she / complained / tired

   _____

5. that he / moved / Mike / had / announced /

   _____

6. said / soccer / played / that she / Alba

   _____

4 Complete the direct and quoted speech sentences with the correct forms of the verbs.

1. "It ___looks___ stormy outside," Luisa said.

   She said that it looked stormy outside.

2. "I walk my dog every day," Greg said.

   He said that he _____ his dog every day.

3. "I'll call you," Marissa told me.

   She told me that she _____ me.

4. "I _____ you," Sarah explained.

   She explained that she could help me.

5. "I _____ at the park," Nidia said.

   She said that she had been skateboarding in the park.

6. "Ling bought a new jacket," Dan said.

   He said that Ling _____ a new jacket.

5 Write the quotes from a website as reported speech.

1. **Katie:** I just read a great book.

   Katie said that she had just read a great book.

2. **Mario:** I studied all night last night.

   _____

3. **Nora:** I'll post photos of the party soon.

   _____

4. **Mia:** I can go to the soccer game on Friday!

   _____

5. **Peter:** I've lost my keys.

   _____

6. **Carol:** I'm ready for vacation.

   _____

7. **Ted:** My cousins will be in town tomorrow!

   _____

8. **Bert:** I went to a great concert on Saturday.

   _____

VOCABULARY Communication methods

1 Fill in the letters to complete the words.

1. s _o_ _c_ _i_ _a_ l n _e_ t w o _r_ _k_ p _o_ _s_ _t_

2. c _ _ _ t _ _ g

3. b _ _ _ _ _ _ t

4. v _ _ e _ _ h _ t

5. _ _ x _ m _ _ _ a g _

6. f _ r _ _

7. _ h _ _ e _ a _ l

8. _ _ _ r o _ _ o _ p _ s _

9. e _ _ i _

2 Write the words from Exercise 1 next to their definitions.

1. A message you put on a social networking page: _social network post_

2. Talking and seeing video of someone computer to computer: _____

3. An online discussion with several people: _____

4. Talking with others in an informal way: _____

5. A way to communicate with someone using only your voice (you can't see the other person): _____

6. A message you send to someone over the Internet that contains a subject line: _____

7. Personal writing on a website that usually shares an experience or opinion and which is usually added to often: _____

8. A short note you type on your phone and send to someone: _____

9. A very short message on a social networking page: _____

3 Check (✓) how often you do these things.

	Often	Sometimes	Never
1. I video chat with my friends or family.			
2. I chat with friends after school.			
3. I make phone calls.			
4. I write social network posts about my day.			
5. I join online forums.			
6. I send my friends text messages.			

GRAMMAR Reported questions

1 Match the direct questions with the reported questions.

1. "When do you eat dinner?" he asked. _d_	a. He asked me if I had eaten dinner.
2. "When did you eat dinner?" he asked. ___	b. He asked me when I had eaten dinner.
3. "When will you eat dinner?" he asked. ___	c. He asked me when I could eat dinner.
4. "When can you eat dinner?" he asked. ___	d. He asked me when I ate dinner.
5. "Did you eat dinner?" he asked. ___	e. He asked me when I would eat dinner.

2 Correct the reported questions.

1. "Why are you tired?" Sandra asked.

   Sandra asked me ~~if~~ *why* I was tired.

2. Haru asked, "Who is your teacher?"

   Haru asked me who was my teacher.

3. Marcos asked, "What have you done today?"

   Marcos asked me what I have done today.

4. "Which sweater did you like?" Trisha asked.

   Trisha asked me which sweater had I liked.

5. Ahmed asked, "Can you help me?"

   Ahmed asked me when I could help him.

6. "Will you come to my party?" Anne asked.

   Anne asked me if I came to her party.

7. "Have you been online today?" asked my mom.

   My mom asked if I am been online today.

8. Dana asked, "Did you do your homework tonight?"

   Dana asked if we had been doing our homework tonight.

3 Write the questions as reported speech.

Dan → Wendy: "When can you video chat?"

1. _Dan asked Wendy when she could video chat._

Mia → Pam: "Did you send me a text message?"

2. _____

Tim → Felipe: "Where did you go on vacation?"

3. _____

Emma → Scott: "Do you chat with Lee a lot?"

4. _____

Huan → Isabel: "How often do you check your email?"

5. _____

Lucas → Victor: "Have you ever written a blog post?"

6. _____

Ben → Shelly: "Which tablet will you buy?"

7. _____

Young-mi → Yolanda: "What computer games can you play?"

8. _____

Unit 9 | 61

CONVERSATION Comparing different accounts of a story

1 Put the words in the correct order to make sentences.

1. what / definitely / happened / that's / not / .
   That's definitely not what happened.

2. that Tina had cheated / had happened, / I asked Kyle / what / and he said / .
   _____
   _____

3. I / that's / what / heard / not / !
   _____
   _____

4. to detention / was assigned / Kyle / according to Jen, / .
   _____
   _____

5. with / you / how / come up / that idea / did / ?
   _____
   _____

6. had posted it / Ricardo said / online yesterday / that Kyle / well, / .
   _____
   _____

2 Complete the conversation with the expressions from Exercise 1.

Lola: We're going to have a great soccer team this year.

Gabe: I know. Kyle is going to be the team captain.

Lola: He is? ¹*How did you come up with that idea?*

Gabe: ² _____
His post said, "I'm so excited to be our soccer team's captain. Go Rangers!"

Lola: Hmm. I don't know about that.
³ _____
She said that he couldn't be captain now. He might not even be able to play on the team because he cheated on a test.

Gabe: ⁴ _____

Lola: Really? How do you know it didn't happen?

Gabe: ⁵ _____
She looked at his answers during the test, but he didn't do anything wrong.

Lola: ⁶ _____!
I heard that *he* cheated off Tina.

Gabe: I don't think so. Hey, here comes Tina now. Let's ask her what happened.

READING TO WRITE

1 Complete Leo's essay with the correct words.

For paragraph 2:

| also | in addition | ✓ for one thing |

For paragraph 3:

| first | finally | in addition |

ONLINE RESEARCH
by Leo Rodriguez

1 Are you like most students? Do you use the Internet for school projects and homework? Doing research online can be easy, but it can also have its share of problems.

2 Online research is extremely convenient. ¹*For one thing*, it can be done at school, in the library, or at home. One writer says that a benefit of online research is that the Internet is available 24 hours a day. It is ² _____ easy to find information on any topic you can imagine, simply by searching for your topic with key words. ³ _____, you can find many kinds of sources online, like newspaper and magazine articles, forums, blogs, and science reports.

3 Although it's convenient, there can be problems with online research. ⁴ _____, anyone can post information online, and this information isn't always true. ⁵ _____, research can be dated, meaning it was posted years ago, and it may not be true anymore. ⁶ _____, some good sources, like magazines, might require you to pay to read them.

4 I believe that doing research online is the best way to research because it's convenient and there is information available on any topic. However, I think people need to be careful. Check facts on several sites to be sure the information is true and check the dates on articles on websites. If used correctly, online research can be a great way to get information about a topic.

2 Read the article in Exercise 1 again. Write the paragraph numbers next to each section below.

_____ A paragraph with arguments against

_____ A conclusion

_____ An introduction

_____ A paragraph with arguments in favor

3 Read the article in Exercise 1 again. Answer the questions.

1. What does Leo use to get the reader's attention?
   _____

2. What reasons does Leo give in favor of online research?
   _____
   _____
   _____

3. What reasons does he give against online research?
   _____
   _____
   _____

4. Overall, does Leo think doing research online is a good idea or a bad one?
   _____

5. What two things does he think people can do to avoid problems with online research?
   _____
   _____

10 Don't Give Up!

VOCABULARY Goals and achievements

1 Put the letters in the correct order to make words about goals and achievements.

1. L E D A   I H T W   _deal with_
2. K L I S L   _____
3. E A F C   _____
4. A L G O   _____
5. E D A R R W   _____
6. R S G E R P S O   _____
7. C R E M P N E F R O A   _____
8. L E H A G C E L N   _____
9. I A E H C E V   _____
10. T T C N M M I O M E   _____

2 Circle the correct words.

1. Josh **challenged** / **achieved** his goal of running 5 kilometers in under 30 minutes.
2. How do you usually **deal with** / **reward** difficult problems?
3. Rita made **progress** / **goal** over the weekend on her school project.
4. Taking care of a pet is a **big commitment** / **skill**.
5. Everyone has to **achieve** / **face** challenges in life.
6. Playing the piano well takes **performance** / **skill** and practice.
7. Aimi's tennis coach **deals with** / **challenges** her with difficult tasks.
8. Raul's **progress** / **performance** at the concert was amazing.
9. The winner of the contest is **faced** / **rewarded** with $1,000.
10. I reached my **goal** / **commitment** of getting 100 percent on a math test.

3 Complete the questions with some of the words from Exercise 1. Then circle the answers that are true for you.

1. How do you usually ___deal with___ challenges?
   a. I face them right away.
   b. I ask friends for their opinions and then face the challenge on my own.
   c. I ask friends and family to help me face challenges.

2. How do you feel about giving a _____ in front of people?
   a. I love it!
   b. It makes me nervous, but I enjoy the challenge.
   c. I hate it!

3. Who or what do you have the biggest _____ to in your life right now?
   a. a friend or family member
   b. a pet
   c. a class or job

4. Which _____ are you best at?
   a. playing a musical instrument
   b. playing a sport
   c. using a computer program

5. Which _____ would you most like to reach?
   a. buying a house or a car
   b. getting a job
   c. finishing school

6. If you won a contest, which _____ would you most like to get?
   a. money
   b. a bicycle or car
   c. a trip to another country

GRAMMAR — Reflexive pronouns

1 Write the correct reflexive pronoun for each subject.

Subject pronoun	Reflexive pronoun
1. I	myself
2. you	/ yourselves
3. he	
4. she	
5. we	
6. they	

2 Complete the paragraphs with reflexive pronouns from Exercise 1.

Hard Work and Rewards

When you work hard, you should reward [1] __yourself__! Look at these examples of how people rewarded [2] _____ for their hard work.

Sheila spent hours studying for a big math test. She passed the test. After the test, she went to the mall and bought [3] _____ a new phone.

Andrew trained for a 5-kilometer race. For several weeks, he only ate healthy food. After the race, he treated [4] _____ to a burger and French fries.

Liv and Rachel wanted to learn Spanish. Liv says, "We decided to teach [5] _____ Spanish instead of taking a class." They spent months learning Spanish together. As a reward, they took a trip to Mexico.

Feng wanted to learn to ski in a weekend. He went on a ski trip, took lessons, and got pretty good. He says, "I set a challenging goal for [6] _____, and I achieved it!" As a reward, he bought some new skis.

Reflexive pronouns with *by*

3 Rewrite the sentences. Add *by* and the correct reflexive pronoun.

1. My little brother can ride a bike.
   My little brother can ride a bike by himself.

2. Can you make dinner?
   _____

3. Anna likes to travel.
   _____

4. We painted our room.
   _____

5. I learned to play the guitar.
   _____

6. Kim and Ed dealt with the problem.
   _____

4 Answer the questions with your own information.

1. What is something you like to do by yourself?
   I like to go to the movies by myself.

2. What is something young children usually can't do by themselves?
   _____
   _____

3. What kinds of things do you usually buy for yourself?
   _____
   _____

4. What is something that people can teach themselves?
   _____
   _____

5. What goals have you set for yourself?
   _____
   _____

6. Do you ever talk to yourself? When?
   _____
   _____

VOCABULARY Emotions related to accomplishments

1 Look at the pictures and complete the crossword.

1 Across: e x c i t e d

ACROSS
1.
6.
8.
9.
10.

DOWN
2.
3.
4.
5.
7.

2 Circle the correct words.

1. My sister learned how to program computers by herself. I'm very **satisfied / (proud) / prepared** of her.

2. Rafael was **miserable / confident / thrilled** that his soccer team won first place.

3. Miya was **nervous / disappointed / calm** before the performance, but she did a great job.

4. I studied a lot and was **excited / prepared / proud** for the test, but it was still difficult.

5. Do you get **excited / miserable / calm** when you get rewarded for something?

6. Farah was **nervous / disappointed / satisfied** that she didn't get a part in the school play.

7. We were **thrilled / miserable / confident** on our ski trip because there wasn't any snow.

8. Are you **proud / prepared / satisfied** with your test score, or do you think you could have done better?

9. I'm **confident / disappointed / nervous** that Jenna is going to win the race. I'll be so happy for her.

10. You are always so **excited / calm / thrilled** before a presentation. Why don't you get nervous?

3 Answer the questions with words from Exercise 1.

1. How do you feel before a test?

   I feel nervous, but if I study, I also feel prepared!

2. How do you feel when you achieve a goal?

   _____

   _____

3. How do you feel when you don't achieve a goal?

   _____

   _____

4. How do you feel before a trip?

   _____

   _____

GRAMMAR Causative *have/get*

1 Read the sentences. Then circle the answer that correctly explains each situation.

1. Joanna took a picture of herself.
   a. (Joanna took her own picture.)
   b. Another person took Joanna's picture.

2. My father has his shirts cleaned every week.
   a. My father cleans his own shirts.
   b. Another person cleans my father's shirts.

3. Terrance got his bicycle fixed.
   a. Terrance fixed his own bike.
   b. Another person fixed Terrance's bike.

4. I usually cut my hair myself.
   a. I cut my own hair.
   b. Another person cuts my hair.

5. Sandra gets her phone updated at TechService.
   a. Sandra updates her phone herself.
   b. Another person updates Sandra's phone.

2 Correct the sentences.

1. I ~~gotten~~ *get* my teeth cleaned twice a year.
2. We had our TV fix at Electric City.
3. Hyo's soccer team had their picture took.
4. Has Linda got her eyes checked?
5. Mr. and Mrs. Simone have had food made for Katy's party last year.
6. Carlos is getting his hair cutting.

3 Put the words in the correct order to make sentences.

1. her skateboard / got / last week / Lilly / fixed
   Lilly got her skateboard fixed last week.

2. delivered / had / we / to our mother / flowers
   _____

3. had gotten / Max / cut / for the picture / his hair
   _____

4. once a year / checked / get / my bicycle / I
   _____

5. his snowboard / painted / red and black / Jack / had
   _____

4 Complete the sentences about what the people got or had done with the correct words. Use the simple past of *have/get*.

get / her car / wash	have / her eyes / check
✓ get / her hair / do	have / his tablet / fix
get / his elbow / examine	have / their dog / clean

1. Mary ___*got her hair done*___ yesterday.

2. Brandon _____ last week.

3. Teresa and Leo _____ on Saturday.

4. Linh _____ last night.

5. Paul _____ on Monday.

6. Janet _____ last month.

CONVERSATION Reassuring someone

1 Match the phrases to make sentences.

1. You've faced ____
2. I think I can ____
3. Try not to ____
4. I'm sure ____

a. help you.
b. you'll do fine.
c. bigger challenges than this.
d. worry about it.

2 Complete the conversation with the expressions from Exercise 1.

Lucia: Hey, Rick. How are you doing?

Rick: Not so good. I just fell off my skateboard.

Lucia: Oh, no. Do you need to have your knee checked?

Rick: No, it's just a small cut. I'm just worried about the skating competition tomorrow.

Lucia: 1 _____
You're a great skater.

Rick: Not worry? That's impossible! You see, I haven't been skating well lately, so I'm not feeling confident at all.

Lucia: 2 _____
You're probably falling because you're nervous.

Rick: Maybe. But I've worked so hard to achieve this goal, and now it seems impossible.

Lucia: Come on, Rick.
3 _____
Remember the time you competed a few months after you had broken your arm?

Rick: Yeah. I did pretty well in that competition. But for some reason, I wasn't nervous like I am now.

Lucia: 4 _____

Rick: Really? How?

Lucia: We'll skate together. We'll pretend it's the competition. Every time you fall, just get up again. We can practice all day if you want to. Before long, I don't think you'll be so nervous.

Rick: OK. You're right. I should keep trying. I won't give up!

READING TO WRITE

1 Complete the sentences with the correct words.

achieve	addition	determined	help

1. I'll need _____ from my mother.
2. In _____, I will check online to see what activities are happening in my neighborhood.
3. I am _____ to do everything by myself.
4. In order to _____ this, I will take a class about web design.

2 Complete the text with the sentences from Exercise 1.

Achieving My GOAL
by Denise Harris

I want to start my own blog about life in my neighborhood.
1 _____

I want to design the webpage, take and post the photos, and write all of the blog posts myself.
2 _____

My computer teacher, Mr. Clark, is teaching a class at the community center this summer. Then I will learn how to take better photos.
3 _____

She's a great photographer. Of course, first I have to get my camera fixed. After I do those things, I'll walk around the neighborhood and take photos of things going on.
4 _____

I'll go to as many events as I can with my camera. Then I'll write stories and post them on my blog with my pictures.

3 Read the text again. Answer the questions.

1. What is Denise's goal?
   _____
   _____

2. What steps will Denise take to achieve her goal?
   - ☑ learn about web design
   - ☐ take a photography class
   - ☐ have her computer fixed
   - ☐ have her camera fixed
   - ☐ learn to take better photos
   - ☐ learn to write better in English
   - ☐ take photos of activities in her neighborhood
   - ☐ take photos of her life at home
   - ☐ find out about activities from her mother
   - ☐ find out about activities online

3. Look at the steps you checked in question 2. Which ones will Denise get help from other people to do?
   _____
   _____
   _____
   _____
   _____

REVIEW UNITS 9–10

1 Circle the correct words.

1. Jana **told** / **announced** me she was nervous about her test.
2. Bob **whispered** / **shouted** loudly at the game. He was thrilled to see his brother play basketball.
3. Luis **explained** / **reminded** that he was disappointed his team lost the soccer game.
4. Jun **complained** / **said** that he was a confident speaker, so I'm sure he was calm before he gave his speech.
5. Tina **suggested** / **reminded** us that we should be prepared for the storm.
6. I was miserable about having to clean the house until Paulina **promised** / **said** to help me.

2 Write the sentences from Exercise 1 under the correct pictures.

1. *I was miserable about having to clean the house until* _____.
2. _____
3. _____
4. _____
5. _____
6. _____

3 Cross out the word that doesn't belong to each category.

1. **Something you type:**
   an email   ~~a phone call~~
   a social network post   a blog post

2. **Something you do online:**
   video chat   send a text message
   join a forum   write a microblog post

3. **A good feeling:**
   excited   proud   miserable   satisfied

4. **A bad feeling:**
   disappointed   miserable
   nervous   confident

5. **Something people sometimes do loudly:**
   shout   announce   whisper   complain

4 Complete the text with the correct words.

✓ achieve	deal with	progress
challenge	face	reward
commitments	goals	skills

Ways to ¹ *Achieve* Success

- ² _____ yourself every day. Then work hard to make ³ _____ so that you can reach your ⁴ _____.
- Learn new ⁵ _____. Teach yourself or take a class to learn something new.
- Keep the ⁶ _____ you make. It's important to do the things you say you'll do.
- ⁷ _____ problems quickly. The longer you wait to fix a problem, the harder it is to ⁸ _____.
- Don't expect to get a ⁹ _____ for everything you do. Sometimes it's enough just to be successful.

5 Write the numbered sentences in the blog as reported speech.

Franco's Blog

Today's post: The future!

Hello, friends. ¹What will you do in the future? ²Goals are important. I want to know what your goals are! ³How are you going to reach them?

Lori: ⁴I want to be a computer programmer. ⁵I'm taking computer classes at school.

Aamir: ⁶I've played soccer for 10 years. ⁷Can you guess my future career?

Kwan: ⁸I went to Mexico on vacation. ⁹I want to improve my Spanish!

1. Franco _asked what we would do in the future_.
2. He said that _____.
3. He _____.
4. Lori _____.
5. She _____.
6. Aamir _____.
7. He _____.
8. Kwan _____.
9. She _____.

6 Complete the sentences with the correct reflexive pronouns.

1. Takeko sang by _herself_ at her last music performance.
2. I'm very proud that I achieved many of my goals by _____.
3. Mindy, you shouldn't be disappointed in _____. You did your best.
4. Josh announced that he would teach _____ to speak Chinese.
5. We promised _____ that we would take a vacation next year.
6. Tim and Carla prepared _____ for a difficult task.

7 Write sentences with causative have/get. Use the simple past.

1. we / get / our hair / cut
   We got our hair cut.
2. Lucia / have / her bike / fix
   _____
3. I / get / my arm / examine
   _____
4. Matt and Lynn / have / their house / paint
   _____
5. Chuck / get / his photo / take
   _____

8 Circle the correct words.

Yin: Hi, Eva. Are you ready for the music performance?

Eva: No, I'm not. I'm so nervous!

Yin: Try not to ¹**deal with** / **(worry about)** it. I'm sure you'll do ²**fine** / **proud**.

Eva: Well, I've practiced a lot, but I just don't want to go first. ³**Chatting with** / **According to** my sister, Hank Patterson went first last year, and he was so nervous that he couldn't play.

Yin: That's not what I ⁴**heard** / **happened**.

Eva: Really?

Yin: Yeah. I asked Hank what ⁵**had faced** / **had happened**, and he said that the audio system wasn't working.

Eva: I see. So, what did he do?

Yin: Well, Hank ⁶**said** / **told** that he didn't realize it at first. So he just played, but no one could hear him. They fixed the system, and he started again. Everything was fine.

Eva: I hope that doesn't happen to me. Now I'm really nervous.

Yin: Don't be! You've faced bigger ⁷**ideas** / **challenges** than this. You're going to be great!

The LONG WINTER

Unit 1 Video 1.1

BEFORE YOU WATCH

1 Look at the pictures from the video. Do you think the sentences are true (*T*) or false (*F*)?

1. These people live in a big city. _____
2. They spend most of their time outdoors. _____
3. They grow their own vegetables. _____
4. They fish in the winter. _____

WHILE YOU WATCH

2 Watch the video. Circle the correct words.

1. In Alaska, it is cold for **three / eight** months of the year.
2. The Kilcher family uses **wood / oil** to heat their home.
3. They put their **food / clothes** in storage.
4. In the winter, they **can / can't** go to a supermarket for food.
5. Atz takes traps for **rabbits / bears** into the forest.

3 Watch the video again. Complete the sentences with the correct words.

| builds | catch | cut down | goes | plan |

1. The Kilchers _____ trees in the summer.
2. They _____ fish in the lake.
3. They _____ their meals for the months ahead.
4. Atz _____ a fire on the lake.
5. He _____ home with a bag of rabbits.

AFTER YOU WATCH

4 Work with a partner. Discuss: Which do you prefer, cold weather or hot weather? What do you like to do outdoors in cold weather? In hot weather?

> I prefer cold weather. I like skiing and ice skating in cold weather. I love swimming in hot weather.

An ISLAND FLOOD

Unit 1 Video 1.3

BEFORE YOU WATCH

1 Look at the pictures from the video. Then match the pictures to the sentences.

a. b. c.

1. These are rice fields on the island of Bali in India. _____
2. People here eat a lot of fish. _____
3. These men are fishermen – they catch fish in the sea. _____

WHILE YOU WATCH

2 Watch the video. Circle the correct words.

1. Life isn't **nice / easy** here.
2. People depend on a few **fish / rice** fields.
3. Years ago, a **flood / storm** destroyed homes.
4. The men knew they needed to **buy / build** a wall.
5. They worked for **three / five** hours.

3 Watch the video again. Match the phrases to make true sentences.

1. At last, _____
2. During the night, _____
3. Last week, _____
4. Years ago, _____

a. water flooded the village.
b. he went fishing.
c. the men went home.
d. the men watched the waters rising.

AFTER YOU WATCH

4 Work with a partner. Describe an extreme weather event in your life. What were you doing when it happened?

> Last summer, there was a big storm. There was thunder and lightning and a lot of rain. I was playing soccer. We ran into the school and closed all the windows.

Get UP and GO!

Unit 2 Video 2.1

BEFORE YOU WATCH

1 Look at the pictures from the video. Circle the correct words.

1. This special bed can wake you **up** / **down** in the morning.
2. It can also pull **off** / **in** your pajamas.
3. They purée the cereal **in** / **on** a blender for breakfast.

WHILE YOU WATCH

2 Watch the video. Check (✓) what the machine can do.

1. ❑ wake you
2. ❑ undress you
3. ❑ make breakfast
4. ❑ shower you
5. ❑ brush your hair

3 Watch the video again. Circle the correct answers.

1. A lot of people say they hate _____.
   a. going to bed   b. waking up   c. getting dressed
2. The machine _____ to wake you up.
   a. shakes you   b. plays music   c. showers you
3. First, they try giving the man some _____.
   a. milk   b. water   c. oatmeal
4. The man _____ the breakfast cereal.
   a. likes   b. loves   c. hates
5. What does the machine give the man at the end?
   a. shoes and socks   b. T-shirt and shorts   c. coat and hat

AFTER YOU WATCH

4 Work with a partner. Describe the differences between your morning routine during the week and on weekends. What do you do, and when?

> During the week, I get up at 6:30. I take a shower and brush my teeth. Then I get dressed. I eat breakfast around 7:00. On weekends, I usually sleep until 9. I wash my face, and then I eat breakfast. Then I get dressed around 10.

Irish DANCING

Unit 2 Video 2.3

BEFORE YOU WATCH

1. Look at the pictures from the video. Do you think the sentences are true (*T*) or false (*F*)?

In Irish dancing, you have to:

1. wear sneakers　　　　_____
2. kick your legs high　　_____
3. hold your hands in the air　_____
4. wear socks　　　　　_____

WHILE YOU WATCH

2. Watch the video. Circle the correct answers.

   1. What does the teacher say to the dancers?
      a. Hurry up!　　　　b. Get up!　　　　c. Pick it up!
   2. This is Julia's ____ time at the World Championship.
      a. first　　　　　　b. third　　　　　c. fourth
   3. Julia won the World Championship ____ years ago.
      a. one　　　　　　b. two　　　　　　c. three
   4. This year the Championship is in ____.
      a. Belfast　　　　　b. London　　　　c. New York City
   5. Julia wins ____ place.
      a. first　　　　　　b. third　　　　　c. fourth

3. Watch the video again. Number the sentences 1–5 in the order that you hear them.

   1. We're on the plane right now.　_____
   2. She dances tall and straight.　_____
   3. I am twelve years old.　　　　_____
   4. Come on! Push it!　　　　　_____
   5. I'm Julia's mom.　　　　　　_____

AFTER YOU WATCH

4. Work with a partner. Do you or your classmates participate in any competitions? How do you prepare for them?

> I'm on the soccer team. We have a game every Saturday. We have to practice three times a week. We have to go to bed early the night before the game and eat a good breakfast in the morning!

Original ART

Unit 3 Video 3.1

BEFORE YOU WATCH

1 Look at the pictures from the video. Complete the sentences with the correct words.

| changed | face | painting |

The Aborigines of Australia have an ancient tradition of _____. Their art is full of symbols and patterns that have not _____ in thousands of years. The dots on this girl's _____ represent rainfall.

WHILE YOU WATCH

2 Watch the video. Are the sentences true (*T*) or false (*F*)? Correct the false sentences.

1. The Aborigines have lived in Australia for 4,000 years. _____
2. The land is very important to the Aborigines. _____
3. Some paintings show where stores are. _____
4. Many symbols in their art have changed. _____
5. Aboriginal body paintings use symbols, too. _____

3 Watch the video again. Check (✔) the sentences you hear.

1. ❏ Australia is an interesting place.
2. ❏ These paintings communicate essential information about the people.
3. ❏ Our whole land is ancient.
4. ❏ Some of these paintings are survival maps.
5. ❏ Everything tells a story.

AFTER YOU WATCH

4 Work with a partner. Make a list of the symbols you see every day. What do they communicate?

I see the recycling symbol on the bins at school. It means you can put your papers there instead of in the garbage.

76 | Unit 3

A WORLD of MUSIC

Unit 3 Video 3.3

BEFORE YOU WATCH

1 Look at the pictures from the video. Then match the pictures to the sentences.

a. b. c.

1. Indian music uses the **tabla**, a kind of drum, and the **sitar**, a stringed instrument. ____
2. An Aborigine in Australia plays the **didgeridoo**. ____
3. **Trumpets** are an important part of the Mexican mariachi sound. ____

WHILE YOU WATCH

2 Watch the video. Circle the correct answers.

1. Mariachi music has been around for ____ of years.
   a. hundreds b. thousands c. millions
2. The Spanish brought instruments like ____ to Mexico.
   a. sitars b. tablas c. guitars
3. The sitar is an ____ instrument.
   a. expensive b. ancient c. English
4. British musicians became interested in Indian music in the ____.
   a. 1950s b. 1960s c. 1970s
5. The didgeridoo is a ____ instrument.
   a. wood b. stringed c. wind
6. Aborigines have played didgeridoos for at least ____ years.
   a. 200 b. 2,000 c. 2,200

3 Watch the video again. Match the nouns and adjectives.

1. ____ mariachi music a. strange
2. ____ the sitar and tabla b. famous
3. ____ kangaroo and koala c. lively
4. ____ didgeridoo d. unusual

AFTER YOU WATCH

4 Work in small groups. Discuss musicians from other countries: Who do you like? Describe their music.

> I really like Lorde. She's from New Zealand. Her music is part pop, rock, and hip hop.

Unit 3 | 77

The AGE of DISCOVERY

Unit 4 Video 4.1

BEFORE YOU WATCH

1 Look at the picture from the video. Complete the sentences with the correct words.

| Atlantic | Pacific | South | Spain |

In 1519, the famous explorer Ferdinand Magellan sailed from _____ across the _____ Ocean. He went around the bottom of _____ America, then crossed the _____ Ocean.

WHILE YOU WATCH

2 Watch the video. Number the events 1–5 in the order they occurred.

1. Magellan sails around South America. ____
2. One of Magellan's ships completes the journey. ____
3. Christopher Columbus discovers the Americas. ____
4. Magellan lives in a castle with the king and queen of Portugal. ____
5. Vasco de Gama sails around Africa to India. ____

3 Watch the video again. Complete the sentences with the correct places.

| Asia | Philippines | Portugal | Strait of Magellan | Spain |

1. Magellan was born in 1480 in _____.
2. Christopher Columbus was looking for _____ in 1492.
3. The king of _____ gave Magellan five boats.
4. The ocean waters in the _____ were very dangerous.
5. Magellan was killed in the _____.

AFTER YOU WATCH

4 Work in small groups. Take turns naming exciting activities you have done and activities you want to do.

> I've gone rafting. I really want to go scuba diving.

Fun in AUSTRALIA

Unit 4 Video 4.3

BEFORE YOU WATCH

1 Look at the pictures from the video. Complete the sentences with the correct words.

camels   sheep   toads

Australia has many different kinds of animals and some very unusual sports. _____ are not easy to ride, but Australians race them. They also have contests to see who can cut a _____'s wool the fastest. In some parts of the country, people paint numbers on these small _____ and race them!

WHILE YOU WATCH

2 Watch the video. Complete the sentences with the correct words.

1. Uluru is a giant _____.
2. Australia has nearly a million wild _____.
3. The cane _____ is poisonous.
4. _____ shearing is a big sport in Australia.
5. Australian rules _____ is the country's favorite sport.

3 Watch the video again. Number the things 1–5 in the order you see them.

1. kangaroos   ____
2. sheep   ____
3. Sydney Opera House ____
4. camels   ____
5. toads   ____

AFTER YOU WATCH

4 Work with a partner. What are some other contests with animals in the world? Make a list, then share it with another pair.

Country	Animal	Contest
Ireland, Scotland, England	dogs	sheep herding

Unit 4 | 79

Creepy CREATURES

Unit 5 Video 5.1

BEFORE YOU WATCH

1 **Look at the picture from the video and read the sentences. Match the words and the definitions.**

1. _____ capture
2. _____ phobia
3. _____ serpent

a. snake
b. catch
c. extreme fear

4. Do you have any phobias? Explain.
   _____
   _____
   _____

This man is <u>capturing</u> a King Cobra. Many people have a <u>phobia</u> of this <u>serpent</u>.

WHILE YOU WATCH

2 **Watch the video. Are the sentences true (T) or false (F)? Correct the false sentences.**

1. The video shows more than eight different kinds of snakes. _____
2. The snake around Jeff Corwin's arm scares him. _____
3. Some King Cobras live near rivers. _____
4. Jeff's friend has never seen a King Cobra before. _____
5. To catch a King Cobra, you must hold its head. _____

3 **Watch the video again. Check (✓) the words you hear to describe the King Cobra.**

1. ❏ nervous
2. ❏ king of the serpents
3. ❏ snake-eater
4. ❏ terrified
5. ❏ awesome

AFTER YOU WATCH

4 **Work in small groups. Make a list of three to four animals that terrify people. Why do you think people are afraid of these animals? Share your list with other groups.**

> 1. lions: They can attack people.
> 2. snakes: A snake bite can be poisonous.
> 3. sharks: A shark might attack you when you're swimming in the ocean.

Calendars of the ANCIENT MAYA

Unit 5 Video 5.3

BEFORE YOU WATCH

1 **Look at the pictures from the video. Circle the correct answers.**

This calendar **use / was used** by the ancient Mayan civilization in Mexico and Central America. Each day **had / has had** a name and a symbol. The Maya **predicted / have predicted** good days and bad days.

2 **Look at the Cimi symbol in the Mayan calendar. What do you think it means?**

_____
_____
_____

WHILE YOU WATCH

3 **Watch the video. Circle the correct answers.**

1. The Mayan calendar showed each **day / week** of the year.
2. The Maya planted on **sunny / good** days.
3. The solar calendar had **18 / 20** months.
4. There were **five / six** bad days in a year.
5. The temple of Kukulkan has **360 / 365** steps.

4 **Watch the video again. Match the phrases to make true sentences.**

1. The Maya _____
2. Each day _____
3. Imix _____
4. Cimi _____
5. Nothing important _____

a. had a symbol.
b. was a good day.
c. watched the sun and moon.
d. happened on bad days.
e. was a bad day.

AFTER YOU WATCH

5 **Work with a partner. Make a calendar for the next week. Use symbols to indicate good days and bad days. Say one good thing that will happen to your partner on the good days, and one bad thing that will happen on the bad days.**

> Next Monday will be a bad day. You will lose your backpack. Next Tuesday will be a good day. You will win tickets to a concert.

Working TOGETHER

Unit 6 Video 6.1

BEFORE YOU WATCH

1 Look at the pictures from the video. Complete the sentences with the correct words.

| business | field | plant | together | vote | weather |

1. The prickly pear is a type of _____ that likes hot _____.
2. These women are working _____ in a _____ in Mexico.
3. The women _____ on how to run their _____.

WHILE YOU WATCH

2 Watch the video. Number the events 1–5 in order.

1. The women started a business. _____
2. The cooperative sells products in the US and Mexico. _____
3. Many men moved away. _____
4. Most people worked in the fields. _____
5. The women voted on how to do things. _____

3 Watch the video again. Circle the correct answers.

1. What did most farms in Ayoquesco grow before 1979?
   a. prickly pear   b. tobacco   c. cactus plants
2. What happened in 1979?
   a. The factory closed.   b. The women earned money.   c. The farms failed.
3. Mexicans add prickly pear to _____.
   a. salads   b. soups   c. both a. and b.
4. In a cooperative, _____ runs the business.
   a. one person   b. a small group   c. everyone
5. In the sentence "A man from the government regularly comes to inspect their factory," to *inspect* means to _____.
   a. photograph   b. examine   c. visit

AFTER YOU WATCH

4 Work with a small group. Imagine that you're going to start a business. Discuss and vote on these questions:

1. What kind of business will it be?
2. Where will it be located?
3. How many people are going to work there?

> We're going to start a restaurant. It will be next to the gym. About 12 people will work there.

82 | Unit 6

Watch Your IDENTITY

Unit 6 Video 6.3

BEFORE YOU WATCH

1 Do you spend a lot of time online? Answer the questions.

1. What personal information do you share online?
   _____
   _____

2. What information should you not share?
   _____
   _____

WHILE YOU WATCH

2 Watch the video. Number the sentences 1–5 in the order you hear them.

1. Sometimes you'll get a message from someone you don't know. _____
2. A criminal just needs your name and some numbers. _____
3. You just have to be aware of who you're adding as a friend. _____
4. Social media is a great way to connect with friends. _____
5. The site will ask for your name. _____

3 Watch the video again. Check (✓) the sentences you hear.

1. ❏ People spend a lot of time online during the day.
2. ❏ Criminals use social media sites, too.
3. ❏ It tells you to go to a website.
4. ❏ They can use that information to get credit cards.
5. ❏ Delete these emails if you get them.

AFTER YOU WATCH

4 Work with a partner. Discuss: What would you do if you discovered that one of your online friends was a fake?

> If I found out one of my friends online was a fake, I'd email him to ask who he was.

> I would delete his or her contact information from all of my social media sites.

Where Does It ALL GO?

Unit 7 Video 7.1

BEFORE YOU WATCH

1 Look at the picture from the video. Answer the questions.

What materials do you think this trash is made of?
If we throw trash on the ground, where does it go?

_____

_____

_____

WHILE YOU WATCH

2 Watch the video. Match the events and the places.

1. The North Pacific Gyre is in _____. a. the Atlantic Ocean
2. There is enough plastic in the gyre to cover _____. b. Hawaii
3. The toys fell into the sea just north of _____. c. South America
4. In 1995, some of the toys wound up in _____. d. Britain
5. Between 1996 and 2000, many of the toys worked their way into _____. e. the Pacific Ocean
6. In 2007, a few of the rubber duckies washed up in _____. f. Texas

3 Watch the video again. Complete the sentences with the numbers you hear.

| ¼ (a quarter) | 29 | 71 | 139 |

1. Oceans cover _____ million square miles of Earth.
2. Water covers _____ percent of the planet.
3. People throw nearly _____ of a million kilos of garbage into the sea every day.
4. A shipment of _____ thousand toys fell into the sea.

AFTER YOU WATCH

4 How much garbage do you produce in a day? Complete the chart, listing everything you threw away yesterday. Share your list with a partner.

#	Item	Material	Where did you throw item(s) away?
2	bottles	plastic	recycling bin

84 | Unit 7

Build IT BETTER

Unit 7 Video 7.3

BEFORE YOU WATCH

1 Look at the pictures from the video. Complete the sentences with the correct words.

| energy | heated | roof | solar | tubes |

1. _____ from the sun is absorbed by these _____ panels.

2. The _____ on the _____ of this building contain water. The water is _____ by the sun.

WHILE YOU WATCH

2 Watch the video. Are the sentences true (*T*) or false (*F*)? Correct the false sentences.

1. There was a tornado in the town in 2007. _____
2. The tornado destroyed 90 percent of the homes and businesses. _____
3. The reflectors always face north. _____
4. The solar panels turn sunlight into heat. _____
5. The solar panels can power the whole building. _____

3 Watch the video again. Circle the correct words.

1. The town was **hit / reduced** by a huge tornado.
2. It was **suggested / decided** to use solar energy.
3. How were the solar tubes **placed / put** in the roof?
4. First, holes were **drilled / made**.
5. Solar panels were **built / rebuilt**.

AFTER YOU WATCH

4 Work in small groups. Discuss what people in your community do to help the environment.

> Most people recycle their bottles and trash. There's a big garden downtown. People plant vegetables and flowers there.

Unit 7 | 85

Land of VOLCANOES

Unit 8 Video 8.1

BEFORE YOU WATCH

1 Look at the picture from the video. Complete the text with the correct words.

| active | cloud | damage | erupt | eruption | warn |

_____ volcanoes can _____ at any time. They produce a _____ of rock and ash. They can kill people and _____ airplanes. Some scientists study these volcanoes and _____ people when there is an _____.

WHILE YOU WATCH

2 Watch the video. Answer the questions yes (*Y*) or no (*N*).

1. Is the region with volcanoes close to Moscow? _____
2. Does Sasha study active volcanoes? _____
3. Can the warning save thousands of airlines? _____
4. Did the volcano erupt a few weeks ago? _____
5. Did small eruptions continue for weeks? _____

3 Watch the video again. Match the phrases to make true sentences.

1. Sasha has visited _____
2. Sasha has taken _____
3. Their warnings can save _____
4. The seismograph had shown _____
5. Sasha and his team had to warn _____

a. activity in one of the volcanoes.
b. the airlines.
c. the volcanoes many times.
d. regular samples from the volcanoes.
e. people's lives.

AFTER YOU WATCH

4 Work in small groups. Discuss: What natural disasters have occurred in the world in the past year? What happened?

> Last year, there was a big flood in Germany. It rained for four days. People had to leave their houses.

Storm CHASERS

Unit 8 Video 8.3

BEFORE YOU WATCH

1 Look at the pictures from the video. Answer the questions.

1. What do you think the men are watching? Where do you think they are?

   _____

   _____

2. What natural disasters can cause this kind of damage?

   _____

   _____

WHILE YOU WATCH

2 Watch the video. Circle the correct answers.

1. Dixie Alley is in the _____ of the United States.
   - a. north
   - b. south
   - c. west
2. The Storm Chasers are _____.
   - a. teachers
   - b. police
   - c. scientists
3. _____ tornadoes are very violent.
   - a. F5
   - b. F15
   - c. F50
4. The Storm Chasers try to _____ people.
   - a. warn
   - b. talk to
   - c. educate

3 Watch the video again. Complete the sentences with the correct numbers.

| 60 | 130 | 180 | 321 | 400 |

1. Every year, tornadoes kill about _____ people.
2. F5 tornadoes have winds higher than _____ kilometers per hour.
3. The F5 stayed on the ground for _____ kilometers.
4. There were over _____ tornadoes in Dixie Alley that day.
5. Unfortunately, _____ people died in the storm.

AFTER YOU WATCH

4 Work in small groups. Discuss: How do people get warnings about extreme weather? What do you think is the best way?

> A lot of people listen to the radio. I also check the weather on the Internet.

Social NETWORKS

Unit 9 Video 9.1

BEFORE YOU WATCH

1 Answer the questions.

1. What Internet sites do you visit most often?
   _____

2. Name two to three popular social media sites.
   _____
   _____

3. What does the number of online "friends" or "followers" someone has tell you?
   _____
   _____

WHILE YOU WATCH

2 Watch the video. Circle the correct answers.

1. The narrator says that _____ changed the way people thought about video.
   a. Facebook   b. YouTube   c. Wikipedia
2. Mark Zuckerberg believes that _____ made Facebook so popular.
   a. college students   b. high school students   c. relationships
3. Zuckerberg explains that the *social graph* is a map of connections between _____.
   a. places   b. people   c. websites
4. Jimmy Wales says that communities can produce _____ of very high quality.
   a. work   b. writing   c. ideas
5. All three men believe that _____ are important.
   a. schools   b. companies   c. communities

3 Watch the video again. Check (✓) the sentences you hear.

1. ❑ Now, anyone with a video can be famous.
2. ❑ The Internet's about connecting individuals.
3. ❑ And, I mean, there are billions of them across the country.
4. ❑ New relationships mean new users.
5. ❑ Wikipedia is now the world's most popular encyclopedia.

AFTER YOU WATCH

4 Work in small groups. Discuss: What social media sites are the best for staying in touch with friends? For sharing photos? For messaging?

> Facebook's OK for staying in touch. I use Instagram for photos, and I use my phone for messaging.

The LANGUAGE of the FUTURE?

Unit 9 Video 9.3

BEFORE YOU WATCH

1 Look at the pictures from the video. Answer the questions.

1. What language or languages do people speak in China?
   _____

2. What are some things China produces?
   _____

WHILE YOU WATCH

2 Watch the video. Are the sentences true (*T*) or false (*F*)? Correct the false sentences.

1. About four billion people live in China.   _____
2. China has the strongest economy in the world.   _____
3. Mandarin has over 40,000 written characters.   _____
4. The Chinese developed a system that uses the Roman alphabet.   _____
5. The narrator asks if Mandarin is the world's number one language now.   _____

3 Watch the video again. Complete the sentences with the words you hear.

1. Everything in China is _____.
2. The country already produces many things, like the _____ you're wearing.
3. But everyone can understand one _____ language: Mandarin.
4. In the late _____, the Chinese developed a system called "Pinyin."
5. There are Chinese people who speak _____ all over the world.

AFTER YOU WATCH

4 Work with a partner. Make a list of things you own or use that are made in China. Do you think your children will speak Mandarin?

1. *backpack*
2. *sneakers*
3. *cell phone*
4. *computer*

Unit 9 | 89

LIFEGUARD and ATHLETE

Unit 10 Video 10.1

BEFORE YOU WATCH

1 Look at the pictures from the video. Complete the sentences with the correct words.

| cool off | lifeguard | rescue | surfboard |

1. On hot days, people go to this beach in Australia to _____.

2. This woman is a _____. She uses her _____ to _____ people from the dangerous waters.

WHILE YOU WATCH

2 Watch the video. Answer the questions about Candice.

1. How many people has Candice rescued?
2. What was her goal when she was 12?
3. What does she say she could not survive without?
4. What is her goal in the Lifesaving Championship?
5. How does she feel about her performance in the first race?

3 Watch the video again. Circle the correct words.

1. Every year, dangerous waters **take / save** the lives of people.
2. If a rescue situation **comes up / goes off**, Candice is the first one out there.
3. Sometimes she must bring people she rescues **out to shore / back to life**.
4. She must put her fears of the ocean **out of her mind / on the table**.
5. The first race is usually her worst because it takes her a bit to **cool off / warm up**.

AFTER YOU WATCH

4 Work with a partner. What are some other life-saving jobs?

> Well, the police save people's lives, and doctors and nurses do, too.

90 | Unit 10

Circus STAR

Unit 10 Video 10.3

BEFORE YOU WATCH

1 Look at the pictures from the video. Do you think the sentences are true (*T*) or false (*F*)?

1. In Russia, the circus is considered an art, like ballet or theater. _____
2. The Russian government owns some of the circuses in Russia. _____
3. Most circus acrobats perform with wild animals. _____
4. Many Russians think that being a circus performer is an excellent job. _____

WHILE YOU WATCH

2 Watch the video. Are the sentences true (*T*) or false (*F*)? Correct the false sentences.

1. Aliona dreams of being a circus director. _____
2. Aliona's last practice doesn't go very well. _____
3. She is performing for the top athletes in Russia's circuses. _____
4. She earns her circus diploma. _____
5. She decides to take her dream job in Moscow. _____

3 Watch the video again. Answer the questions about Aliona.

1. What must Aliona do in four weeks? _____
2. What happens during her last practice? _____
3. What is she offered after her performance? _____
4. What does she decide to do? _____

AFTER YOU WATCH

4 Work with a partner. Discuss: What was a goal you accomplished when you were very young? What challenges did you face?

> I really wanted to learn how to ride a bike. At first, I fell a lot, and I was a little scared of hurting myself. But now, I ride my bike everywhere!

Notes

Notes

Credits

The authors and publishers acknowledge the following sources of copyright material and are grateful for the permissions granted. While every effort has been made, it has not always been possible to identify the sources of all the material used, or to trace all copyright holders. If any omissions are brought to our notice, we will be happy to include the appropriate acknowledgements on reprinting.

p. 2 (1): Shutterstock Images/Michael Wick; p. 2 (2): Shutterstock Images/Menno Schaefer; p. 2 (3): Shutterstock Images/Ragnisphoto; p. 10 (CR): Alamy/©Tetra Images; p. 21 (TL): Alamy/©Juice Images; p. 25 (TL): Alamy/©Keith Morris; p. 27 (TR): Getty Images/Manfred Rutz; p. 28 (BR): Alamy/©Maria Galan; p. 38 (CL): Getty images/Roy Mehta; p. 44 (1): Alamy/©Ruslan Kudrin; p. 44 (2): Shutterstock Images/Elena Elisseeva; p. 44 (3): Shutterstock Images/Gtstudio; p. 44 (4): Shutterstock Images/Quang Ho; p. 44 (5): Shutterstock Images/Sophie McAulay; p. 44 (6): Shutterstock Images/Coolkengzz; p. 44 (7): Alamy/©Paul Debois; p. 44 (8): Shutterstock Images/Yevgeniy11; p. 49 (TR): Shutterstock Images/Mila Supinskaya; p. 55 (TL): Alamy/©Acumen images; Back cover: Shutterstock Images Images/Fluke Samed.

Front cover photograph by Alamy/©Martin Strmiska.

The publishers are grateful to the following illustrators:
Janet Allinger p. 6, 8, 34, 40, 68; David Belmonte p. 4, 16, 17, 42, 43, 70; Galia Bernstein p. 18 (BR), 20, 23, 45, 46; Anni Betts p. 5, 37, 39, 66; Nigel Dobbyn p. 12, 26, 30, 33, 50, 54, 62; Mark Duffin p. 18 (1-10), 52; Q2A Media Services, Inc. p. 9, 11, 28, 50 (1, 2, 4, 5, 9), 56, 60, 61, 76; Jose Rubio p. 14, 31, 47, 48, 67.

All video stills by kind permission of Discovery Communications, LLC 2015.